ALWAYS DIVIDED, NEVER UNITED

AND OTHER STORIES DURING A TIME OF PANDEMICS AND POLITICS

BY J.P. PRAG

> **The book is on my kitchen table.** *Neglected masterpieces of the twentieth century*, it says in italic script under the title. Laura was a "modernist", we are told in the inside flap. She was "influenced" by the likes of Djuna Barnes, Elizabeth Smart, Carson McCullers – authors I know for a fact that Laura never read. The cover design isn't too bad, however.
>
> *The Blind Assassin*, pg. 545
> Margaret Atwood

OPENING SALVO

WHAT IS A DAY?

Here I sit at the very end of 2021 staring at this screen.

A little over a year ago, what you are holding in your hands was not the plan. But as with everything during our time of pandemics and politics, things quickly changed. What started out as just a one-off story slowly blossomed into several narratives, a series, and now an entire book.

To my surprise, we have chronicled a span of time and how it affected not only humankind in general, but also individual people—myself included. This was a unique point in history with the COVID-19 pandemic raging, a political turnover that was disputed by some and abused by others, and a world that would not stop spinning for either of these situations... or anything else, really.

Throughout this tome, you will find many different approaches on how to express these ideas. Several chapters are locked into a point-in-time to keep them in a specific context, while others are more broadly focused and have been adjusted with new information that has surfaced since their progenesis. Some intervals have been massively edited and modified; many others have only been lightly touched.

This is all meant to tell one cohesive saga. Each distinct segment and overarching part may feel like its own stand-alone feature—and that is intentional as well—but there is a larger thesis for you to discover. Please enjoy, learn, and open your mind to the possibilities.

J.P. Prag
December 28, 2021, Revised March 8, 2022

TABLE OF CONTENTS

OPENING SALVO **3**
   What is a Day? 4
   Table of Contents 5

PART 1: POLITICAL TRAPS **7**
   Always Divided, Never United 8
   That's Not Treason :-(.... 22
   Future Policies of the Republican Party 36
   Liz Cheney & Friends are Not Leaving the Republican Party 66
   Left-Leaning Social Libertarian 84

PART 2: LIFE, DEATH, AND COVID-19 .... **97**
   Did I Have COVID-19? 98
   Mandatory COVID-19 Vaccine 114
   Yelling Fire in a Vaccination Clinic 138
   My Family is Underground 150
   Eulogy for my Dad 160

PART 3: SCIENCE AND CONSEQUENCES **167**
   Environmentalism: Worst Case Scenario 168
   The Vegan Extinction 180
   Forget Mars, Let's Colonize Venus 196

PART 4: AMENDING THE FUTURE **215**
   Complete Overhaul: Electing the President of the United States 216
   How to Stop Voter Suppression... Permanently 238
   Fix Congress? No, Demolish It! 254
   Part-Time // Citizen Legislature 278
   Ending the Tyranny of Mitch McConnell 306
   Demand More than Justice 322

PART 5: PEOPLE AND THE CENSUS **351**
   One More Seat at the Table 352
   2022+ Implications for 2020 Failings 368
   Race and Ethnicity are Meaningless Human Constructs 388

PART 6: APPROACH **407**
   Do 10 Minutes of Research 408
   Empathy // Rediscovered 422
   Agreeing with my Enemy 430

AFTERWARDS **443**
   About the Author 444
   Other Works 445
   Dedications and Notes 446
   Version History 447
   Copyrights and Disclaimers 448

PART 1: POLITICAL TRAPS

ALWAYS DIVIDED, NEVER UNITED

No President has ever received a "mandate" to govern; all elections have been very close.

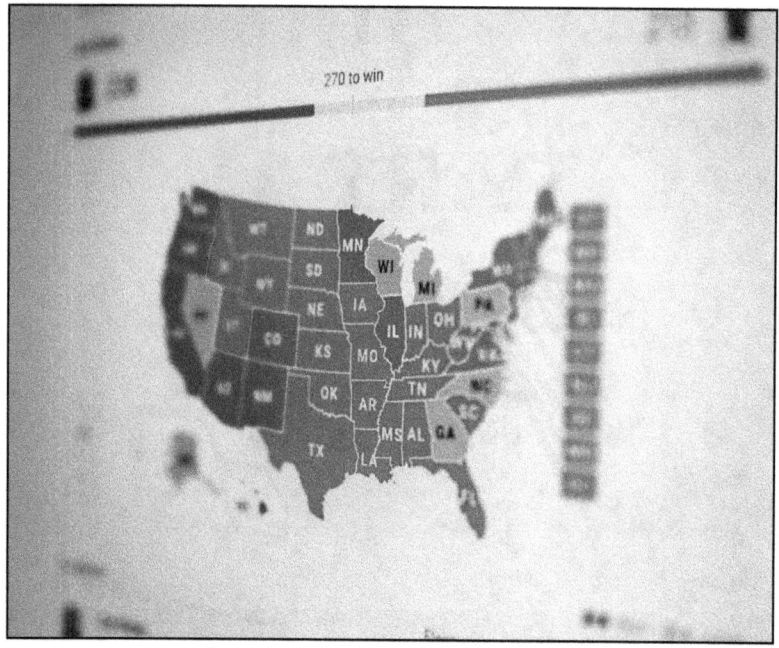

*Photo by **Clay Banks**[1] on **Unsplash***

---

[11] HTTPS://UNSPLASH.COM/@CLAYBANKS

» KEY POINTS

- *Having just over 52% of the popular vote demonstrated that then President-elect Joe Biden did not have a mandate from the people.*

- *However, he was not alone as very few Presidents have ever had more than 55% of the popular vote.*

- *From a Presidential race perspective, we are not any more divided today than any other point in history.*

> **NOW, THIS CAMPAIGN IS OVER. WHAT IS THE WILL OF THE PEOPLE? WHAT IS OUR MANDATE?**
>
> **... I BELIEVE THAT THIS IS PART OF THE MANDATE GIVEN TO US FROM THE AMERICAN PEOPLE.**
>
> *EXCERPTS FROM PRESIDENT ELECT JOE BIDEN'S VICTORY SPEECH, NOVEMBER 7, 2020*

Then president-elect Joe Biden believed he had the will of the people. Or, in his words, he had a "mandate" to govern and perform in a certain way. While there is no reasonable, fact-based, reality-grounded argument that showed that Mr. Biden did not win the 2020 Presidential election, that is far and away from saying he had a mandate from the people.

By mid-December 2020, standing President and first-runner-up Donald Trump had amassed over 74.2 million votes in his favor according to the **COOK POLITICAL REPORT NATIONAL VOTE TRACKER**[2]. While this paled in comparison to the over 81.3 million for Mr. Biden, it did confirm there was a massive pool of people who voted against Mr. Biden. Additionally, there were another 2.9 million people who voted for neither candidate. All told, Mr. Biden had about 52% of the vote among those who actually cast a ballot.

---

[2] HTTPS://COOKPOLITICAL.COM/2020-NATIONAL-POPULAR-VOTE-TRACKER

Photo by LUKE STACKPOOLE[3] on UNSPLASH

And of course, that is the rub. According to the **UNITED STATES CENSUS BUREAU**[4], there were approximately 235.4 million people over the age of 18 in the United States at the end of 2019. Using that number as the denominator, Mr. Biden had less than 35% of the voting-age population cast their ballots for him (never mind people who are not eligible to vote due to debatable State and Federal laws). Now, to be fair, plenty of people who did not vote may have voted for him anyway but were in a noncompetitive State—one way or another—and therefore were dis-incentivized to vote. On the other hand, plenty of people also voted for him not out of preference, but out of dis-preference for Mr. Trump and the other options.

Suffice to say, no matter which way you slice it, Joe Biden did not have a clear mandate of the people. But this is no

---

[3] HTTPS://UNSPLASH.COM/@WITHLUKE

[4] HTTPS://DATA.CENSUS.GOV/CEDSCI/TABLE?Q=S2901&G=0100000US,.04000.001&TID=ACSST1Y2019.S2901&HIDEPREVIEW=TRUE

indictment against him nor a challenge to whatever his agenda may be. On the contrary, this is a defense of these results because:

NO PRESIDENT IN HISTORY HAS *EVER* HAD THE WILL OF THE PEOPLE.

First off, let us take a look at "modern elections". We already know there are two elections—2000 and 2016—where the eventual Electoral College winner did not receive the majority of the popular vote. In 2000, the winner George W. Bush received 47.9% of the popular vote compared to first runner up Al Gore who received 48.4%. Similarly, in 2016 Donald Trump received 46.1% to Hillary Clinton's 48.2%. Yet, are these numbers that different than other recent elections?

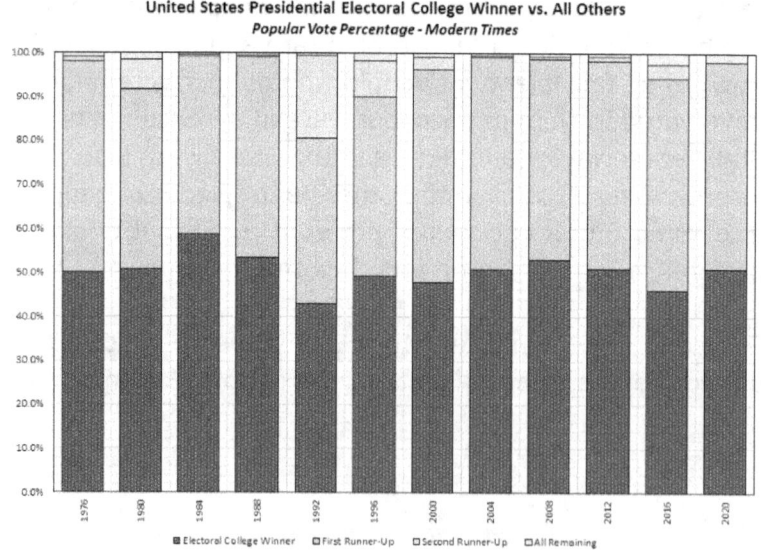

The chart above (and all other charts in this story) shows the popular vote percentage for the Electoral College winner in purple, the first runner up in orange, and second runner up in a lighter orange/yellow, and all others in a pale yellow; or in ever lightening shades if viewing in monochrome. As can be clearly seen, in the 12 elections since 1976, only one saw a candidate even get close—but not surpass—60% of the popular vote. In other words, we are a divided nation, at least when it comes to electing a President. The results are no different than any other election in our recent past.

Photo by OBIE FERNANDEZ[5] on UNSPLASH

Just to be clear how little mandate the Presidents have had, in Bill Clinton's first term in 1992 he received just 43.0% of the popular vote (the fourth lowest in history). At the same time, in the end he received 68.8% of the Electoral College vote! Even in his second term election

---

[5] HTTPS://UNSPLASH.COM/@OBIEFERNANDEZ

four years later his popular vote percentage did not reach half the voters, petering out at 49.2%. The best results over the "modern" timeframe go to Ronald Reagan's second term in 1984 with a *whopping* 58.8%. Other than that, every other election has been around or below 50%—whether it was Barack Obama, George H.W. Bush, Jimmy Carter, or anyone else.

Thus far, then, we can see that—at least recently—there has been a clear divide. No eventual winner in modern times has carried a true super majority of the people. But what about for all time?

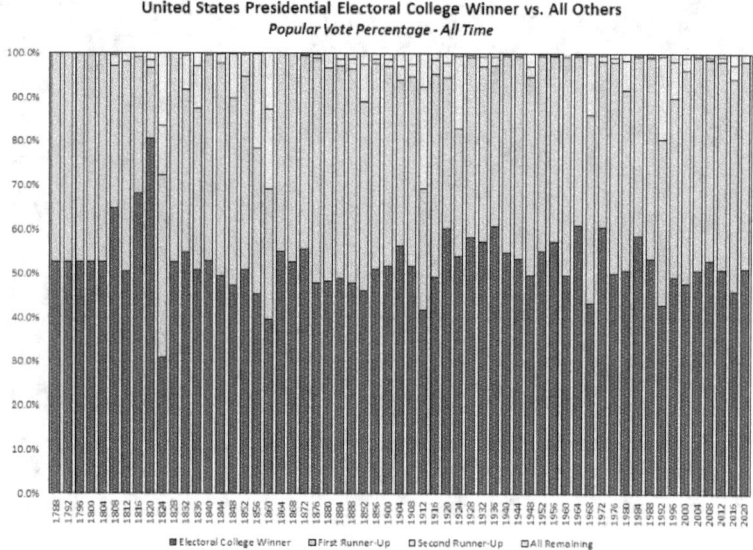

Well, this is where things get a bit complicated. Sure, you could say in 1820 James Monroe received 80.6% of the popular vote. Or you could look at the opposite direction for the next election in 1824 where the House of Representatives picked John Quincy Adams to be the President even though he lost both the popular and Electoral College votes (30.9% and 32.2%, respectively).

However, we need to remember a few things. First off, large swaths of Americans—people of color, women, natives, non-landowners—were barred from voting in general. Next, widespread use of popular voting to determine the actions of Electors did not come until later. For that, we need to zoom in on the point after the last time the people did not directly vote for President: the 1876 vote where Colorado's Legislature chose instead of the people.

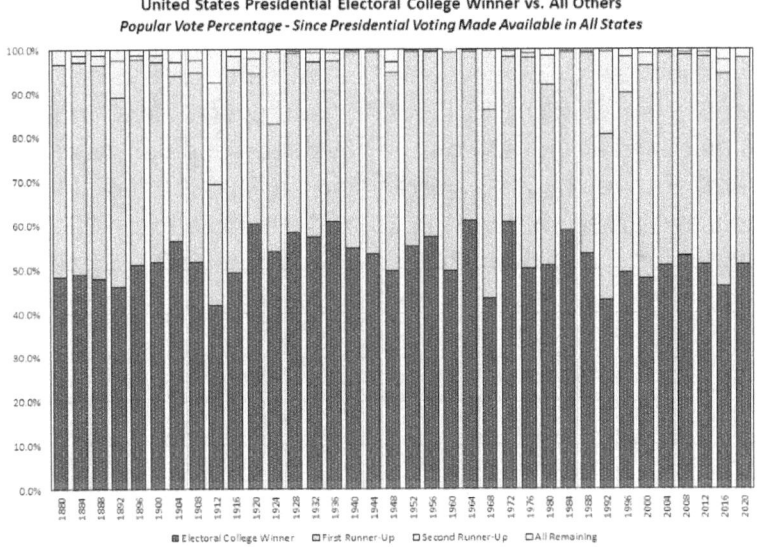

All right, we still know that people were being disenfranchised from their vote (and many still are), but at least we have a viable comparison point of all States picking their Electors based upon the results of that popular vote. And what happened right away in that first election? James Garfield *barely* squeaked by with just 48.3% of the popular vote, a dead heat with his main competitor Winfield Scott Hancock. While accuracy in the count is not as verifiable as today, it is safe to say the margin between the two was less than 2,000 votes.

However, just as today, Mr. Garfield was able to take 58.0% of the Electoral College votes just because of which States he carried, not how many people voted for him across the entire nation.

And similar to today, there were fights over fairness and who had a mandate and what Presidents thought the people told them to do. Since 1880, the average popular vote percentage for the eventual winner has been 52.1%, including the unofficial 2020 counts. Over the 36 elections since 1880, only 10 (27.8%) have had the Electoral College winner carry 55.0% or more of the popular vote. If we look at all 59 elections, that number only jumps up another small bit to 15 (25.4%). And even among those, in elections after 1820 only 4 have seen popular vote numbers break 60%—Warren Harding in 1920, Franklin Roosevelt (second term) in 1936, Lyndon Johnson in 1964, and Richard Nixon (second term) in 1972. Since then, not a single candidate has cracked that barrier.

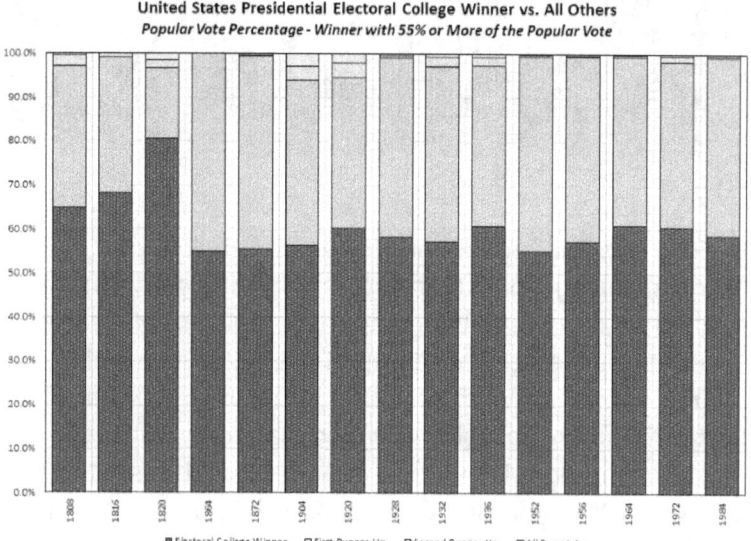

United States Presidential Electoral College Winner vs. All Others
Popular Vote Percentage - Winner with 55% or More of the Popular Vote

That is right, disgraced former President Richard Nixon was the last one who could have potentially said he had a mandate, or at least a clear majority of voters. He certainly swept the Electoral College with 96.7% of that vote. Ronald Reagan was the last president to perform as well as Mr. Nixon in the Electoral College. That said, while in 1980 and 1984 Mr. Reagan took 90.9% and 97.6% of the Electoral College, he still only had 50.8% and 58.8% of the popular vote, respectively. This is another reason why looking at political maps of the country that assign a single color to a State—like the one at the top of this chapter—are so misleading.

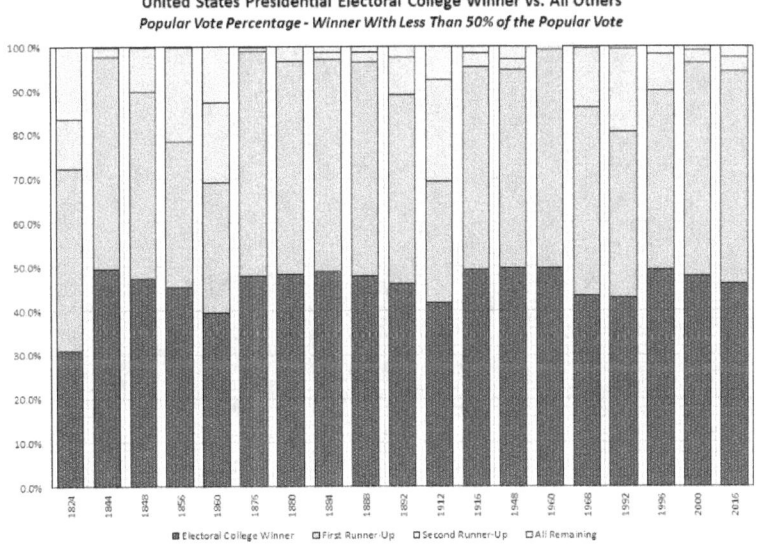

What is actually clear is that the opposite situation is more likely to happen. On 19 occasions (32.3%) the eventual Presidential winner had less than or equal to 50% of the popular vote. Thirteen (36.1%) of those have come since 1880. This includes the election of 1912 where Woodrow Wilson (first term) received just 41.8% of the popular vote—the least since Abraham Lincoln's first term in 1860 with 39.7%. The aforementioned 1992 Election of Bill Clinton was the next one to come close to this low number.

After tumultuous elections in 1876 and 1880, things kept getting worse. This was a country that still had festering wounds from the Civil War. It did not help when, in 1888, Benjamin Harrison became the next President to win the Electoral College while losing the popular vote with 47.8% compared to incumbent Grover Cleveland's 48.6%. The Electoral College, being what it is, awarded 58.1% of the vote to Mr. Harrison.

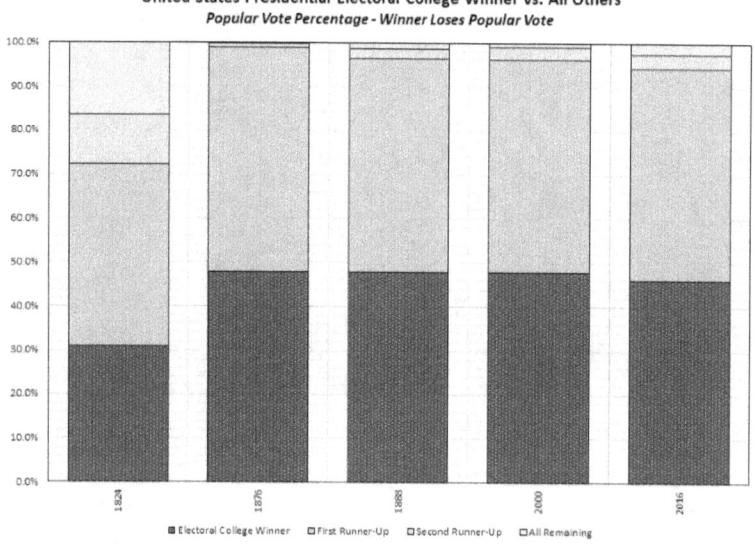

The next election would seem to make things worse when Grover Cleveland re-won the White House with just 46.0% of the popular vote to Benjamin Harrison's 43.0% and James Weaver's 8.5%. One could say this was a time even more split and separated than now, and the country could have easily fallen back into Civil War.

Despite the rhetoric of today, we are not nearly as divided as that. While there are chasms, they are not as insurmountable. Though people back then feared the worst was yet to come, circumstances actually shifted to more just solutions instead. Since that time, the **19th Amendment** was ratified in 1920 that extended full voting rights to all sexes. In 1964, the **24th Amendment** removed racist policies like a poll tax from being used to deny people the right to vote. Just a year later in 1965 the **Voting Rights Act** became the law of the land in an attempt to make sure all minority groups could not be denied their privileges to cast a ballot—and was further amended in 1970, 1975, 1982, 1992, and 2006. After that, in 1971, the **26th Amendment** lowered the voting age to 18 for all elections in the country.

Photo by *UNSEEN HISTORIES*[6] on *UNSPLASH*

This is the story that demonstrates that as we have expanded voting rights to all people and more individuals

---

[6] HTTPS://UNSPLASH.COM/@UNSEENHISTORIES

have felt comfortable expressing their political opinions, we have not become any more divided. We are the same as many points in the past and—on average—throughout all history. No, then President-elect Joe Biden did not have a mandate, and should not have acted as if he did. However, he was not alone as no one in his position has ever had one. Times may feel like we are on the precipice and we could not be more at odds, but that is always true. There is no single person who can encompass and represent the dreams of a nation as vast and diverse as our own.

And, perhaps, that is for the best.

"Voting as easy as Shopping" postcard c. 1910 by **Unknown author**[7], Public domain, via Wikimedia Commons.

---

[7] HTTPS://COMMONS.WIKIMEDIA.ORG/WIKI/FILE:%22VOTING_AS_EASY_AS_SHOPPING%22_POSTCARD_C._1910.JPG

THAT'S NOT TREASON :-(

Unfortunately, trying to circumvent democracy is not a crime

Photo by VISUALS[8] on UNSPLASH

---

[8] HTTPS://UNSPLASH.COM/@VISUALS

» KEY POINTS

- *Was signing on to a lawsuit to throw out the results of the Presidential Election by disenfranchising over 10 million voters—like 126 members of the House of Representatives did—a betrayal of America?*

- *Crimes like "treason", "sedition", "rebellion", "insurrection", and "advocating overthrow" all require an act of violence or asking for violence, which this action did not do.*

- *Even testing other laws and the Oath of Office, there was nothing illegal or un-Constitutional about attempting to usurp democracy for one's own personal or party gain.*

In one of the most surreal of the lawsuits contesting the results of the 2020 Presidential Election seen by December of the same year, the State of Texas sued four fellow States over their results. While the word "unprecedented" is tossed around to the point of being trite, this one truly was because Texas Attorney General Ken Paxton was trying to disenfranchise the legally cast ballots of over 10 million people. No one else in Mr. Paxton's office would even sign off on the suit, so he filed it by himself. However, that did not mean he did not gain support and friends.

PLEASE NOTE THAT MR. PAXTON, ACCORDING TO THE TEXAS TRIBUNE[9], "**HAS BEEN UNDER INDICTMENT FOR MORE THAN FIVE YEARS ON SECURITIES FRAUD CHARGES BUT HAS YET TO STAND TRIAL**" **AND IS UNDER INVESTIGATION BY THE FBI FOR USING** "**THE POWER OF HIS OFFICE TO BENEFIT A POLITICAL DONOR**" **AFTER A SET OF WHISTLEBLOWER COMPLAINTS.**

That support came shortly after he filed his brief directly to the Supreme Court. There, **126 MEMBERS OF THE HOUSE OF REPRESENTATIVES**[10] [see the link in the footnote to view

---

[9] HTTPS://WWW.TEXASTRIBUNE.ORG/2020/11/17/TEXAS-KEN-PAXTON-FBI/
[10] HTTPS://WWW.MERCURYNEWS.COM/2020/12/12/LIST-THE-126-CONGRESS-MEMBERS-19-STATES-AND-2-IMAGINARY-STATES-THAT-BACKED-TEXAS-SUIT-OVER-TRUMP-DEFEAT/

their names] signed on board to try to change the will of the majority—as slim as that majority may have been in some cases—of the people of Georgia, Michigan, Pennsylvania and Wisconsin to Texas' own. This behavior has been described by many adjectives, none too flattering except by diehard supporters of President Donald Trump who wanted him to rule no matter the reality, consequences, or appearances.

Photo by **ANTHONY GARAND**[11] on **UNSPLASH**

Thankfully, on Friday December 11, 2020 the Supreme Court unanimously rejected hearing the case (although two justices said they would have heard it just because, but Texas and friends would have lost anyway). The main reason they stated was that Texas lacked any standing and could not show in any way that they were harmed. Just because they did not like the candidate the other States chose, it does not mean they were hurt. And even if there was fraud on such a massive scale that it could

---

[11] HTTPS://UNSPLASH.COM/@GARAND

have changed the results in four States (there was not, just to be *VERY* clear), the States are responsible for reviewing their own results and those local courts would be the venues to have those fights. Although the Supreme Court did not comment on it, those cases did already happen at the State level and moved up through the federal appeals process, all affirming the results. Whatever small issues there were—and there are always some—none would have made the slightest difference to the statewide and national results.

After this opinion, on Sunday December 13, 2020 Chris Wallace, on his Fox News show, asked one of those 126 their thoughts. Louisiana Representative and House Minority Whip Steve Scalise was unperturbed and unrepentant. Even though Chis Wallace took him to task in an unflattering interview, Mr. Scalise still posted the interview segment on his own YouTube page:

HTTPS://YOUTU.BE/HZFYLDN7ZZW

Speech like this and the general sign-off on an attempted—no matter how far-fetched—bloodless coup prompted New Jersey Representative Bill Pascrell to send a letter to House Speaker Nancy Pelosi on the same day as the Supreme Court ruling, stating in part:

> **I CALL ON YOU TO EXERCISE THE POWER OF YOUR OFFICES TO EVALUATE STEPS YOU CAN TAKE TO ADDRESS THESE CONSTITUTIONAL VIOLATIONS THIS CONGRESS AND, IF POSSIBLE, REFUSE TO SEAT IN THE 117ᵀᴴ CONGRESS ANY MEMBERS-ELECT SEEKING TO MAKE DONALD TRUMP AN UNELECTED DICTATOR.**

This would be a wildly extreme response, just as wildly extreme as the original Texas lawsuit was. But did Mr. Pascrell have a point? In his reasoning, Representative Pascrell invoked the **14ᵗʰ Amendment, Clause 2**:

> **NO PERSON SHALL BE A SENATOR OR REPRESENTATIVE IN CONGRESS... SHALL HAVE ENGAGED IN INSURRECTION OR REBELLION AGAINST THE SAME...**

Thus, the argument he was making was that by supporting this lawsuit they had committed insurrection or rebellion. That brings up the question of what does "insurrection" and "rebellion" mean? Can "speech" be "insurrection" or "rebellion"? Is the act of using the tools of the system against itself an act against the organism? First, let us turn to **U.S. Code, Title 18 § 2383** to see if we can get a clearer definition:

> **WHOEVER INCITES, SETS ON FOOT, ASSISTS, OR ENGAGES IN ANY REBELLION OR INSURRECTION AGAINST THE AUTHORITY OF THE UNITED STATES OR THE LAWS THEREOF...**

Well, that was no help! Without getting too deep into the various cases, the Courts have made clear that both "insurrection" and "rebellion" require an act of violence or force, or at least asking for violence or force to be used. Therefore, neither Mr. Scalise nor his cohorts would be guilty of that. What, then, about "treason"? After all, that was the argument Mr. Pascrell was making: that these people had betrayed the country.

Photo by *JOSHUA SUKOFF*[12] on *UNSPLASH*

---

[12] HTTPS://UNSPLASH.COM/@JOSHUAS

Treason is the only crime that is written into the original Constitution. By **Article 3, Section 3, Clause 1**:

> TREASON AGAINST THE UNITED STATES, SHALL CONSIST ONLY IN LEVYING WAR AGAINST THEM, OR IN ADHERING TO THEIR ENEMIES, GIVING THEM AID AND COMFORT.

And just as before, we also have the law via **U.S. Code, Title 18 § 2381:**

> WHOEVER, OWING ALLEGIANCE TO THE UNITED STATES, LEVIES WAR AGAINST THEM OR ADHERES TO THEIR ENEMIES, GIVING THEM AID AND COMFORT WITHIN THE UNITED STATES OR ELSEWHERE, IS GUILTY OF TREASON...

Both these definitions require either levying war themselves or giving aid to enemies of the United States. Though some enemies may have had indirect benefits due to these actions, one could not make the argument that any member of Congress was giving them aid. Nor could it be said they were making war against the United States. On the contrary, while they attempted to co-opt the United States for their own purposes, they were using the tools that are built into the law and Constitution. No treason had been committed.

Where does that leave us? If it is not "treason", could it be "sedition"? According to **U.S. Code Title 18 § 2384**:

> **IF TWO OR MORE PERSONS IN ANY STATE OR TERRITORY, OR IN ANY PLACE SUBJECT TO THE JURISDICTION OF THE UNITED STATES, CONSPIRE TO OVERTHROW, PUT DOWN, OR TO DESTROY BY FORCE THE GOVERNMENT OF THE UNITED STATES, OR TO LEVY WAR AGAINST THEM, OR TO OPPOSE BY FORCE THE AUTHORITY THEREOF, OR BY FORCE TO PREVENT, HINDER, OR DELAY THE EXECUTION OF ANY LAW OF THE UNITED STATES, OR BY FORCE TO SEIZE, TAKE, OR POSSESS ANY PROPERTY OF THE UNITED STATES CONTRARY TO THE AUTHORITY THEREOF...**

Flags wave in front of the Washington Monument in Washington, D.C. on December 31, 2019. Photo by J.P. Prag

Sedition, unlike treason, does require two or more people to be working together in a conspiracy. Here, we do have that. However, once again, the law is actually clear: there must be an "act of force". Going to the Supreme Court is not an "act of force" because having a judiciary that is equally powerful to the Legislative and Executive Branches is a Constitutional right. That would seem to leave us with only one recourse. Is this "Advocating overthrow of Government"? **U.S. Code Title 18 § 2385** provides a definition of that:

> WHOEVER KNOWINGLY OR WILLFULLY ADVOCATES, ABETS, ADVISES, OR TEACHES THE DUTY, NECESSITY, DESIRABILITY, OR PROPRIETY OF OVERTHROWING OR DESTROYING THE GOVERNMENT OF THE UNITED STATES OR THE GOVERNMENT OF ANY STATE, TERRITORY, DISTRICT OR POSSESSION THEREOF, OR THE GOVERNMENT OF ANY POLITICAL SUBDIVISION THEREIN, BY FORCE OR VIOLENCE, OR BY THE ASSASSINATION OF ANY OFFICER OF ANY SUCH GOVERNMENT; OR
>
> WHOEVER, WITH INTENT TO CAUSE THE OVERTHROW OR DESTRUCTION OF ANY SUCH GOVERNMENT, PRINTS, PUBLISHES, EDITS, ISSUES, CIRCULATES, SELLS, DISTRIBUTES, OR PUBLICLY DISPLAYS ANY WRITTEN OR PRINTED MATTER ADVOCATING, ADVISING, OR TEACHING THE DUTY, NECESSITY, DESIRABILITY, OR PROPRIETY OF OVERTHROWING OR DESTROYING ANY GOVERNMENT IN THE UNITED STATES BY FORCE OR VIOLENCE, OR ATTEMPTS TO DO SO; OR
>
> WHOEVER ORGANIZES OR HELPS OR ATTEMPTS TO ORGANIZE ANY SOCIETY, GROUP, OR ASSEMBLY OF PERSONS WHO TEACH, ADVOCATE, OR ENCOURAGE THE OVERTHROW OR DESTRUCTION OF ANY SUCH GOVERNMENT BY FORCE OR VIOLENCE; OR BECOMES OR IS A MEMBER OF, OR AFFILIATES WITH, ANY SUCH SOCIETY, GROUP, OR ASSEMBLY OF PERSONS, KNOWING THE PURPOSES THEREOF —

And that is the issue with all of these adjectives that have been used to describe the actions of these members of the House of Representatives: not a single one of them has—by signing on to this case—used or asked others to use force or violence. Yes, some had made implied and outright threats of violence, but not by attaching their names to this fruitless case. Just to rub more salt in the wounds, they were not attempting to "overthrow" the government. In reality, they were looking to take control and create a continuation of government; in other words, they were looking to support, and not remove, the government.

No matter how disingenuous that may be, they had not committed "insurrection", "rebellion", "treason", "sedition", or "advocating overthrow". However, there is one last area to consider. **Article 6, Clause 3 of the Constitution** requires an oath or affirmation be taken to protect the Constitution. **U.S. Code Title 5 § 3331** lays out the oath as:

> **I, [YOUR NAME HERE], DO SOLEMNLY SWEAR (OR AFFIRM) THAT I WILL SUPPORT AND DEFEND THE CONSTITUTION OF THE UNITED STATES AGAINST ALL ENEMIES, FOREIGN AND DOMESTIC; THAT I WILL BEAR TRUE FAITH AND ALLEGIANCE TO THE SAME; THAT I TAKE THIS OBLIGATION FREELY, WITHOUT ANY MENTAL RESERVATION OR PURPOSE OF EVASION; AND THAT I WILL WELL AND FAITHFULLY DISCHARGE THE DUTIES OF THE OFFICE ON WHICH I AM ABOUT TO ENTER.**

Long story short, violation of the oath is a crime and

there are punishments for that violation—including fines, removal from office, and imprisonment. **U.S. Code Title 5 § 7311** and **Title 18 § 1918** lay out the punishments and further expound on what would be a violation. The first couple of clauses are the same as we have seen before; attempting or advocating for overthrowing the government. We know that is not what was done here. But that leaves us **Clauses 3 and 4**:

> (3) PARTICIPATES IN A STRIKE, OR ASSERTS THE RIGHT TO STRIKE, AGAINST THE GOVERNMENT OF THE UNITED STATES OR THE GOVERNMENT OF THE DISTRICT OF COLUMBIA; OR
>
> (4) IS A MEMBER OF AN ORGANIZATION OF EMPLOYEES OF THE GOVERNMENT OF THE UNITED STATES OR OF INDIVIDUALS EMPLOYED BY THE GOVERNMENT OF THE DISTRICT OF COLUMBIA THAT HE KNOWS ASSERTS THE RIGHT TO STRIKE AGAINST THE GOVERNMENT OF THE UNITED STATES OR THE GOVERNMENT OF THE DISTRICT OF COLUMBIA.

So, had these members of the House of Representatives engaged in a "strike" against the government? Had they refused to perform their duties? In this particular instance, the answer is "no". Their duty of certifying the results of the Presidential Election had, at that point in time, not yet happened. And even if they voted against certification, that would still be doing their duty. If they refused to show up to debate and vote, it might be a "strike". But here, acting outside of Congress, they had not committed any crime.

Trying to disenfranchise over 10 million voters may be described using adjectives like:

- Unethical
- Unscrupulous
- Self-serving
- Contemptible
- Reprobate
- Ignoble
- Callous
- Virulent
- Egomaniacal
- Anti-democratic
- Anti-American

That all said, there is nothing illegal or un-Constitutional about attempting to usurp democracy for one's own personal or party gain, distasteful as that may be. And the fault for that lies right in the heart of our Constitution itself.

*Photo by **Gayatri Malhotra**[13] on **Unsplash***

---

[13] HTTPS://UNSPLASH.COM/@GMALHOTRA

FUTURE POLICIES OF THE REPUBLICAN PARTY

Once founded to stop the spread of slavery, how far will the future Republican Party be from these ideals?

Photo by **JAMES HAMMOND**[14] on **UNSPLASH**

---

[14] HTTPS://UNSPLASH.COM/@JAMESMHAMMOND

» Key Points

- *The Republican Party was formed with progressive policies on personal freedoms, labor and wage protections, protecting immigrants, unifying people across many beliefs, and much more.*

- *After gaining near monopolistic political control for over 70 years, the Republican Party became an entrenched establishment that changed its values in order to maintain that power.*

- *As the Republican Party continues to evolve, it will have an agenda that differs greatly from what Republicans even from a few years ago would consider sacrosanct.*

On May 17, 1860, an only six-year-old political party published their second ever platform which commenced (courtesy of the UNIVERSITY OF CALIFORNIA SANTA BARBARA "THE AMERICAN PRESIDENCY PROJECT"[15]):

> THAT THE HISTORY OF THE NATION DURING THE LAST FOUR YEARS, HAS FULLY ESTABLISHED THE PROPRIETY AND NECESSITY OF THE ORGANIZATION AND PERPETUATION OF THE... PARTY, AND THAT THE CAUSES WHICH CALLED IT INTO EXISTENCE ARE PERMANENT IN THEIR NATURE, AND NOW, MORE THAN EVER BEFORE, DEMAND ITS PEACEFUL AND CONSTITUTIONAL TRIUMPH.

Thus began an agenda that laid out broad goals that the members of this party felt expressed a moral imperative to protect this nation and all its people from the demagogues of the political machinery that were only interested in maintaining their power. Among those ideals were:

---

[15] HTTPS://WWW.PRESIDENCY.UCSB.EDU/DOCUMENTS/REPUBLICAN-PARTY-PLATFORM-1860

- **Personal Freedom:** *That the normal condition... of the United States is that of freedom: That, as our [forefathers]... ordained that "no persons should be deprived of life, liberty or property without due process of law," it becomes our duty, by legislation, whenever such legislation is necessary, to maintain this provision of the Constitution against all attempts to violate it...*

- **Labor and Wages:** *...[T]o encourage the development of the industrial interests of the whole country... we [support] policy... which secures to the workingmen liberal wages, to agriculture remunerative prices, to mechanics and manufacturers an adequate reward for their skill, labor, and enterprise, and to the nation commercial prosperity and independence.*

- **Social Welfare:** *...[T]hat the federal government ought to render immediate and efficient aid...*

- **Immigration:** *[The] party is opposed to any... legislation by which the rights of citizens hitherto accorded to immigrants from foreign lands shall be abridged or impaired; and in favor of giving a full and efficient protection to the rights of all classes of citizens, whether native or naturalized, both at home and abroad.*

- **Environmentalism:** *That appropriations by Congress for river and harbor improvements of a national character... are authorized by the Constitution, and justified by the obligation of Government...*

- **Partisanship:** *...[W]e invite the co-operation of all citizens, however differing on other questions, who* *substantially agree with us in their affirmance* (sic) *and support.*

- **Human Rights:** *That we brand the recent [actions of our government], aided by perversions of judicial power, as a crime against humanity and a burning shame to our country and age; and we call upon Congress to take prompt and efficient measures for the total and final suppression of that [terrible act]…*

- **Federal Police Power:** *…[W]e denounce the lawless invasion by armed [federal] force[s] of the soil of any state or territory, no matter under what pretext, as among the gravest of crimes.*

And finally, the Party stated:

> …[N]O… MEMBER OF CONGRESS [FROM OUR PARTY] HAS UTTERED OR COUNTENANCED THE THREATS OF DISUNION SO OFTEN MADE BY [THE OPPOSITION] MEMBERS, WITHOUT REBUKE AND WITH APPLAUSE FROM THEIR POLITICAL ASSOCIATES; AND WE DENOUNCE THOSE THREATS OF DISUNION, IN CASE OF A POPULAR OVERTHROW OF THEIR ASCENDENCY *(SIC)* AS DENYING THE VITAL PRINCIPLES OF A FREE GOVERNMENT, AND AS AN AVOWAL OF CONTEMPLATED TREASON, WHICH IT IS THE IMPERATIVE DUTY OF AN INDIGNANT PEOPLE STERNLY TO REBUKE AND FOREVER SILENCE.

These policies and more as laid out made this political party very popular among the northern States and fairly despised in the south. And amazingly, this was the Republican Party of 1860—far and away from the platform of the Republican Party today. What happened to this progressive party?

» BECOMING THE GRAND OLD PARTY

Is it odd to read about a Republican Party that supported wage protections? One that point blank stated a preference for social welfare? A party that wanted to expand and shelter immigrants and make sure they had the full protection of the law? A group of people who called out with disgust the use of police powers on innocent civilians and dared to point out that their own country had committed "a crime against humanity"?

*Photo by **RONDA DARBY**[16] on **UNSPLASH***

The Republicans used this platform to quickly rise to power in the legislatures of States and the Federal Government—to the point where with this declaration they gained control of both chambers of Congress and put Abraham Lincoln in the White House. As discussed

---

[16] HTTPS://UNSPLASH.COM/@RONDA

EARLIER, though, Lincoln gained the Presidency with just 39.7% of the popular vote (though it is fair to again note that popular voting for President was not universal among all States and that many, many people were disenfranchised from their vote due to race, gender, land-ownership status, and various other reasons).

After the Civil War, Republicans controlled the Presidency almost exclusively—save for a couple of brief sojourns for Grover Cleveland and Woodrow Wilson—until Franklin Delano Roosevelt rose to prominence in the 1930s. Over the same timeframe, Republicans held domination over both chambers of Congress 64% of the time and at least one chamber another 22%, meaning they had some level of legislative power at least 86% of the time.

In other words, the Republican Party became the establishment. All of the issues the original party rallied against, all of the sins that the entrenched Democrats committed, all of the problems associated with being in power for power's sake came to fruition within the party itself. As such, the roles of the two major parties completely reversed over time.

Well, completely reversed is perhaps a bridge too far. Many of the original policies have been maintained by the Republican Party, such as promoting States' governments above the Federal one and consistent support for unabridged rights to bear arms. However, even stalwart policies like these are quite in flux today. Look no further than when the FCC under President Donald Trump rolled back Net Neutrality rules. The State of California implemented its own rules (similar to what they had done with emission standards in the past), and the Federal Government and Republicans sued to stop it. They said that the State had no right to implement a policy on its own and that the will of the Federal Government—even the absence of promoting a will—triumphed.

It is fairer to say that the policies of the Republican Party have transformed over time. This is not necessarily a rebuke on what those policies were or have become, but more a study on how fundamentally opinions can alter and mutate over time. The reasons are varied, but at the end of the day it comes down to one thing: voters. The modern and future Republican Party will espouse whatever they believe will get them the most votes; not a thesis of ideas for people to rally around and let the chips fall where they may.

As such, on this day in March 2021, we must ask:

WHAT WILL THE REPUBLICAN PARTY BELIEVE IN NEXT?

» NEXTGEN POLITICS

In order to understand and project what Republican policies will be, we have to understand what demographics they are building the party around. Without getting too deep into the numbers, **PEW RESEARCH CENTER**[17] has made it clear that although white people—especially men—with lower levels of post-secondary education are making up less of the population, they are making up a much larger proportion of Republican and Republican-leaning voters. Because of this, the Republican Party has embraced a form of populism that

---

[17] HTTPS://WWW.PEWRESEARCH.ORG/POLITICS/2020/06/02/IN-CHANGING-U-S-ELECTORATE-RACE-AND-EDUCATION-REMAIN-STARK-DIVIDING-LINES/

decrees that these groups are being suppressed and forgotten at the expense of others. This will be the basis for their policies, but often in surprising ways with tertiary benefits.

At the same time, the party cannot depend upon this group because it is shrinking as a percentage of the total population and further aging and dying out. A totally different type of coalition must be built around this group while at the same time not disenfranchising them. This commences with a particular set of people they made significant headway with starting in 2016.

» UNIONS

Members of unions—especially in midwestern States with large or formerly large industrial bases—used to be the bastion of the Democratic Party. Republicans have made it clear that they are not proponents of organized labor and believe in full free-market economies, even in staff negotiations. Despite this, nearly half of households that had members in a union supported Trump in 2016. Aside from Democrats assuming they had this vote and did not put in much effort to court them, there was and still is a growing gap between union leadership and line workers. The workers continue to lose out on benefits for their membership while not seeing any sacrifice from their leaders or understanding of their plights.

And this is the wedge that Republicans can entrench themselves into. Their position can be restated that they are pro-union in a way that union leadership cannot be there for the workers. Protectionist policies are one thing they offered at the time, and they could continue to propose a suite of government intervention programs to protect and support union members. In order to be "for the people" and "for the workers", they must at least *claim* that they can offer more as a partner than the members are getting from their own infrastructure and the Democrats—whether they intend to do so or not.

Photo by **EHIMETALOR AKHERE UNUABONA**[18] on **UNSPLASH**

At the same time, there is an added benefit of reaching new people. While the general image of white men in factory unions is a prevailing one, it is largely incorrect. According to the **BUREAU OF LABOR STATISTICS 2020 REPORT ON UNION MEMBERS**[19]:

> **BLACK WORKERS REMAINED MORE LIKELY TO BE UNION MEMBERS THAN WHITE, ASIAN, OR HISPANIC WORKERS.**

---

[18] HTTPS://UNSPLASH.COM/@THEEASTLONDONPHOTOGRAPHER
[19] HTTPS://WWW.BLS.GOV/NEWS.RELEASE/PDF/UNION2.PDF

And that number has risen from 11.2% in 2019 to 12.3% in 2020. The same is true with Latinx workers going from 8.9% to 9.8%. Appealing to the core base of white workers now will have a secondary benefit of peeling off some minority voters that tend to vote in much higher proportions for Democrats. And being a blind spot for Democrats is another benefit in which a plotting Republican Party has succeeded in the past, and they could do so again.

UNION AFFILIATION BY STATE

	20+% of workers union members
	15–19.9% of workers union members
	10–14.9% of workers union members
	5–9.9% of workers union members
	0–4.9% of workers union members

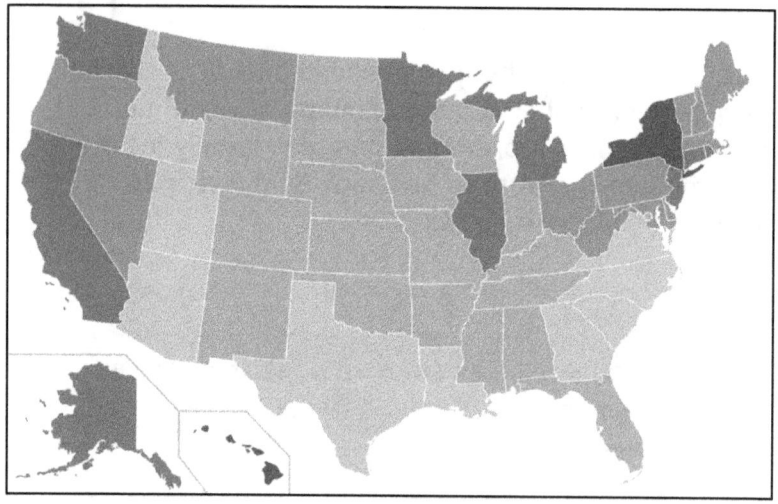

MARGINALCOST, CC BY-SA 4.0[20], via Wikimedia Commons.

---

[20] HTTPS://CREATIVECOMMONS.ORG/LICENSES/BY-SA/4.0

Even though union membership is at the lowest in Republican strongholds in the South and Center, one must remember: it is not about capturing everyone. The only important thing—as far as the Party is concerned—is to get more votes than their opponents. When margins across States are less than 10,000 votes, even a small shift here could have a massive impact.

» IMMIGRATION

In order to appeal to Latinx voters, though, it will take more than support for workers. Rhetoric among Republican candidates trends towards unabashedly anti-Hispanic sentiment and as such the group tends to reject the party en masse. Except Hispanic people are not monolithic and come from an array of backgrounds and cultures. As **PEW RESEARCH CENTER NOTED IN OCTOBER 2020**[21], voters of Cuban descent are more likely to lean Republican 58% to 38% versus all other Hispanics that are the opposite at 32% to 65%.

To put it another way, Republicans have had great success with Cubans. As a specific example, it was Cuban voting patterns in Florida that gave the State handily to Donald Trump in 2020. Other Latinx groups with people originating or descended from places like Mexico, Ecuador, and Venezuela are places where Republicans can make inroads. Overall, many in the Latin world tend to be more religious and conservative in their beliefs, which would align them closer to the current Republican Party. Further, a significant proportion grew up in rough situations whether it was economic collapse, perceived socialism gone wrong, or violent conditions. In any of these situations, it makes a case for a strong government that can protect people and their values.

---

[21] HTTPS://WWW.PEWRESEARCH.ORG/FACT-TANK/2020/10/02/MOST-CUBAN-AMERICAN-VOTERS-IDENTIFY-AS-REPUBLICAN-IN-2020/

What is keeping Republicans from gathering a greater share of these groups is their stance on immigration and their treatment of people trying to escape those conditions. That said, it would not take substantial mental gymnastics for Republicans to change their tune here. They can—and will—say that they were not against immigration; just that they were against undocumented (a.k.a. "illegal", but they won't use that term in the future) immigrants. Instead, they will present policies that will create easier paths for people to come to America to work and perhaps stay and become citizens. They will portray the Democrats as the ones who want lawlessness and chaos at the border while they want to give people a path they can understand and follow.

Photo by *Greg Bulla*[22] on *Unsplash*

Meanwhile, it is not just to gain voters from Latin countries, but also due to another issue facing America.

---

[22] HTTPS://UNSPLASH.COM/@GREGBULLA

Currently, the birthrate is below replacement (i.e., on average a woman is having less than two children) and it is trending further downward. At some point in the near future, we will need immigrants just to replace those workers that were lost. And imagine if those workers came here on a government program created and supported by Republicans, and then join unions!

Of course, Hispanic groups are not the only ones an immigration path like this will appeal to. Many eastern European and former Soviet bloc countries have very similar cultures when it comes to religion and conservatism. These countries are often at odds with Western Europe on how the European Union should be run and how to protect their people and interests. Expanding a similar program to these types of people will further allow them to be "pro-immigrant" while also having a sizable amount of those immigrants be white Europeans, thus not disenfranchising the core base.

» ANTI-DISCRIMINATION

Speaking of that core base of older, whiter, more male people—as noted that group is shrinking in the country and over time will come closer to being a true minority. While America is "minority majority", that is only by adding up vastly different groups together. And white people are not singular in their cultures and beliefs, either, and that is the argument that the Republican Party will make.

While the Republican Party was founded mostly to stop the spread of slavery and to dismantle it where it existed, once in power they failed to stop the spread of discrimination. Further, as time went on, the party became the progenitor of discriminatory laws and actions. Today, the Republican Party would never say they are for laws that discriminate, but they do say they are against laws like Affirmative Action and policies like extending Title IX protections to all gender and sexual identities. The reason for this, they claim, is that it causes an affront to religious freedoms, and that for some reason one part of the first Amendment ranks higher than another part.

Photo by **SHARON MCCUTCHEON**[23] on **UNSPLASH**

This is where their populist message to those who feel disenfranchised will find a new turn. Instead of fighting against anti-discrimination laws, they will instead embrace them as a weapon against Democrats. Here, they will say that these shrinking groups are being marginalized and need all the same protection of the laws that minority groups get. The argument will expand to how—in order to have "fairness", "an even playing field", and "equal opportunity"—that all people must be treated the same. Instead of fighting against laws to limit discrimination, they will battle for those laws to include

---

[23] HTTPS://UNSPLASH.COM/@SHARONMCCUTCHEON

their core constituents so that they are "not lost in a changing America".

» PERSONAL FREEDOMS

Expounding further on discrimination, in 1856, the **REPUBLICAN PLATFORM**[24] stated:

> **THAT, WITH OUR REPUBLICAN FATHERS, WE HOLD IT TO BE A SELF-EVIDENT TRUTH, THAT ALL MEN ARE ENDOWED WITH THE INALIENABLE RIGHT TO LIFE, LIBERTY, AND THE PURSUIT OF HAPPINESS, AND THAT THE PRIMARY OBJECT AND ULTERIOR DESIGN OF OUR FEDERAL GOVERNMENT WERE TO SECURE THESE RIGHTS TO ALL PERSONS UNDER ITS EXCLUSIVE JURISDICTION...**

It would seem, then, that the Republican Party from the get-go has been about protecting all people no matter their demographics, conditions, or preferences. Except, of course, they have not. As noted, they have fought relentlessly against gender identity and sexuality equality, created legislation that marginalized and unduly impacted people of color, passed massive regulations and programs to control what people see and consume, and have been actively involved in witch-hunts against people even for their political thoughts.

Despite this, there have been areas where Republicans as a party have still fought vehemently for personal freedom. This has been about freedoms of speech (even

---

[24] HTTPS://WWW.PRESIDENCY.UCSB.EDU/DOCUMENTS/REPUBLICAN-PARTY-PLATFORM-1856

hateful speech), religion, commerce, and property. Yet even these stalwarts of Republican core values will come to an end and be replaced with a moralistic dictatorial approach.

Photo by **MATT SEYMOUR**[25] on **UNSPLASH**

---

[25] HTTPS://UNSPLASH.COM/@MATTSEYMOUR

In order to fight the expansion of populations in liberal centers—especially cities—they will endorse policies that control how land can be used and developed. To "protect women", they will try to pass laws like Switzerland, France, Denmark, the Netherlands, and Austria have that say how women can dress (these countries all have **APPROVED BANS ON FULL FACE COVERINGS LIKE BURQAS**[26]). Other situations will include limiting grants for artistic expressions they find "offensive", and trying to eliminate existing art the same way statues of slave holders and Confederates have been removed in the early 2020s.

The bottom line is, the Republican Party will no longer even pretend they believe in "personal freedom" and instead will replace it with the "moral imperative" to help people live a "better life".

» Gun Control

As discussed earlier, since 1856 the Republican Party has been an adamant supporter of the 2nd Amendment right of keeping and bearing arms. While not often thought of as a civil rights issue, gun owners and those who desire to own firearms are expressing their interpretation of what the 2nd Amendment means and how it aligns to the freedom of individuals. We are not here to discuss the merits of that, just note for over 165 years Republicans have made it clear that the government should have no say in gun ownership.

Of course, that will have to change.

In order to be the party of the "moral center", Republicans must acknowledge that there are "others"

---

[26] HTTPS://WWW.NPR.ORG/2021/03/07/974630640/SWITZERLAND-APPROVES-BAN-ON-FACE-COVERINGS-IN-PUBLIC

who are not in this center, and therefore cannot be trusted. And there is one civil right they have been able to successfully restrict and uphold in many courts: **voting**. Convicted felons, even after serving a full sentence, can be disenfranchised from their vote by the way the law is written and how the courts have interpreted the Constitution. States and Territories that have these types of systems are shown below for you to make you own judgement on what particular areas are mostly covered versus those that are not:

MAP SHOWING DISENFRANCHISEMENT LAWS BY STATE

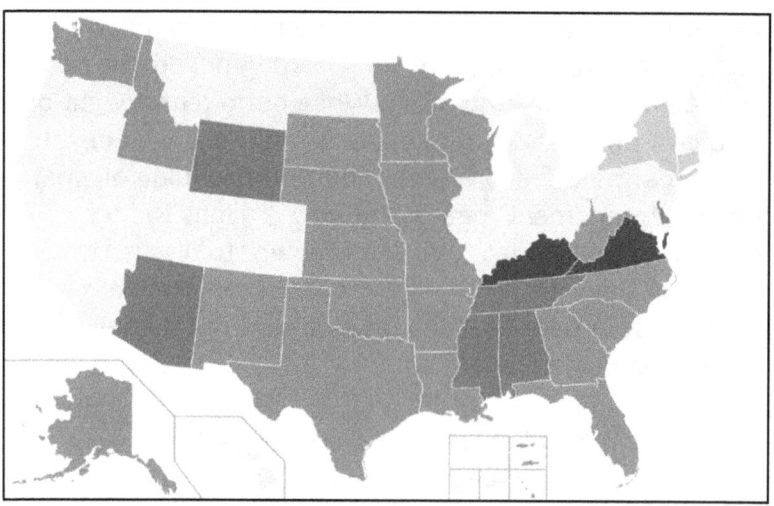

JayCoop, CC BY-SA 4.0[27], via Wikimedia Commons.

---

[27] HTTPS://CREATIVECOMMONS.ORG/LICENSES/BY-SA/4.0

Further, if we look at the percentage of the population that are disenfranchised in these States and Territories based upon the laws, we see this:

MAP SHOWING ESTIMATED DISENFRANCHISEMENT BY STATE

	Less than 0,5%
	0,5% - 1%
	1,5% - 2,5%
	2,5 - 3,5%
	3,5% - 4,5%
	4,5% - 5,5%
	5,5% - 8,5%
	8,5% - 9,5%
	More than 9,5%

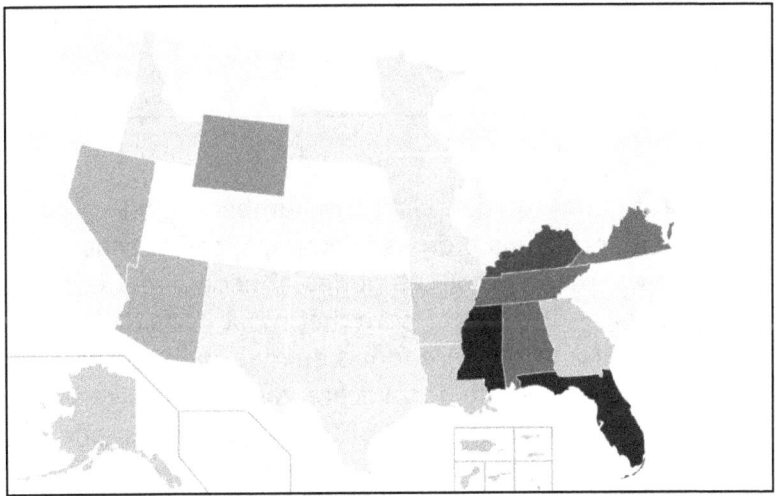

JANKÜHN, CC BY-SA 4.0[28], via Wikimedia Commons.

Ergo, if one civil right can be restricted for being a former felon, certainly another right could be constrained for the "safety" of all and to protect that "moral center". Of course, we then need to ask what populations are

---

[28] HTTPS://CREATIVECOMMONS.ORG/LICENSES/BY-SA/4.0

disproportionately incarcerated in the United States (not to mention that the United States has the largest percentage of its population in prison and jail in the world to begin with):

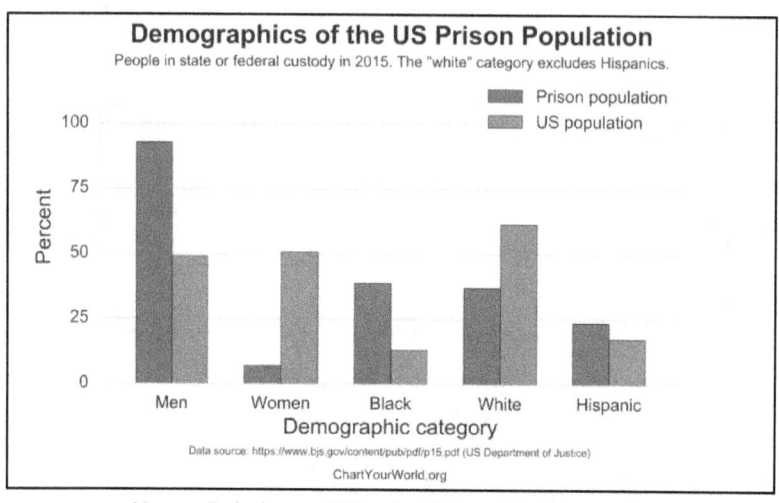

MorganRehnberg, CC0, via Wikimedia Commons.

Again, not going too deep into the numbers—and acknowledging this is a gross oversimplification that glosses over many other categories of people and various demographics—it is fair to note that most people of color who are incarcerated were found guilty of nonviolent crimes. Further, people of color are vastly more likely to be arrested for and convicted of the same crimes, and serve longer sentences compared to their white counterparts.

That is not the nuanced discussion or argument the Republican Party will be looking to have. Instead, they will want to extend restrictions on civil rights—including gun ownership that they have fought so hard for their entire existence—for "dangerous convicted criminals". It just so happens that doing so would disproportionately impact people of color, which would once again soothe that base from which they are building the party.

» FEDERALISM AND REGULATION

To implement the removal of rights like this, the Republican Party could continue to work on laws and regulation on a State-by-State basis. They have successfully been able to make the most impact at the State level for decades, which in turn helped set the direction at the Federal level. Since the Republican Party has always stood for States' rights, it seems a natural progression to do so.

Except we have already covered examples such as with California and the FCC where the Republican party is trying to use Federalism to push their desires downward from the top. And it is not stopping on that issue as they have already tried and are currently trying to do the same for issues like environmentalism (more on this later), abortion access, the definition of marriage, and more. One particular area they will zone in on will be voting logistics and rights because—demographically—they need to control where and how people vote in order to ever hold a majority at the Federal level again. Natural voting patterns would not eliminate Republicans from serving any particular Federal office, but their numbers would be significantly limited without the gerrymandering that has been further expanding in the 2020s.

As discussed above, using Federalism to create new definitions of protected classes of people will also be on their agenda. In similar protectionist themes, they will advocate for growing Federal policing agencies—which would contrast the *"well regulated Militia"* that the **2nd Amendment** specifically lays out. So here again Republicans would want to take power away from the

States (or at least some of the States) and confer that into the Federal government.

This, of course, can only lead to one thing: regulation. In order to implement policy and force others to follow it, one must have regulation and agencies to enforce and prosecute those decrees. We are seeing this come to fruition now in the Republican Party's fight against "cancel culture". Members of Congress and State legislatures are trying to create rules around how social media and online communication work. They say it is about "freedom of speech" except the Republican Party of yesteryear would have protected a private company since "free speech" is about public settings and relates to the government not restricting it; certainly not how a private company acts. But if they want to push this definition, it means they want regulation and Federal enforcement.

Photo by **C DUSTIN**[29] *on* **UNSPLASH**

And this is what happens when you define yourself as morally superior. If you are and you want others to act

---

[29] HTTPS://UNSPLASH.COM/@DIANAMIA

the way you believe they should act, then you are going to regulate them and use the tools of the Federal government to do so. Since the Republican Party will want to be that "moral center", then they will be the biggest proponents of regulation and Federal interference.

» WELFARE AND ENVIRONMENTALISM

> "TONIGHT, WE RENEW OUR RESOLVE THAT AMERICA WILL NEVER BE A SOCIALIST COUNTRY."
>
> *PRESIDENT DONALD TRUMP DURING HIS STATE OF THE UNION ON FEBRUARY 5, 2019*

> "WE WILL PROTECT MEDICARE AND SOCIAL SECURITY. WE WILL ALWAYS AND VERY STRONGLY PROTECT PATIENTS WITH PRE-EXISTING CONDITIONS. AND THAT IS A PLEDGE FROM THE ENTIRE REPUBLICAN PARTY."
>
> *PRESIDENT DONALD TRUMP DURING THE REPUBLICAN NATIONAL CONVENTION ON AUGUST 28, 2020*

The United States of America is a socialist country. We have a program that is literally called "Social Security" that is the very definition of socialism. Any program that the government runs by taking money from some people to give a benefit to many or all others is socialism—such as building and maintaining roads or having a standing armed forces.

However, when the Republican Party rallies against "socialism" they are really saying they are against "social safety net" programs. Except, apparently, they do care about making sure ones that large swaths of their constituents use are maintained, robust, and available. Suffice to say, the Republican Party of today is for socialism in certain situations that are beneficial to them.

So why would it stop there?

Yet, directly providing socialist programs to people would not mesh with the Republican brand. Instead, they will work within a framework they can find more palatable. For instance, instead of more regulation and stick diplomacy to get employers to pay employees more (i.e., minimum/living wage, protections for independent contractors, etcetera), they would want to take a more "carrot" approach. This would come in the form of subsidies and tax breaks for companies that meet criteria such as paying a higher average wage. They would present this as an incentive for private companies that keeps the government out of their affairs. In reality, this would amount to corporate handouts instead of to the people, but in either case it would still be *welfare*.

On the same subject of business, the Republican Party will have to change their tune on environmentalism. Green energy is a large and growing industry in America and already many forms of it are cheaper than fossil fuel alternatives. As economies of scale continue, eventually it will not be cost efficient for companies and people not to use renewable sources whenever and wherever possible. Continuing to provide subsidies to fossil fuel companies with large foreign holdings and ownership will not only be anti-competitive, it will become a national security concern.

This is where Republicans can easily turn and embrace policies much closer to right wing governments elsewhere in the world. Protectionist policies require that the country not be dependent on foreign organizations for energy and similar production. If an important slice of the pool of potential voters are isolationists, then the Republican Party must embrace companies that can produce all of our needs domestically. Expect to see a full embrace of the business of environmentalism.

Photo by **KARSTEN WÜRTH**[30] on **UNSPLASH**

» GOVERNMENT SPENDING

Subsidies to businesses cost money. Building infrastructure and removing fossil fuel use from the grid and homes costs even more money. Regulating States, expanded Federal programs, supplementary Federal policies, more Federal police—everything previously discussed is going to cost money.

---

[30] HTTPS://UNSPLASH.COM/@KARSTEN_WUERTH

Fiscal conservatism is already dead in the Republican Party. Even without the COVID-19 Pandemic (which is an emergency situation that should not be considered in any statistics), Republicans have used their time in control of Congress and the White House cutting taxes and increasing spending. For instance, the military and adjacent activities already amount to nearly $1 trillion (with a 'T'!) and is growing annually, even though the country is not officially at war anywhere.

Of course, they are not solely to blame for this, but it is a matter of factual record that there has not been a balanced budget since FY2001, and that one did not work out due to 9/11 and the recession that followed.

The only way to pay for all this without cutting costs elsewhere and not increasing taxes is with either novel revenue generating mechanisms or taking on more debt. And this is what the story of the Republican Party will be: not one of even discussing cutting spending (except to programs that go against their moral imperative), but to one that explains why they are better at managing novel revenue sources and debt.

» COURT REFORM

Even with all of these pivots away from historical and current policies, the trends are not in favor of the Republican Party. Not that they are in any danger of going extinct any time soon (save a complete schism), but changing demographics are ushering in new places of Democratic control. Look no further than the flip of the Senate seats in Georgia in the 2020/2021 runoff election from Republican to Democrat to see where and how things are changing. Even in a State like Texas the demographics and voting patterns are moving further away from Republican control.

This is not the case everywhere, but it certainly is in a lot of key areas. What this will lead to is Executive control being nearly monopolized by Democrats in various States and at the Federal level, which in turn gives the Democrats control of appointing judges to the courts. Although Republicans have been amazingly successful in getting their desired judges appointed—especially from January 2017 to January 2021—even those people will eventually move on, retire, die, or leave their positions for any variety of reasons. The longer Democrats control things at the Presidential and Governor levels, the more they will be able to replace conservative judges with liberal ones, thus impacting the long-term direction of the country.

Photo by **DAVID VEKSLER**[31] on **UNSPLASH**

---

[31] HTTPS://UNSPLASH.COM/@DAVIDVEKSLER

In order to mitigate the "liberal agenda" of "packing the courts" with their picks, the Republican Party will embrace reforms on the Judicial Branch. This will come in the form of term limits for judges and the ability for legislatures to overrule court decisions. Basically, it will be a way to "re-balance" the co-equal branches so that one—the legislature—is a little more equal than the other two.

» Party On

Is it difficult to imagine a Republican Party that supports unions, has an open immigration policy, wants to expand the classes of protected people, tells people how to live their lives, pushes gun control legislation, creates and implements new regulations, and embraces welfare and environmentalism? Is it just as difficult to align the Republican Party of the 2020s with the one that put forth its manifestos in 1856 and 1860?

At the end of the day, like any organization or person, the Republican Party has the right to define itself in any way it pleases. The Party has evolved over time to what it is today, and will continue to metamorphosize going forward. Where it will land after this is beyond our purview, but rest assured that so long as it exists the Republican Party will always become something else.

If you are looking for a political party that is fiscally conservative, respects and protects the rights of individuals and their property, wants the government out of your daily life, and believes your local government is more important than the Federal one—the Republican Party of today is most likely not for you.

The future Republican Party certainly is not.

*A female African Bush Elephant in Mikumi National Park, Tanzania. Photo and description by **MUHAMMAD MAHDI KARIM**[32], **GFDL 1.2**[33], via Wikimedia Commons.*

---

[32] HTTPS://COMMONS.WIKIMEDIA.ORG/WIKI/FILE:AFRICAN_BUSH_ELEPHANT.JPG
[33] HTTP://WWW.GNU.ORG/LICENSES/OLD-LICENSES/FDL-1.2.HTML

LIZ CHENEY & FRIENDS ARE NOT LEAVING THE REPUBLICAN PARTY

But maybe they could be convinced if Joe Manchin & friends left the Democratic Party with them

Liz Cheney (R-WY) spoke to a small crowd at the American Legion in Buffalo, Wyoming on October 26, 2013 during what would become a failed attempt to gain the Republican nomination for the United States Senate. She would later win a seat in the House of Representatives in 2016, a seat she has successfully defended through her current term in the Congress that sat in 2021. Photo by **MILONICA**[34], **CC BY-SA 3.0**[35], via Wikimedia Commons.

---

[34] HTTPS://COMMONS.WIKIMEDIA.ORG/WIKI/FILE:LIZ_CHENEY_IN_BUFFALO_WYOMING.JPG

[35] HTTPS://CREATIVECOMMONS.ORG/LICENSES/BY-SA/3.0

» Key Points

- *Representative Liz Cheney (R-WY) had once again gained the ire of her Party by accepting a position from Speaker Nancy Pelosi (D-CA) to investigate the attack on the United States Capitol Building on January 6, 2021.*

- *She was not the only one in the Republican Party who had been censured and humiliated as the conference moved further away from their values; nor was this a uniquely Republican problem as there were those in the Democratic Party like Senator Joe Manchin (D-WV) who buck unilateral, partisan action.*

- *In the end, these politicians shared more in common with each other than their contemporaries— not in policy, but in the approach to government, conversation, compromise, and duty to the country above self and Party.*

> I'M NOT THREATENING ANYBODY... WHAT I'M SAYING IS, IT WAS SHOCKING TO ME THAT IF A PERSON IS A REPUBLICAN, THEY GET... THEIR COMMITTEE ASSIGNMENTS FROM THE REPUBLICAN CONFERENCE. FOR [SOMEBODY] TO ACCEPT COMMITTEE ASSIGNMENTS FROM [DEMOCRATIC] SPEAKER PELOSI... {SHRUGS}
>
> HOUSE MINORITY LEADER KEVIN MCCARTHY (R-CA) STATED THIS ON JULY 1, 2021 IN RELATION TO REPRESENTATIVE LIZ CHENEY ACCEPTING A POSITION ON THE JANUARY 6TH SELECT COMMITTEE TO INVESTIGATE THE INSURRECTION AT THE UNITED STATES CAPITOL BUILDING ON THAT NAMED DAY IN 2021.

After Republican Senators ensured that no 9/11-style bipartisan commission would be created to explore the attack on the United States Capitol Building that occurred on January 6, 2021, House of Representatives Speaker Nancy Pelosi (D-CA) used her position to put forward an investigation run solely by her chamber. On June 30, 2021, that vote finally came to fruition with the House voting 222–190 to create the **January 6th Select Committee**. All of the votes for the Committee came from Democrats (none voted against it), as well as just 2 Republicans: Liz Cheney (R-WY) and Adam Kinzinger (R-IL). It should be noted that 19 Republicans did not vote at all, giving an implicit agreement without it getting on the record. Four positions at the time were vacant, split evenly between Democrats and Republicans.

One person that definitely voted against the Committee was Pelosi's corresponding California Representative Kevin McCarthy (R-CA), who was also House Minority Leader. By the next day, reports were leaking out that McCarthy had a meeting with his fellow House Republicans and threatened that anyone who took a position on the Committee from Pelosi was in danger of losing all of their dearly held spots. Yet despite that warning, one woman would not be deterred and gladly accepted her position as the only Republican—as of early July 2021—appointed to the Committee by Pelosi:

> **I'M HONORED TO BE ON THIS COMMITTEE. WE HAVE AN OBLIGATION TO HAVE A THOROUGH, SOBER INVESTIGATION OF WHAT HAPPENED LEADING UP TO JANUARY 6TH AND THE ATTACK ON THE CAPITOL THAT DAY.**
>
> *REPRESENTATIVE LIZ CHENEY (R-WY) ON JULY 1, 2021 ADDRESSING REPORTERS AFTER THE ANNOUNCEMENT OF THE JANUARY 6TH SELECT COMMITTEE (CLARIFIED FOR PAUSES AND TRANSITIONS).*

This was not the first time that Cheney had gained the ire of her Party. At the second impeachment for President Donald Trump for his alleged role in the attacks, Cheney voted with nine other House Republicans in favor of impeachment. After this, she survived votes for removal from leadership and committee positions, censure from her own Party in her State, and other intimidations. As she not only remained unapologetic but downright hostile to the idea of supporting Donald Trump in any way, the former President's supporters eventually got to enough of the remaining House Republicans and they voted to remove her from her position of power on May 12, 2021. Despite the constant recriminations and humiliations, Cheney would not back down.

President Joe Biden and Vice President Kamala Harris met with a bipartisan group of lawmakers to discuss infrastructure on April 12, 2021, an effort that eventually failed and required creating a different working group. Even after that new group came to an agreeable solution, all members immediately faced push-back from their own parties. These people legitimately wanted to work together, but their own parties were making it impossible. Photo and base-description by THE WHITE HOUSE[36], Public domain, via Wikimedia Commons.

Once word got out that Cheney had accepted a position from Pelosi, McCarthy was quick to speak to the press:

36
HTTPS://COMMONS.WIKIMEDIA.ORG/WIKI/FILE:PRESIDENT_JOE_BIDEN_MEETS_WITH_A_BIPARTISAN_GROUP_OF_HOUSE_AND_SENATE_MEMBERS.JPG

> **AS YOU KNOW HOW CONGRESS WORKS: YOU GET ELECTED BY YOUR DISTRICT, AND YOU GET YOUR COMMITTEES FROM YOUR CONFERENCE... I DON'T KNOW IN HISTORY WHERE SOMEONE WOULD GO GET THEIR COMMITTEE ASSIGNMENTS FROM THE SPEAKER AND EXPECT TO HAVE THEM FROM THE CONFERENCE AS WELL. *{SHRUGS}***

McCarthy has made it clear through his many shrugs—he does not believe Republicans and Democrats should work together. Republicans manage themselves, Democrats manage themselves, and at no point shall the two meet. Of course, the only reason why Congress works this way is because of those like McCarthy who do not see their fellow Congresspeople as co-workers and patriots but as competitors and anti-Americans. And let us be clear, among those in power across the entire political spectrum are people like McCarthy; this is hardly a Republican-only position. However, Cheney is not one of those people. As she stated during that same press briefing:

> **I THINK IT'S CLEAR TO ALL THE PEOPLE ON THE [JANUARY 6TH SELECT] COMMITTEE THAT OUR OATH TO THE CONSTITUTION, OUR DUTY, OUR DEDICATION TO RULE OF LAW, AND THE PEACEFUL TRANSFER OF POWER, HAS TO COME ABOVE ANY, ANY CONCERN ABOUT PARTISANSHIP OR ABOUT POLITICS. AND I THINK THAT'S, THAT'S HUGELY IMPORTANT.**

Despite hearing McCarthy's position and comments from other people like him, when asked by a reporter if she believed she would be removed from her committee assignments, Cheney quickly responded:

> **I HAVE NOT BEEN [REMOVED FROM MY COMMITTEE ASSIGNMENTS]. BUT AGAIN, MY OATH, MY DUTY, ALL OF OUR OATHS AND OUR DUTY IS TO THE CONSTITUTION AND THAT WILL ALWAYS BE ABOVE POLITICS.**

By early July 2021, liberals of all stripes and other non-conservatives were salivating at this apparent falling out between top Republicans. Imagine that after being repudiated so many times that Cheney would switch teams and join the Democratic Party! She could have further tip the scales in the Democrat's favor and be a major talking point against Republicans in the then forthcoming 2022 mid-term elections (an election in which her own position would be up for grabs). Perhaps she would be like a crack in an iceberg that eventually gives way to a swath of disenfranchised Republicans looking for a new home? After all, there have been a handful of others in history who have switched sides. Why not her? And why not a deluge to come after her?

» QUEEN OF THE CONSERVATIVES

Those who believed Liz Cheney was about to join the Democratic Party had not paid attention to what her actual views were. Cheney's stances are conservative through-and-through with little room for interpretation.

On her own campaign website and the official House page she proudly touts positions and legislation that include:

- Protections for coal, oil, and natural gas producers;

- Creating exceptions for farms from environmental laws and policies;

- Repealing the Affordable Care Act in its totality;

- Hawkish action in Afghanistan, Russia, China, and other places;

- Furthering a financial stance that began with the 2017 Tax Cut and Jobs Act;

- Allowing conceal and carry for any and all arms, including those crossing State lines; and

- Extreme prejudice against undocumented immigrants, even refugees.

These are not the positions of someone who intends to be part of the Democratic Party of the 2020s! All right, if she could not fit in with the Democratic Party, where does she belong? While her viewpoints are conservative, that is not what the Republican Party of the 2020s is either. That conference has become populist and Trumpist, not anywhere in line with Cheney's ideas of how politics should work. After all, the Republican Party is the one moving further away from the right side of the spectrum to somewhere else entirely. As shown above, Cheney is as traditionally conservative as someone can be, yet her own party despises her instead of rallying to her cause. All she portends to want is to put the country before her own party, but at the same time use her politics to inform her final decisions and actions. Unfortunately for her, her biggest sin is just not falling in line enough.

Representative Liz Cheney (R-WY, right) posted a praiseworthy message on Twitter about President Donald Trump with this photo on September 29, 2018. Despite later protests, she voted in line with Trump's positions nearly 93% of the time while both were in office. **OFFICIAL WHITE HOUSE PHOTO AND BASE-DESCRIPTION BY JOYCE N. BOGHOSIAN**[37], *Public domain, via Wikimedia Commons.*

And Cheney was not the only one who found herself at odds with her own party. For instance, Senator Lisa Murkowski (R-AK) had also voted against many of her colleagues and joined Democrats in various actions, including to convict President Trump during his second impeachment trial. Like Cheney, she has been censured, threatened, cajoled, and experienced many worse actions. Those who have been treated like this have moved on in the past, including recent history.

---

[37] HTTPS://COMMONS.WIKIMEDIA.ORG/WIKI/FILE:PRESIDENT_DONALD_TRUMP_SIGNS_AN_APPROPRIATIONS_BILL.JPG

On July 8, 2019, then Representative Justin Amash (R-MI) submitted his resignation from the Republican Conference to none other than Mr. McCarthy and Ms. Cheney. At first he was an Independent but later went on to join the Libertarian Party. Days before his official resignation, he posted an **op-ed in the Washington Post**[38] stating in part:

> **These are consequences of a mind-set among the political class that loyalty to party is more important than serving the American people or protecting our governing institutions. The parties value winning for its own sake, and at whatever cost. Instead of acting as an independent branch of government and serving as a check on the executive branch, congressional leaders of both parties expect the House and Senate to act in obedience or opposition to the president and their colleagues on a partisan basis.**

At that point in time, anti-oligopolists thought this was the dam-breaking moment—that others would follow, the Republican party would schism between classical conservatives and Trump loyalists, and that there would be no way they could hold things together. Yet, hold-it-together is exactly what happened! No one followed Amash and he opted not to run for Congress or any other position, instead fading off as if he never existed.

---

[38] https://www.washingtonpost.com/opinions/justin-amash-our-politics-is-in-a-partisan-death-spiral-thats-why-im-leaving-the-gop/2019/07/04/afbe0480-9e3d-11e9-b27f-ed2942f73d70_story.html

In the end, it should be no surprise. Despite Congresspeople like Murkowski being vocal about their views in contrast to the Republican and/or Trump mainstream, that does not stop them from keeping the party together no matter what. For instance, during the nomination of Brett Kavanaugh to the Supreme Court, Murkowski made it abundantly clear that she would not vote for him. But when Senator Steve Daines (R-MT) could not attend the vote because he wanted to be at his daughter's wedding, things changed. Instead of voting "nay" and causing either a split vote or a potential loss (more on this later), she instead voted "present" so as to offset the missing Daines. Despite all the convictions she claimed, at the end of the day Murkowski still did the Republican Party's bidding.

And that is where those hoping to see the Republican Party fall apart or split in two are completely missing the bigger picture. In reality, the one thing that is keeping the Republicans together and the main thing they have in common is that they do not want the Democratic Party and its most liberal wing to have absolute control. If the Republican Party split in half or even 90/10, Democrats would win every single competitive race (so long as they stayed united, too). Sure, there would be a fair amount of both types of Republicans in Congress and almost all other positions of government around the country, but they would lose any semblance of power or direction at the Federal level.

That is why Cheney, Murkowski, and all of the people like them will not leave the Republican Party. Even should they lose their primaries or main elections, they will only attempt to come back as Republicans again. Even if the Republican Party continues to drift further from their conservative values, they believe they will have a better chance to change the Party's direction than to try to make a go of it alone.

» THE OTHER JOE

However, they are not exactly alone; Democrats have their own rogues to contend with. In the early days of President Biden's first term, that has been embodied by none other than Senator Joe Manchin (D-WV). Manchin has almost single-handedly—though sometimes with the help of others like Kyrsten Sinema (D-AZ)—kept the Democrats from pushing through all of their desires without a single Republican vote being needed.

Senator Joe Manchin (D-WV, left) was the only non-Republican Senator to vote for the confirmation of Associate Supreme Court Justice Brett Kavanaugh (right). Photo on July 30, 2018 by the OFFICE OF SENATOR JOE MANCHIN[39], Public domain, via Wikimedia Commons.

---

[39] HTTPS://COMMONS.WIKIMEDIA.ORG/WIKI/FILE:JOE_MANCHIN_AND_BRETT_KAVANAUGH.JPG

This was hardly the first time that Manchin had bucked his own party. For instance, he was the only non-Republican Senator to vote for the confirmation of the aforementioned Kavanaugh. As discussed above, without his actions and those of Murkowski, Kavanaugh would not be on the Supreme Court today. While Democrats on a national level may be shocked and frustrated by a person like this, those who come from single-party dominated States are not. For context, although Rhode Island's General Assembly (the legislature) is 88% Democrat, bills still have the same difficulties moving forward as those in Congress. Lacking a strong Republican Party, instead Democrats encompass a wide range of beliefs that seem quite at odds with the national Party—including having members that are against legalizing marijuana, are anti-choice on abortion, and have a tax policy that is extremely pro-business. A non-liberal Democrat is actually quite common in these situations.

Yet Manchin's actions had Republicans salivating for a switch just the same as Democrats felt they could potentially count on Cheney's defection. To deflate everyone, Manchin appeared on Fox News on July 1, 2021 and had this to say:

> **IF SWITCHING A PARTY, OR WHETHER YOU HAVE A 'D' BY YOUR NAME OR AN 'R' BY YOUR NAME CHANGES WHO YOU ARE AS A PERSON, THEN YOU'RE IN THE WRONG PROFESSION.... [H]AVING THE D OR R BY MY NAME OR CHANGING AND GOING FROM ONE TO ANOTHER, I'VE NEVER CONSIDERED THAT.**

Further, Manchin went on to say about those who had switched parties:

> [I]T'S ALL ABOUT YOU AND NOT ABOUT THE OATH YOU TAKE TO THE OFFICE, THE OATH TO THE CONSTITUTION, TO PROTECT AND DEFEND. THAT SHOULDN'T BE A PARTY AFFILIATION; THAT SHOULD BE ALL OF US....

Senator Joe Manchin (D-WV, right) smiles onstage with Senator Lisa Murkowski (R-AK, left), and former Senator Kelly Ayotte (R-NH, center) at the Citizens for Responsible Energy Solutions event on September 27, 2019. These three have more in common with each other than most anyone else in their parties. Photo and base-description by the UNITED STATES SENATE—OFFICE OF LISA MURKOWSKI[10], Public domain, via Wikimedia Commons.

40

HTTPS://COMMONS.WIKIMEDIA.ORG/WIKI/FILE:LISA_MURKOWSKI,_KELLY_AYOTTE

Do those words sound familiar? They are almost the exact same ones that Cheney used in describing her position. You see, Manchin, Cheney, and people like them in both major parties have more in common with each other than the extremes of their own caucuses. Truth be told, they do not have to share policies in order to work together. Contrary, they actually revel in their differences and believe in the importance of debate to find common or unexplored ground. They do not want to be locked away behind walled gardens of their own sycophants, but instead want the challenge of finding a solution by working from common facts.

If we return to Amash's op-ed in the Washington Post, he said in part:

> **MOST AMERICANS ARE NOT RIGIDLY PARTISAN AND DO NOT FEEL WELL REPRESENTED BY EITHER OF THE TWO MAJOR PARTIES. IN FACT, THE PARTIES HAVE BECOME MORE PARTISAN IN PART BECAUSE THEY ARE CATERING TO FEWER PEOPLE, AS AMERICANS ARE REJECTING PARTY AFFILIATION IN RECORD NUMBERS...**
>
> **NO MATTER YOUR CIRCUMSTANCE, I'M ASKING YOU TO JOIN ME IN REJECTING THE PARTISAN LOYALTIES AND RHETORIC THAT DIVIDE AND DEHUMANIZE US. I'M ASKING YOU TO BELIEVE THAT WE CAN DO BETTER THAN THIS TWO-PARTY SYSTEM—AND TO WORK TOWARD IT.**

_AND_JOE_MANCHIN_AT_CITIZENS_FOR_RESPONSIBLE_ENERGY_SOLUTIONS_EVENT_IN_2019_02.JPG

This is the *real* possibility. People like Cheney and Manchin respect each other and want to work together in the best interest of America, not in the best interest of themselves. We do not have to agree with either one's policy positions and they do not have to agree with each other to make it happen. Said Manchin in the same Fox News interview:

> **I BELIEVE IN THE DEMOCRATIC PRINCIPLES THAT I GREW UP WITH AND HOW I WAS RAISED, AND I BELIEVE TO RESPECT EVERY ONE OF MY REPUBLICAN FRIENDS BECAUSE THEY HAVE A COMMITMENT AND I RESPECT THAT.**

This is the real opening. Cheney and friends do not fathom leaving the Republican Party because they do not want to destroy any future for their conservative views. Manchin and his friends do not want to leave the Democratic Party for similar reasons related to liberalism and because they see switching teams as self-serving instead of country-serving. But what if they left *together*?

What if instead of hoping the Republican or Democratic Party broke apart so the other could dominate, we had both break apart to create a viable Third party? What if instead of just trying to get the occasional defector to switch sides or go out as a lone wolf, a new potentiality was set up? Imagine a Party that is neither Liberal nor Conservative, but is American-focused. The priority of this Party would be to the truth, not what is going to get them the most votes from a shrinking pool of turned-off citizens. As stated by the people mentioned in this article and many more, their duties would be upholding the Constitution, debating and passing laws through vigorous discussion, and being a check against uncontrolled executive action.

And if Republicans and Democrats left their conferences together, at the same time, their "damage" would be equal. How many might go? It is not most, and it is certainly not even half of each party. Perhaps, at best, it would be a quarter of each. Still, once they left, the largest Third Party in United States history would suddenly exist, and that would only attract more politicians and voters. After all, both the Democratic and Republican Parties came into existence because the incumbent, dominant Parties of their days fell apart under their own weight, impudence, and extremism.

Now is the time for that to happen again. Even President Joe Biden fits more in the category of this potential Party than the current and future Democratic one. There are a significant number of malcontents who only want this one strange thing:

TO WORK TOGETHER FOR A BETTER AMERICA, NO MATTER THEIR OTHER DIFFERENCES.

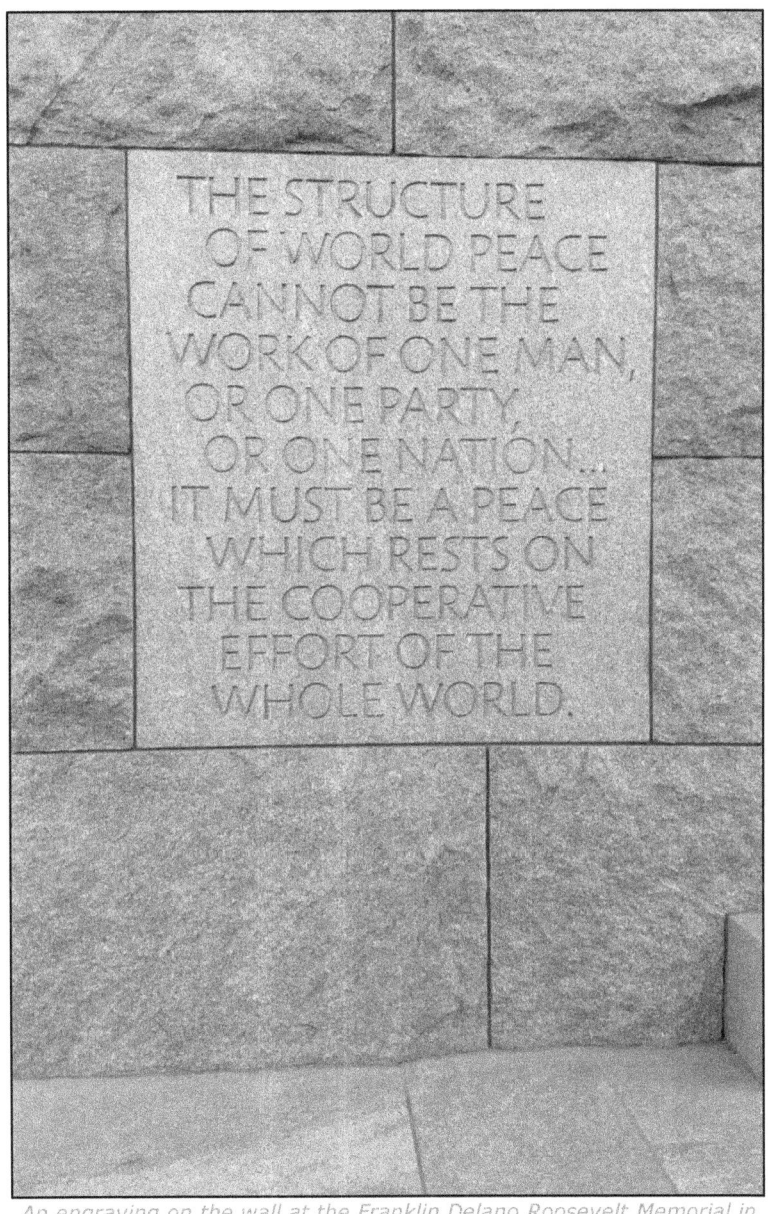

An engraving on the wall at the Franklin Delano Roosevelt Memorial in Washington, D.C. features a quote from the same that states, "The structure of world peace cannot be the work one man, or one Party, or one nation... it must be a peace which rests on the cooperative effort of the whole world." Photo by J.P. Prag on December 31, 2019.

LEFT-LEANING SOCIAL LIBERTARIAN

Debunking the Myth of the Two-Party System

A map from 1856 entitled "Reynolds's Political Map of the United States" that shows free and slave states and populations. Image and description by **REYNOLDS**[41], *Public domain, via Wikimedia Commons from Library of Congress collection.*

---

[41] HTTPS://COMMONS.WIKIMEDIA.ORG/WIKI/FILE:REYNOLDS%27S_POLITICAL_MAP_OF_THE_UNITED_STATES_1856.JPG

» Key Points

- *The Republican and Democratic Parties— along with the media that follow them—perpetuate a lie that they are the only two choices in town.*

- *This lie is used to keep particular politicians in control; and the media rich in viewers and advertising dollars. An "Us vs. Them" never-ending war is good for those groups, though not the citizenry as a whole.*

- *People who do not subscribe to either major Political Party far outnumber those who do and therefore have all of the power, if only they would take it.*

Headlines on CNN, Fox News, and all their brethren proclaim horror! The citizens of the United States are losing faith that democracy is safe in this country. Republicans blame Democrats, Democrats blame Republicans, and each act as if they represent at least half of all people—if not some secret super majority that is not speaking up. On September 15, 2021, **CNN RELEASED THE RESULTS OF A POLL**[42] on the subject including one tidbit they keep using in many subsequent pieces:

> **AMONG REPUBLICANS, 78% SAY THAT BIDEN DID NOT WIN...**

Well, that sounds downright terrifying. If nearly 8 out of every 10 Republicans believe the **Big Lie** that Joe Biden did not legitimately win the office of President of the United States, then there must be a massive danger of nearly 130 million people (~332 million people from the 2020 Census * 50% being Republicans * 78% who do not believe Biden won) ready to take up arms, revolt, and install their dictator-in-chief Donald Trump. Oh, and just forget that people under 18 represent over 22% of the total population; or that this is totally based on "a sample of 2,119 adults initially reached by mail" (a group certainly as diverse as the entire nation because 100% of the population definitely responds to random pieces of junk mail); or that **ACCORDING TO PEW RESEARCH**[43] only

---

[42] HTTPS://WWW.CNN.COM/2021/09/15/POLITICS/CNN-POLL-MOST-AMERICANS-DEMOCRACY-UNDER-ATTACK/INDEX.HTML
[43] HTTPS://WWW.PEWRESEARCH.ORG/FACT-TANK/2020/10/26/WHAT-THE-2020-ELECTORATE-LOOKS-LIKE-BY-PARTY-RACE-AND-ETHNICITY-AGE-EDUCATION-AND-RELIGION/

29% of registered voters identify as Republicans.

» Bunk Beds

Wait... what was that last one? Only 29% of *registered voters* identify as Republicans? And that number has been dropping for years. For the most recent national election in November 2020, the Census Bureau **RELEASED A BREAKDOWN OF THE VOTING AGE POPULATION**[44] and how many of them are registered voters. As a summary:

- **Voting Age Population:** 252 million
- **Registered to Vote:** 168 million
- **Actually Voted:** 155 million

*A Trump supporter shouts "Get a job!" to an anti-Trump protester on March 4, 2017. Photo and description by **FIBONACCI BLUE FROM MINNESOTA, USA**[45], **CC BY 2.0**[46], via Wikimedia Commons.*

---

[44] HTTPS://WWW.CENSUS.GOV/DATA/TABLES/TIME-SERIES/DEMO/VOTING-AND-REGISTRATION/P20-585.HTML

[45] HTTPS://COMMONS.WIKIMEDIA.ORG/WIKI/FILE:TRUMP_SUPPORTER_CONFRONTS_ANTI-TRUMP_PROTESTERS_%2832912421710%29.JPG

[46] HTTPS://CREATIVECOMMONS.ORG/LICENSES/BY/2.0

If we plug in the numbers of those who categorically did vote with our more accurate Republican counts, we have already dropped from 130 million to 35 million, or 73% less. Of course, that is if we really believe the results of this survey which—if you cannot tell—I do not. Are there millions of people who erroneously believe the 2020 Presidential Election was stolen from then President Donald Trump? Yes, and it is troublesome, but it is not the imminent danger these news sources and bloggers are heralding it to be.

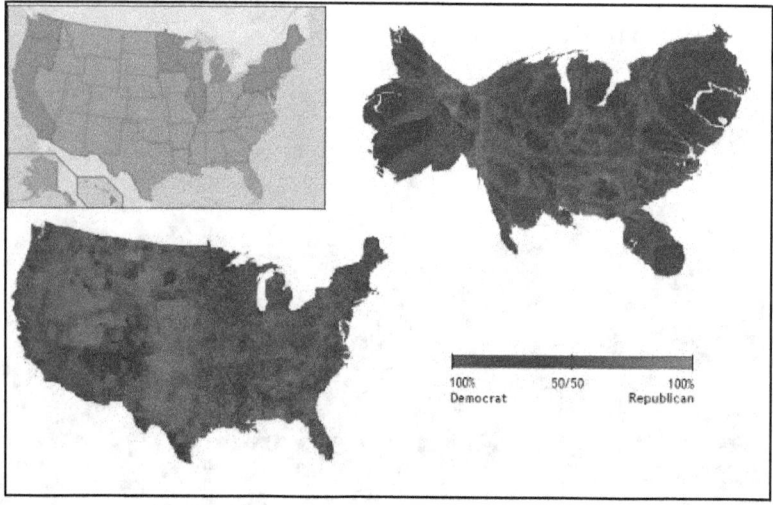

Composite image of maps from the 2004 Presidential election to show how deceptive each can be. Counterclockwise from top left: standard map of winner by state; range of votes by county; resizing the country for population density. Picture and description produced by Zscout370[47], CC-BY-2.0[48], via Wikimedia Commons.

Let us pretend for a moment that the 35 million number is accurate. That would mean that roughly 10–11% of Americans are complete goofballs (to put it mildly). When

---

[47] HTTPS://COMMONS.WIKIMEDIA.ORG/WIKI/USER:ZSCOUT370
[48] HTTPS://COMMONS.WIKIMEDIA.ORG/WIKI/TEMPLATE:CC-BY-2.0

placed into those terms, I find that number totally acceptable. To be clear: goofballs deserve representation, too. There is no reason they should be excluded from society and government; their political opinions are just as valid as yours and mine. But do you know who else deserves representation? The majority of people who are not Republicans or Democrats.

Returning to that same Pew Research poll, not only did 29% of respondents identify as Republicans, but 33% said they were Democrats and 34% said they were Independent (leaving 4% who identified as a specific third party like Green, Libertarian, or others). That would mean the largest Political Party in the United States is **No Political Party**. If we combine data sets, we get something more like this:

	Voting Age Population (In Millions)	Percentage
Non-Voters	84.0	33%
No Political Party	57.2	23%
3rd Party	6.7	3%
Subtotal Non-Oligopoly	*147.9*	*59%*
Democrats	55.5	22%
Republicans	48.8	19%
Subtotal Oligopoly	*104.3*	*41%*
Total	**252.3**	**100%**

Data table showing that people who do not prescribe to either major party in America are by far the largest proportion of potential voters.

In other words, the two major Political Parties in the United States that control 99% of all available elected and appointed positions (the very definition of an oligopoly) are supported by only 41% of voting-age people. The real largest group in the United States are non-voters—who often do not vote because they feel their voice will make no impact—followed by unaffiliated people. Combined together, everyone not aligned with a principal Political Party outnumber those who are by almost 42%.

This is the real **Big Lie**: that there are only two Political Parties in the United States and you must align to one or the other. In the media and in the government, this lie is told over and over again for the purposes of maintaining power and creating hysteria about "the other" in order to have viewers and sell advertisement. These Parties hold supremacy for no good reason other than we allow the lie to live, even though in plain numbers it is not even remotely true. If we told the real story and let people know they not only have choice, but have the power, then we could have a wide span of Parties representing us in all areas of government. Unfortunately, that truth provides no benefit to anyone but the actual citizenry.

» TELL ME WHAT TO DO

Even the so-called non-partisan study centers help perpetuate the lie. In the same Pew Research report from above, the authors presented the results of their survey forcing people into either Democrat or Republican buckets. Doing that made 49% of respondents Democrats and 44% Republicans (with 7% still refusing to join either). Pew also has a **RESEARCH QUIZ**[49] that is supposed to help undecided voters understand where they stand. I took that quiz and ended up with this result:

---

[49] HTTPS://WWW.PEWRESEARCH.ORG/POLITICS/QUIZ/POLITICAL-TYPOLOGY/

IDEOLOGICAL PLACEMENT

Distribution of Disaffected Democrats and the overall public on a 10-item scale of political values. Learn more about the scale.

Disaffected Democrats make up 14% of the population.

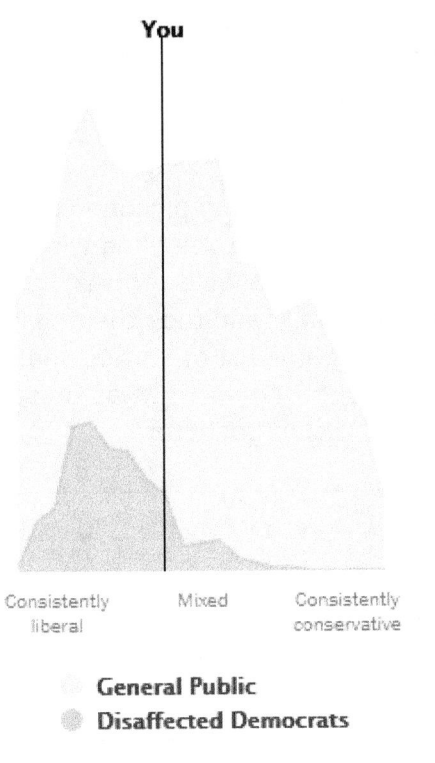

General Public
Disaffected Democrats

Results from the Pew Research Political Quiz that shows I am on the fringe of a fringe, but still somehow aligned with a major Political Party.

And here it is in plain text. While trying to understand where I stood on highly complex political issues, Pew—the premier research institution in the entire world—handed me a tool that would only place me on a two-dimensional scale that ranged from **"Core Conservative"** to **"Solid Liberal"**. In other words, they were going to decide whether I was a Republican or Democrat, and which type of sub-group I am a part of within that overarching assemblage. Apparently, I am a **"Disaffected Democrat"**, and even on the far edge of that one. What separates me from the more traditional **"Opportunity Democrats"** and **"Solid Liberals"** is that "[i]n contrast to other Democratic-oriented groups, a majority (63%) characterizes government as 'almost always wasteful and inefficient.'"

I was not satisfied with being pigeonholed into one of the major Parties and wanted something with more breadth across the entirety of available choices. As such, I headed over to **I SIDE WITH...**[50] and took their political quiz. While it gave me a large list of Parties and by what percentage I aligned with each, I was most amused with seeing these two results together:

Results from isidewith.com that shows I support two completely opposite Political Parties in equal measure.

---

[50] HTTPS://WWW.ISIDEWITH.COM/POLITICAL-QUIZ

Apparently, I support both **"Big Government"** and **"Small Government"** at the same time. Libertarians and the American Solidarity Party are polar opposites in every way, yet the survey would have me believe I support both equally. This contradiction made me laugh, but also made me doubt the veracity of these results. Surely I could not be so contradictory, at least not to that degree. As such, I turned my attention to **9Axes**[51] which focuses more on where one stands on categories of issues instead of on Political Parties, allowing me to make the leap myself from beliefs to political alignment:

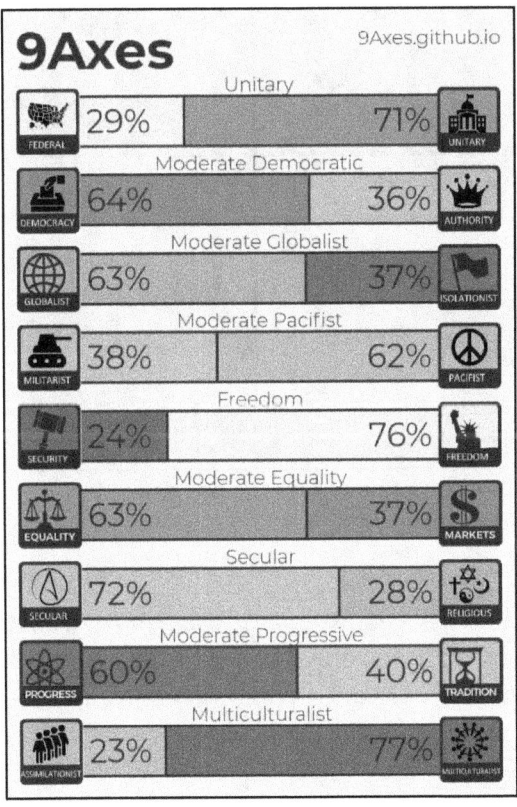

Results from 9Axes that is probably more accurate to my beliefs, but does not offer much help in what I am supposed to do with this data.

---

[51] HTTPS://9AXES.GITHUB.IO/INSTRUCTIONS.HTML

This one was interesting and helped me see where I stood on specific issues, but it is so opaque that I cannot actually take anything away from it in terms of which type of candidates to support. So that brought me to **THE POLITICAL COMPASS**[52] which wanted to give me a direction:

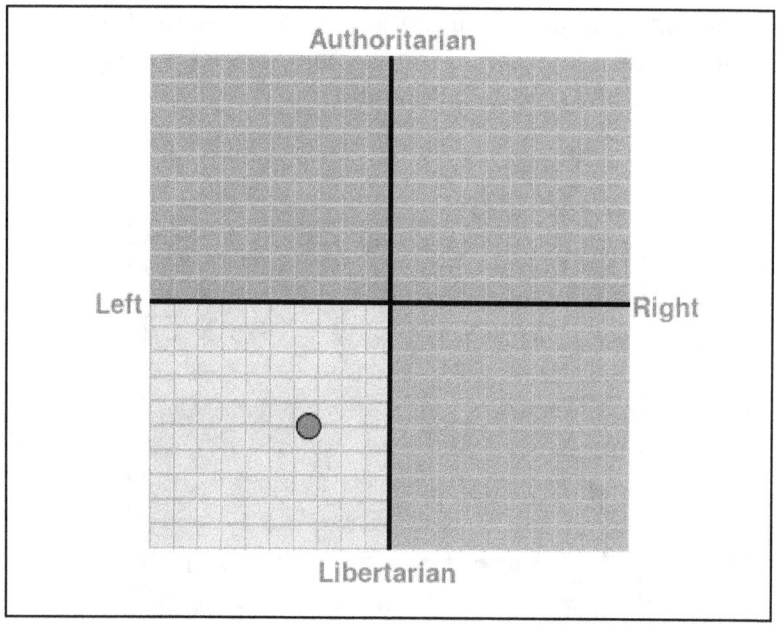

Results from The Political Compass that was founded because the Left/Right two-dimensional scale only captures economic beliefs, not social beliefs.

Thankfully, there it is. Reading through my results and using this chart it is clear as mud: I am a left-leaning social libertarian. Glad we could tidy that up.

» GOING TO THE POLLS

At the end of the day, it does not matter what any of

---

[52] HTTPS://WWW.POLITICALCOMPASS.ORG/TEST

these charts say about me, you, and the population as a whole. They are interesting instruments, but all they help point out is the same as what we have seen from the surveys: the Republican and Democratic Parties do not align nor represent the majority of Americans, even among those who belong to and identify with those Parties. We must stop believing their lie that only serves to benefit the elected instead of the electorate. Picking a candidate that most aligns to your matrix is not a wasted vote. What is a waste is using your unique voice to support the politician that is the least-worst of a couple of bad choices, or not bothering to show up at all.

PART 2: LIFE, DEATH, AND COVID-19

DID I HAVE COVID-19?

I will never know if I had or will get SARS-CoV-2

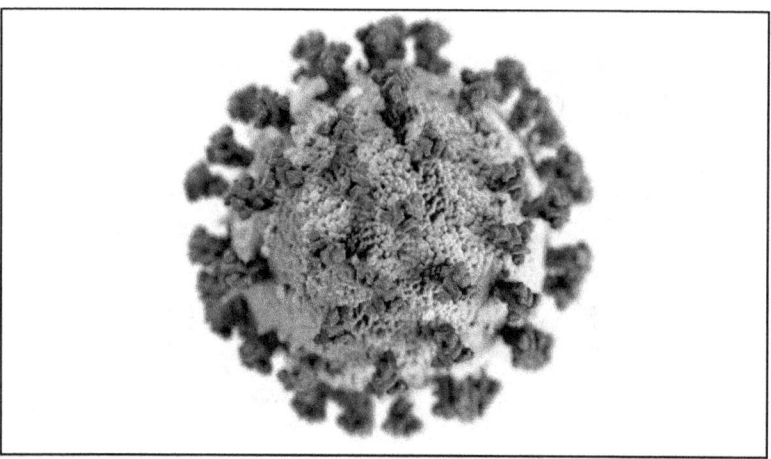

*Photo by **CDC**[53] on **UNSPLASH***

---

[53] HTTPS://UNSPLASH.COM/@CDC

» **KEY POINTS**

- *Although I have had horrific, mysterious infections and direct exposure to COVID-19, no test has ever given me anything but a negative result.*

- *Every step along the way has only left me with more questions and potentialities with little to no answers.*

- *Now that I am fully vaccinated, will there ever be any way to know if I ever had COVID-19, or if I get it now?*

I CAN ALWAYS TELL WHEN I AM ABOUT TO GET SICK.

Although I rarely come down with anything, once or twice a year I feel my lips get completely dry. No matter how much I drink, how much lip balm I apply, how much I steam and try to hydrate—my lips will just not stay moist. From there, the symptoms may move up into my sinuses and head. Other times, they will instead dive into my throat and maybe chest. In either situation, it is annoying and difficult to work; but in the past it rarely stopped me in my tracks. Even after all of this, I can still count on one hand the number of times I have been taken out of commission. Before the COVID-19 Pandemic, I was one of those people that literally had to be dragged off the worksite against my will. It was not in my nature to give in to disease.

While now I am much more cognizant of infection vectors and my potential to spread pain, suffering, and even death to others, that was not the case just a short while ago. On January 1, 2020, I started to have that feeling in my lips. By the end of the day, my throat felt completely closed in. But it did not matter; I was on a combined vacation and research trip (though mostly the former) in Washington, D.C. with my partner. We had been there since December 27, 2019, walking everywhere to take in the city and visit all of the sites. During that week, we put 50 miles on our feet, wearing ourselves down and lowering my immune-resistance.

Looking at the pictures now, I cringe thinking about the crowds of strangers from all over the country and world tightly packed together. There are plenty of photos of us touching everything, things everyone else was touching, too. There were no face masks, no gloves, no disinfectant, and no regular hand washing aside from trips to the bathroom. Picking up some illness seemed quite likely to happen, so I was not that surprised. Besides, we had a packed flight home the next day, so what else was there to do but tough it out and carry whatever I had back with us, infecting who knows how many others along the way?

Photo by **GIACOMO CARRA**[54] on **UNSPLASH**

» SOMETHING IS TERRIBLY WRONG

Over the weekend after returning home, things continued to get worse. This was some truly tenacious infection, but I was determined to just beat it on my own. Despite how horrible I felt, I kissed my partner goodbye as she went into the office (I worked from home anyway, so it was no difference for me) and started to go about my day. Except

---

[54] HTTPS://UNSPLASH.COM/ @GIACOMOCARRA

I could not. Suddenly, I could not keep anything down and my body was rebelling against me. I was feverish and felt like I had food poisoning. My entire being was wracked with pain and I could barely move.

When I could move, I called my doctor's office to get an emergency appointment. Then, I called my partner to come home and take me to the appointment. She was amazed that I had called and knew something must have been terribly wrong for me to ask for help like this. All I could say is that I had never had an illness like this—I was sick in a way I had never experienced before.

So there I was, more ill than I had ever been, just sitting in a waiting room with other people hoping to be seen. When the doctor brought me out back, he examined me without donning a mask saying he, too, had just gotten over something similar. He was seeing several patients like this and was hearing rumors of some type of respiratory disease going around. As such, he prescribed me an anti-inflammatory to ease the symptoms, and after a couple of days it mostly worked. Effects lingered for a while, but after a few weeks I was more-or-less back to normal. Still, I was shaken by the experience and the mysterious illness.

What, exactly, did I, the doctor, and those other people have? Even over the next couple of months I could not completely shake what had happened to me. But life moved on and so did I. After all, although it had caused me quite a bit of trouble, my partner was completely unaffected; she never displayed any symptoms at all. If I did not transfer it to her, then certainly it was not that big of a deal. The idea of an asymptomatic carrier had never occurred to me.

» THE DAY THE EARTH STOOD STILL

My illness was far in the back of my memory when we went to New Orleans for a wedding on March 6, 2020. Yes, we had started to hear the warnings from the CDC and WHO about a potential pandemic, but it seemed fairly contained. Others were not as sure as our once fully-booked flights ended up losing a third of the passengers. At the airport, I started to see people wearing masks and wondered what they could possibly do.

Photo by **EDWIN HOOPER**[55] on **UNSPLASH**

The wedding went off well even with some noticeably missing guests. There was even a little parade for everyone to participate in! We stayed tightly packed with many guests and the usual throngs of the French Quarter during our free time when not involved in wedding activities. Despite some of the weirdness around the airports, it was an enjoyable, carefree time.

---

[55] HTTPS://UNSPLASH.COM/@EDWINHOOPER

Then, shortly after we got back, the bride was diagnosed with this mysterious thing called COVD-19. The recently married couple had only alerted some of the older guests and we found out through one of those. But as the days went on, others quickly joined them in going down for the count. Some of those people continued to have symptoms and effects long after the initial infection. But I felt nothing. As a matter of fact, I felt perfectly fine despite all of the same confines and high-contact situations.

How had I avoided COVID-19? Or did I? Was I an asymptomatic carrier? Did I get infected at all? Or, was that mysterious illness I had in January COVID-19? Did I have anti-bodies and was I protected? And if I was protected, for how long?

Tests for COVID-19 were spotty at best and only available to people with the worst symptoms. I was fine, so there was no way for me to get one. The lockdown had begun and all I would ever receive were unanswerable questions.

» Somewhere Not the Supermarket

As the lockdown started in earnest (and thankfully we had by happenstance bought a large amount of toilet paper a few weeks beforehand), we set up shop at home. Since my office was already there, it was not a big transition for me other than getting used to having my partner home during the day. We only went places together, and that was usually just the supermarket as infrequently as possible. Still, my father was going through a health crisis and I was trying to help him, so I did have my own trips to doctors, hospitals, and nursing homes for him.

My father actually caught COVID-19 in January 2021, two days before he was supposed to get his first shot of the vaccine. When I was sick that prior January, after I got back from New Orleans, and during all these other times, I could hardly avoid him. It was before regular mask wearing, before social distancing, before everything. He never displayed any illness like mine or like COVID-19 at that point, so maybe I did not infect him? Or maybe he did get it and was asymptomatic the first time, while the second time was much worse? Even then, with the drug regimens they had available by that point, he was mostly recovered in just a couple of days. His other health issues could easily be confused with COVID-19, even the long-lasting ones, so it was impossible to say where he stood.

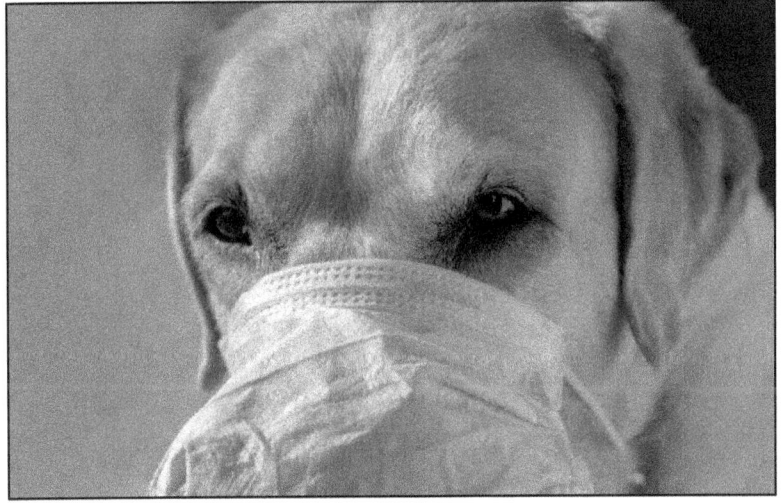

Photo by STEFAN HEESCH[56] on UNSPLASH

Prior to all that, though, in May 2020 I went in for my regular PCP appointment. I had not seen my doctor since that January bout and he brought no further insight to the table. However, he did tell me a serology test—a blood test—to detect COVID-19 anti-bodies had become available just the week beforehand. It was so new that

---

[56] HTTPS://UNSPLASH.COM/@NORDFRIISK

there was no code in the computer to order it, so he had to hand write it out. I wanted the test both for my own peace of mind to understand where I stood and because—at that time—physicians were recruiting people with anti-bodies in order to help develop treatments for others. If I could assist in any way, I wanted to.

When the tests came back, I was negative for anti-bodies. But—as this very new test warned—there was a large chance of false negatives. Also, since they did not know (and still do not know) how long anti-bodies lasted, it was possible I had been infected and they were now gone. Thus, once again, I was left with questions.

If the illness I had in January was COVID-19, were all my anti-bodies gone? Had I gotten it in March and was in the same situation? Or had I not had it at all? Or was the test just a false negative? No answers were forthcoming, so like everyone else I went deeper into lockdown.

» EMERGING FROM THE CAVE

The rest of the Spring, Summer, and beginning of Autumn 2020 went on the same as it did with most conscientious people. We social distanced from everyone, we made limited trips for supplies, we built our life around our house and walks in the woods. Our masks got fancy and fun while we stayed relatively healthy. Avoiding the rest of humanity does have some tertiary benefits.

Yet in October I developed some type of chest congestion. I let it go on for over a week and half before I even considered trying to make an appointment with my doctor. Much like many people, I avoided even going to my doctor in order to stay out of small, enclosed spaces and away from others. Finally, I gave in. While there, I asked if I should seek out a COVID test. My doctor seemed unconcerned with my symptoms being COVID-related and said I could if I wanted to, but offered me no assistance or guidance on how to get an appointment. I thought they would set one up, but it was not to be. Even the medical office did not really know how it was done.

He prescribed me a steroid and it helped somewhat, but even today I still feel like I have not completely gotten over it. Instead, I just learned to live with it and work around it on the bad days. Most days are fine, but every once in a while I feel that same compression. If no answers are coming, I figured I would just manage. Maybe I have not learned any lessons?

Meanwhile, I began hunting down my first COVID-19 tests. Everywhere I sought was booked up for days in advance with no slots visibly available. I was advised to sit at the computer at midnight or 5am to see if a spot opened and try to grab it. Amazingly, I was able to find one at a CVS in what is considered a "bad area" a few miles away. It was a drive-through experience where I had to swab my own nose. Once I dropped off my swab in a slot outside the building, it became a waiting game of when the lab would get back to me.

Though the news was filled with people waiting over seven days for results, I got mine back in two. The results were clear as day: **NEGATIVE**. Yet how accurate was the test? Again, there was not an insignificant chance for false negatives, including a big question whether I administered the test to myself correctly. More so, the time frame mattered when you took the test. Take it too soon and you do not have enough of the virus to pick up. Take it too late and you have the opposite problem as anti-bodies clear your system. Had I just missed the window in the days it took to book an appointment? Or are my symptoms perhaps just left over from my earlier infection, so there is nothing to detect? Still, they may not be related at all. How can I possibly know?

» Testing, One, Two, Testing

As we rolled in to 2021, testing started to become more readily available. There were even some walk-up locations that did not require appointments! On January 13th and 14th, I was able to get next day and same day testing—both the Rapid kind and the more accurate PCR type. Both of those tests came back fast and negative.

Photo by **Michael Marais**[57] on **Unsplash**

The governor of my State started encouraging people to get tested regularly, especially while waiting for vaccine availability to come to the masses. At that moment, the timeline had me getting my first shot in June, so my expectations were low. Beginning February 12, 2021, I

---

[57] HTTPS://UNSPLASH.COM/@MICHAEL_MARAIS

proceeded to get tested on a near weekly basis, varying between Rapid and PCR testing, even picking locations based upon my errands. It just became a regular thing I did as I was out and about doing other stuff. Every single time the results came back the same: negative.

In reality, the testing availability was such that I could have gone daily! But why bother? Most of my time was spent at home interacting with no one else but my partner. If we were going to see anyone (outside, masks on), we would get tested en route. It was just life.

» Vaccines are named for Cows

My partner worked administratively in a medical field and was able to get leftover vaccine at the end of the day pretty early on. Originally she struggled with the decision, but I encouraged her to do it. She was not stealing a vaccine from anyone; she was making sure it was not wasted and protecting herself and our loved ones while doing so. With each shot of the Pfizer vaccine, she had almost no reaction, just a little tiredness the next day.

People around us slowly became eligible and went through their own tribulations. Some people's side-effects were worse than others, but no horror stories. Finally, on April 14, 2021 I became eligible and received my first dose of the Moderna vaccine. Within a few minutes, the back of my head went numb, my blood pressure shot up 30%, and my body temperature soared. I could not stop sweating despite the coolness of the large mass vaccination site I was in.

The EMTs on hand monitored me and after about 45 minutes my vitals returned to near normal. After sitting outside for another half hour or so, I felt perfectly fine. I then walked the two miles home, including stopping off at the supermarket and carrying grocery bags on my shoulders. It seemed to me that it was nothing.

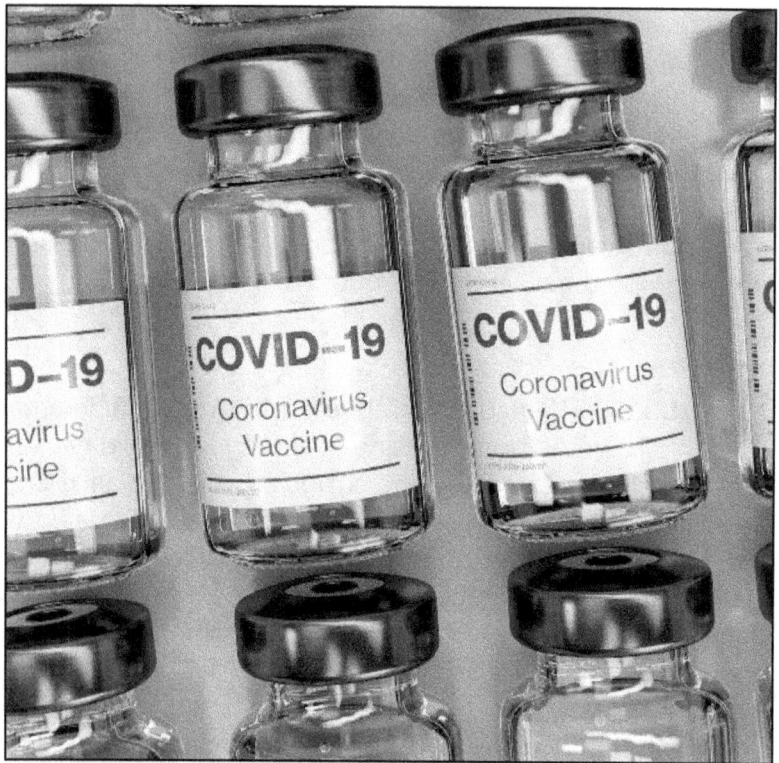

Photo by **DANIEL SCHLUDI**[58] on **UNSPLASH**

However, six hours later, I could not move my arm. It was not pain (although there was plenty of that, too); it was immobilization. It took a couple of days before that subsided, but otherwise I was fine.

The second shot would be a different story entirely.

Four weeks later, I received that second shot and had no immediate reaction. I took a much longer walk home

---

[58] HTTPS://UNSPLASH.COM/@SCHLUDITSCH

doing a bunch of errands I planned around the jab. Many hours later, my arm hurt but it was nowhere near as bad as the first dose. Overnight and through the next few days, though, things turned horrid. I got full flu symptoms, including fever, pain, delirium, lethargy, nausea, vomiting, and plenty more. I once again had to call my partner to return home from work (her office had pulled everyone back in months prior) to help take care of me. Eventually it all passed, but I felt as sick as I had nearly 18 months prior. It was like I had come full circle.

Why was my immune-response so bad with this shot? And why was it so similar to how I felt in January 2020? Could a prior infection of COVID-19 have impacted how the vaccine affected me? Or was it totally unrelated to that and just due to any number of factors from my blood type to body chemistry to genetic makeup? There were no answers coming; I had no way to know.

Despite my poor reaction, two weeks after my last dose I was considered "fully vaccinated". At the time, it was a question whether a booster would be in my and everyone else's future. Still, with what was considered complete protection and waning cases, my regimen of testing slowed down and eventually stopped, except in some specific cases. Overall, it seemed like our world was starting to take a turn for the better.

Of course, as with everything pandemic-related, things continued to evolve. When the variants began to rapidly spread and there were questions about the long-term efficacy of the vaccines, I returned to testing every week or two, never getting a positive result even when I had close contact with someone who did. Further, I received the first of what may be many booster shots in the years to come. Though it was only a half dose compared to my first two shots, my body's reaction to it was the same. At least I was prepared.

What is more, even if I am infected after this point, I stand a high probability of never knowing. According to Dr. Anthony Fauci—director of the U.S. National Institute of Allergy and Infectious Diseases (NIAID) and generally the face of the federal government's response to the outbreak—on CBS's **Face the Nation** on May 16, 2021:

> **EVEN THOUGH THERE ARE BREAKTHROUGH INFECTIONS WITH VACCINATED PEOPLE, ALMOST ALWAYS THE PEOPLE ARE ASYMPTOMATIC, AND THE LEVEL OF VIRUS IS SO LOW, IT MAKES IT EXTREMELY UNLIKELY, NOT IMPOSSIBLE BUT VERY, VERY LOW LIKELIHOOD THEY ARE GOING TO TRANSMIT IT.**

Thus, whether I have been infected in the past or not, whether I had any anti-bodies of my own or not, whether any of these test results were accurate—I could still get infected between now and forever and never know.

It is frustrating. Did I have COVID-19? Will I get it?

There is only one thing I am confident about: that I do not and most likely will never know.

Photo by **LUKE JONES**[59] on **UNSPLASH**

---

[59] HTTPS://UNSPLASH.COM/@LUKEJONESDESIGN

Mandatory COVID-19 Vaccine

Does any President have the legal authority to require everyone in America be vaccinated?

President Joe Biden signs the Saves Lives Act which authorized the Department of Veterans Affairs to provide COVID-19 vaccines to veterans and their families on March 24, 2021 in the Oval Office at the White House. **Official White House Photo and description by Adam Schultz**[60], Public domain, via Wikimedia Commons.

---

[60] HTTPS://COMMONS.WIKIMEDIA.ORG/WIKI/FILE:P20210324AS-0040_%2851129996706%29.JPG

» Key Points

- The 1905 court case Jacobson v. Massachusetts seems to give the right to mandate vaccines, but does it apply to the Federal Government?

- Even if it does, would this Congress pass a law to make it possible? Or can existing law be bent enough to fit the purpose? And what compulsion mechanisms are legally available?

- Then, of course, are the questions of whether the Courts would allow such actions to continue and what could be done to stave them off long enough to make an impact anyway before any rulings are made?

> **IT IS WITHIN THE POLICE POWER OF A STATE TO ENACT A COMPULSORY VACCINATION LAW, AND IT IS FOR THE LEGISLATURE, AND NOT FOR THE COURTS, TO DETERMINE IN THE FIRST INSTANCE WHETHER VACCINATION IS OR IS NOT THE BEST MODE FOR THE PREVENTION OF [THE DISEASE] AND THE PROTECTION OF THE PUBLIC HEALTH.**
>
> *SUPREME COURT DECISION IN JACOBSON V. MASSACHUSETTS, 197 U.S. 11*[61]
> *FEBRUARY 20, 1905*

By mid-July 2021, the United States of America had vaccinated about 48% of its total population against COVID-19, coming in at 14th in the world by that measure. This number was not nearly enough to stop community spread and reach herd immunity, which most likely is around 80%. While the United States was by far the largest country (both by area and population) in the top 15, there was great disparity across the land. At the top of the list was Vermont at 66% of its total population and on the complete opposite end was Alabama at 31%.

And it was not from lack of access or unavailability of vaccines for the most part, even in the most rural places in America (though some of this did exist, especially on Tribal Lands). Where nearly 8,000 people were dying

---

[61] HTTPS://SUPREME.JUSTIA.COM/CASES/FEDERAL/US/197/11/

around the world every day due to COVID-19 and other countries were begging for doses, within the United States it was necessary to turn to monetary lotteries and literally knocking door-to-door in the hopes of getting vaccination rates up. At that juncture and against all odds, the issues were mostly related to hesitancy, one that was mired in personal politics of various kinds.

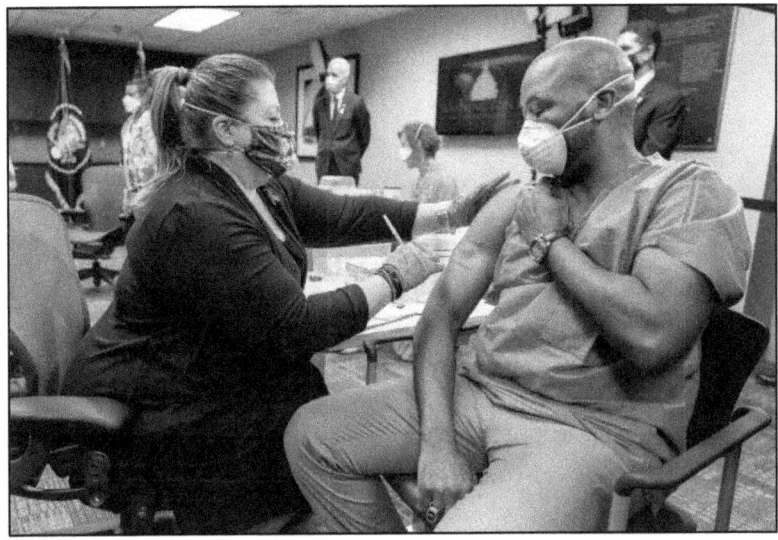

Nurse Denise Boehm administers a COVID-19 vaccine to U.S. Army Staff Sgt. Marvin Cornish during a briefing on the vaccine process with President Joe Biden on March 8, 2021, at the Washington D.C. Veterans Affairs Medical Center. Official **WHITE HOUSE PHOTO AND DESCRIPTION BY ADAM SCHULTZ**[62], Public domain, via Wikimedia Commons.

This is why there was such a difference between States and even sub-divisions within States. For instance, at the time, Georgia's Chattahoochee County topped the entire country with almost its entire population vaccinated. On the other end of the State in Long County just 3% were fully vaccinated. The statistics went deeper into towns

---

[62] HTTPS://COMMONS.WIKIMEDIA.ORG/WIKI/FILE:P20210308AS-0440_%2851102027353%29.JPG

and cities themselves with great differences between neighborhoods. Each one of these pockets—whether the size of a country, State, county, city, or block—allowed SARS-CoV-2 to mutate and spread variants. The numbers were clear: in areas with lower vaccination rates there were more variants, more cases, and more deaths.

Thus, the question became: what more could be done? The carrot was not doing the trick, so was it time for the stick? If it was, was there a potential stick to leverage?

» Past Prologue

Based upon the quote at the top of this chapter from the Supreme Court Decision in *Jacobson v. Massachusetts*, it appears that since 1905 it has been legal to compel people to be vaccinated against their will. As such, it would seem that President Joe Biden could have just signed an Executive Order to use "the police power of the state" to forcibly jab people in the arms against their will in the name of "prevention" and "public health". Just before that statement, the decision noted:

> **THE LIBERTY SECURED BY THE CONSTITUTION OF THE UNITED STATES DOES NOT IMPORT AN ABSOLUTE RIGHT IN EACH PERSON TO BE AT ALL TIMES, AND IN ALL CIRCUMSTANCES, WHOLLY FREED FROM RESTRAINT, NOR IS IT AN ELEMENT IN SUCH LIBERTY THAT ONE PERSON, OR A MINORITY OF PERSONS RESIDING IN ANY COMMUNITY... SHOULD HAVE POWER TO DOMINATE...**

The precedents set in this case have been used many

times since, including on June 12, 2021 for the case "*21–1774—Bridges, et al. v. Houston Methodist Hospital et al.*" In this trial, Houston Methodist Hospital in Texas required all employees to be vaccinated for COVID-19 by a certain date otherwise they would lose their employment. Those who had been suspended and were about to be fired sued to prevent that, but they were stopped in their tracks by the Federal Court that forcefully ruled in favor of their employer. Judge Lynn N. Hughes of the *United States District Court Southern District of Texas* stated in part in her **OPINION**[63]:

> [PLAINTIFF] ALSO ARGUES THE INJECTION REQUIREMENT VIOLATES PUBLIC POLICY. TEXAS DOES NOT RECOGNIZE THIS EXCEPTION TO AT-WILL EMPLOYMENT, AND IF IT DID, THE INJECTION REQUIREMENT IS CONSISTENT WITH PUBLIC POLICY. THE SUPREME COURT HAS HELD THAT (A) INVOLUNTARY QUARANTINE FOR CONTAGIOUS DISEASES AND (B) STATE-IMPOSED REQUIREMENTS OF MANDATORY VACCINATION DO NOT VIOLATE DUE PROCESS.

With that statement she placed a footnote to the aforementioned *Jacobson v. Massachusetts* case. Ten days later, the majority of those in the class were let go or resigned with very little recourse, at least in the short term. It would seem, then, that nothing would block the way from taking a more direct approach to increase vaccination rates.

---

[63] HTTPS://WWW.GOVINFO.GOV/CONTENT/PKG/USCOURTS-TXSD-4_21-CV-01774/PDF/USCOURTS-TXSD-4_21-CV-01774-0.PDF

However, there are several factors within this case and the United States judicial system that may not give the President that type of carte blanche decision making.

» COLLECTING THE STONES

At the top of the list is the question of whether President Biden, any future President, and the Executive Branch in general have any authority over vaccine mandates and enforcement. First off, within the decision of *Jacobson v. Massachusetts* it stated:

> THE SAFETY AND THE HEALTH OF THE PEOPLE... ARE, IN THE FIRST INSTANCE, FOR THAT [STATE] TO GUARD AND PROTECT. THEY ARE MATTERS THAT DO NOT ORDINARILY CONCERN THE NATIONAL GOVERNMENT. SO FAR AS THEY CAN BE REACHED BY ANY GOVERNMENT, THEY DEPEND, PRIMARILY, UPON SUCH ACTION AS THE STATE IN ITS WISDOM MAY TAKE...

In other words, the courts recognized the "*State's right*" to use its police power to make a vaccine mandate, but specifically called out the "*National Government*" as one that is not normally involved in such things. True to these words, coming in to the 2020s, all 50 States and most of the Territories had laws that compelled at least some type of vaccination—although the majority had exceptions for things like deeply held religious beliefs. On its website, the *Center for Disease Control and Prevention* (CDC) noted how it was completely dependent upon States for enforcement of their decrees and guidance.

Despite this, in November 2021, President Biden signed an executive order directing the *Occupational Safety and Health Administration* (OSHA) to require COVID-19 vaccinations for the vast majority of American workers. It was a novel interpretation of OSHA's vested powers, but one the Supreme Court found lacking and struck down by mid-January 2022—while at the same time upholding a similar decree for healthcare workers.

On April 6, 2021, President Joe Biden posted this image on Facebook saying: "This afternoon, I stopped by a vaccination clinic at the Virginia Theological Seminary. It's an example of the kind of partnerships we're seeing around the country—people coming together across different faiths to serve those most in need. It's America at its best." Photo by **THE WHITE HOUSE**[64], Public domain, via Wikimedia Commons.

Yet, this was not the only path President Biden could have taken. There was, perhaps, a better option; one that could still be implemented by this or another President in any ongoing or future pandemic.

64

HTTPS://COMMONS.WIKIMEDIA.ORG/WIKI/FILE:PRESIDENT_JOE_BIDEN_STOPS_BY _A_VACCINATION_CLINIC_AT_THE_VIRGINIA_THEOLOGICAL_SEMINARY.JPG

On April 2, 2021, the *Congressional Research Service* (CRS)—another agency of the Federal Government itself—released a report aptly titled **STATE AND FEDERAL AUTHORITY TO MANDATE COVID-19 VACCINATION**[65]. A surprisingly succinct read, the report begins Section 2 with this clear statement:

> **EXCEPT IN CERTAIN LIMITED CIRCUMSTANCES, INCLUDING IN THE IMMIGRATION AND MILITARY CONTEXTS, NO EXISTING FEDERAL LAW EXPRESSLY IMPOSES VACCINATION REQUIREMENTS ON THE GENERAL POPULATION.**

Thus, at first glance, it would appear that nothing could have been done because *Jacobson v. Massachusetts* specifically stated that the compelling power must come from "legislative enactment". Without any federal-level legislation, neither President Biden, any future President, nor any of the Executive Departments and agencies would have authority to take any actions, not to mention forceful or punitive ones.

Further, the makeup of Congress in the 2020s meant the chances of getting legislation through that would create a vaccine mandate were slim at best. Even with an evenly divided Congress or one with a Democratic majority, there were enough hesitant members of the caucus to not guarantee passing a mandate of any kind through some type of reconciliation or filibuster-breaking method.

---

[65] HTTPS://CRSREPORTS.CONGRESS.GOV/PRODUCT/PDF/R/R46745

That all said, this case being more than 115 years old means the Court at that time was not privy to later laws and decisions. Congress has been able to use the Commerce Clause of the Constitution to pass a large number of public health laws and agencies to enforce them. As a matter of fact, this authority was used just one year after this case to pass the *Pure Food and Drug Act*, which eventually gave way to the *Food and Drug Administration* (FDA) that still exists in the 2020s. This particular usage of the Commerce Clause has been upheld by the Supreme Court, so the Federal Government could—in theory—create some type of vaccine mandate around it. Says the CRS report:

> ACCORDING TO [THE SUPREME COURT]... THE COMMERCE CLAUSE DID NOT EMPOWER CONGRESS "TO REGULATE INDIVIDUALS PRECISELY BECAUSE THEY ARE DOING NOTHING." WHILE IT IS UNCERTAIN WHETHER THIS CONCLUSION CONSTITUTES BINDING PRECEDENT, IT SUGGESTS THAT A DIRECT FEDERAL MANDATE ON INDIVIDUALS TO RECEIVE A VACCINE MAY BE SUSCEPTIBLE TO CHALLENGE BECAUSE SUCH MANDATES COULD BE CONSTRUED AS COMPELLING INDIVIDUALS WHO ARE "DOING NOTHING" TO ENGAGE IN THE COMMERCIAL ACTIVITY OF RECEIVING A SPECIFIED HEALTH CARE SERVICE. ON THE OTHER HAND, A FEDERAL MANDATE THAT REQUIRES VACCINATION AS A CONDITION TO ENGAGE IN EXISTING ECONOMIC ACTIVITIES, SUCH AS EMPLOYMENT OR INTERSTATE TRAVEL, MAY RAISE FEWER [C]ONSTITUTIONAL CONCERNS.

So perhaps Congress could have created a law that met this narrow definition, although as already established the Congress of the 2020s was highly unlikely to do so. But what if they already did and just did not know it? In the CRS examination, the authors note that **Section 361** of the *Public Health Service Act* (PHSA) gives the *Health and Human Services Department* (HHS) and CDC the unique and specific power:

> [T]O MAKE AND ENFORCE REGULATIONS NECESSARY "TO PREVENT THE INTRODUCTION, TRANSMISSION, OR SPREAD OF COMMUNICABLE DISEASES FROM FOREIGN COUNTRIES INTO THE STATES OR POSSESSIONS, OR FROM ONE STATE OR POSSESSION INTO ANY OTHER STATE OR POSSESSION."

That certainly sounds like Congress has written a law that gives those agencies the necessary power. Therefore, based upon that, the President could in turn write an Executive Order to tell those agencies to enact this policy.

Despite that, even here the President could run into a wall. The law requires the action to be "necessary" and the Courts use a test of "reasonableness" to determine what that actually is. While it might be easier to argue for a quarantine being "necessary" to stop transmission, it is a much larger ask to force someone to put something into their body against their will. If transmission can be stopped by other means or if the harm is not high enough for the Courts to consider the actions "reasonable", then there is no way this could be used. Says Anastasia Boden—Senior Attorney at the Pacific Legal Foundation—

in part from a blog post on **APRIL 14, 2021**[66]:

> GOVERNMENT ACTIONS MUST BE REASONABLE UNDER ANY CIRCUMSTANCES, AND WHAT IS DEFINED AS REASONABLE MAY CHANGE BASED ON THE FACTS. IT DOESN'T MEAN THAT WHEN THERE'S AN EMERGENCY, THE GOVERNMENT SUDDENLY HAS MORE POWER AND THE COURTS MUST SIMPLY DEFER TO THAT POWER. THERE IS NO WORLD IN WHICH THE GOVERNMENT SHOULD ENJOY THE RIGHT TO BE UNREASONABLE—EVEN IN A PUBLIC HEALTH EMERGENCY.

Each situation has to be looked at on its own merits. Earlier within the same posting, Ms. Boden made an equally salient point:

> [JACOBSON V. MASSACHUSETTS] STEMMED FROM A SMALLPOX OUTBREAK IN NEW ENGLAND AT A TIME WHEN THE DISEASE WAS STILL HIGHLY LETHAL. AT THE HEIGHT OF SMALLPOX EPIDEMICS IN THE LATE 1800S, FATALITY RATES REACHED AS HIGH AS 80%, AND EVEN THOSE WHO WERE INFECTED AND RECOVERED WERE LEFT WITH NASTY, PERMANENT SCARRING.

Thus what Ms. Boden is supposing here is that due to smallpox's potential for harm, the Courts found the

---

[66] HTTPS://PACIFICLEGAL.ORG/CAN-THE-GOVERNMENT-FORCE-YOU-TO-GET-A-VACCINE/

vaccine requirement was reasonable. Is that the same for COVID-19 or other diseases that are far less lethal and dangerous in the long term? While most may say "yes", it is no guarantee that the Courts would agree. There is a lot of risk here.

Soldiers in the Maryland Army National Guard use the soldiers' backs in front of them to fill out their medical paperwork to receive the COVID-19 vaccine at the U.S. Capitol Complex in Washington, D.C., on January 14, 2021. National Guard Soldiers and Airmen from several states had traveled to the District to provide support to federal and district authorities leading up to the 59th Presidential Inauguration. U.S. National Guard photo and description by **SGT. CHAZZ KIBLER/29TH MOBILE PUBLIC AFFAIRS DETAC**[67], Public domain, via Wikimedia Commons.

But let us assume for now that the Courts do agree, or at the very least put off a decision until action has been taken for months without any type of injunction. What, then, could those actions be? Returning to Ms. Boden:

---

[67] HTTPS://COMMONS.WIKIMEDIA.ORG/WIKI/FILE:MARYLAND_NATIONAL_GUARD_%2850863555917%29.JPG

> *JACOBSON* DID NOT SAY THAT THE GOVERNMENT COULD HOLD YOU DOWN AND STICK A NEEDLE IN YOUR ARM. IT SAID THE GOVERNMENT COULD, UNDER CERTAIN CIRCUMSTANCES, PASS A LAW REQUIRING YOU TO GET A VACCINE OR PAY A $5 FINE (ABOUT $150 IN TODAY'S DOLLARS). SO, THE DECISION DOESN'T NECESSARILY SUPPORT THE IDEA THAT VACCINATION CAN BE LEGALLY COMPELLED.

And there is the real rub. The original case dealt with a Massachusetts law that said local (town/city level) health agencies could impose a vaccine requirement using the fine system if they felt it was necessary. That is exactly what happened, and one man—who did not meet any of the exceptions in the law—was fined and did not think he should have to pay. At the end of the day, all the Supreme Court did was force him to hand over $5; he never did get vaccinated for smallpox.

Physically forcing someone to do an action is most likely not going to hold up in any Court. Besides, mandates are meaningless without an enforcement mechanism. For that, the aforementioned CRS report highlights:

> UNDER SECTION 368 OF THE **PHSA**, VIOLATORS OF REGULATIONS ISSUED UNDER SECTION 361 ARE SUBJECT TO STATUTORY PENALTIES OF UP TO ONE YEAR IN JAIL OR A FINE..., OR BOTH.

D.C. Firefighter and EMT Gerald Bunn receives a shot from RN Elizabeth Galloway during an event with President Joe Biden, celebrating the 50 millionth COVID-19 vaccination on February 25, 2021, in the South Court Auditorium in the Eisenhower Executive Office Building at the White House. *OFFICIAL WHITE HOUSE PHOTO AND DESCRIPTION BY ADAM SCHULTZ*[68], *Public domain, via Wikimedia Commons.*

Specifically, the report notes that there are other statutes of the law related to sentencing that the CDC has incorporated in the past and could use again that:

> **SUBJECT[S] VIOLATING INDIVIDUALS TO A FINE UP TO $100,000 IF THE VIOLATION DOES NOT RESULT IN DEATH, OR A FINE OF UP TO $250,000 IF THE VIOLATION RESULTS IN A DEATH.**

---

[68] HTTPS://COMMONS.WIKIMEDIA.ORG/WIKI/FILE:P20210225AS-0626_%2851012507228%29.JPG

With these laws, it appears as if HHS and CDC can fine and potentially jail people for non-compliance. This would give the President and the rest of the Executive Branch the enforcement mechanisms necessary to carry out a vaccine mandate for the masses.

Based upon all of this we can say that **IF**:

- Existing Federal Law can be wrought for this purpose;

- States do not try to override this with their local and more relevant police power over people; and

- The Courts do not put in any type of injunction or rule that the approach is unreasonable;

Then the President could maybe, possibly write an Executive Order directing HHS and the CDC to make vaccines a requirement (with certain exceptions due to health or deeply held religious beliefs) and to fine and arrest those who refuse to do so, especially if their actions result in someone else's death.

» Ordering a Side of Fries

Of course, we have been basing all of this logic on a Supreme Court case that was decided in 1905. It is important to remember that opinions of the Court are not law; they are interpretations of the law and the Constitution. Says Sarah Fujiwara, MD in the *American Medical Association (AMA) Journal of Ethics* in April 2006 (**Virtual Mentor. 2006;8(4):227–229. doi: 10.1001/virtualmentor.2006.8.4.hlaw1–0604.**[69]):

---

[69] https://journalofethics.ama-assn.org/article/mandatory-vaccination-legal-time-epidemic/2006-04

> **THE COURT FOLLOWS THE DOCTRINE OF *STARE DECISIS*, WHICH DIRECTS IT TO FOLLOW EXISTING JUDICIAL DECISIONS WHEN THE SAME POINTS ARISE IN LITIGATION UNLESS THERE IS SUFFICIENT JUSTIFICATION FOR DEPARTING FROM PRECEDENT. IN THIS CASE THE *JACOBSON* COURT'S RULING HAS STOOD—NOT ALLOWING A SINGLE INDIVIDUAL TO REFUSE VACCINATION WHILE HE OR SHE REMAINS WITHIN THE GENERAL POPULATION ON THE GROUNDS THAT TO MAKE SUCH AN EXCEPTION WOULD STRIP THE LEGISLATIVE BRANCH OF ITS FUNCTION TO CARE FOR THE PUBLIC HEALTH AND SAFETY WHEN THREATENED BY EPIDEMIC DISEASE.**

Therefore we can assume that any President would have a decent chance of prevailing in the Courts at the lowest and appeals levels. Those Courts are bound by this precedent and, frankly, during the COVID-19 pandemic, President Biden only needed to delay any decision long enough to increase COVID-19 vaccination rates. Even should the Supreme Court have overturned his position and made the government refund and cancel all of the fines, he may already have coerced enough people into getting vaccinated to make all the difference in the world.

During Biden's first year, the Supreme Court was not set to start hearing cases until October 4, 2021 and the docket was already rather full. If he had acted much earlier, and somehow the case against the President, HHS, and CDC went through all appeals levels before then (*Jacobson v. Massachusetts* took three years to reach the Supreme Court), the Court may not have had a spot available to hear the case. Even if they did, a ruling would not have been expected until May or June 2022.

True, the Supreme Court could have, in the short term, put a preliminary injunction in place if it looked like the plaintiffs would suffer irreparable harm, but the lineup of the Supreme Court in 2021 seemed less likely to do so. They had already let many contentious programs—such as those related to border control—continue even when they later ruled them against the law or found the actions to be un-Constitutional. Given that their own precedent was that vaccines could be mandated so long as there was legislation to back them up, and the worst that could happen was someone paid a fine (i.e., easily repairable harm), then they would most likely have let the program continue until they made a ruling. The reasons for striking down the mandate related to OSHA were technical; there was no decision on mandates in general. Again, that is why the mandate for healthcare workers was allowed to stay in place—it met their procedural limitations.

Given that, even if the groundwork is shaky, the President may as well attempt to make the vaccine for COVID-19 or some similar future disease mandatory. The worst that could happen is that the Supreme Court will find the President overreached his power and force the government to give back or cancel any fines and maybe pay the lawyer fees of the plaintiffs. It would hardly be a rounding error in the budget of the United States Federal Government. In the meantime, while the Courts were considering the merits, the program could continue, meaning the President should be able to push a large number of hesitant people into getting vaccinated, which is the whole point. Mandates are not about collecting money or putting people in jail; they are about using a medical tool to stop the spread of a dangerous organism, end people needlessly dying, and allow America to have some semblance of normalcy.

President Biden tours the Viral Pathogenesis Laboratory in Bethesda, MD on February 11, 2021. OFFICIAL WHITE HOUSE PHOTO AND DESCRIPTION BY ADAM SCHULTZ[70], Public domain, via Wikimedia Commons.

Yet there is a risk in going before any Supreme Court, nonetheless the ideologically skewed version of the early 20202s. While the hope is that the Courts would rule narrowly on just the President's actions, there is nothing stopping them from having a much broader opinion. The Supreme Court could say the decision in 1905 under Chief Justice Melville Weston Fuller was in error and that no legislature can enforce a vaccine mandate of any kind for any reason. Many of the justices on the Supreme Court in 2021 had expressed a great interest in revisiting past decisions and deciding them in totally different ways.

And we must be fair about this because some opinions do

---

[70] HTTPS://COMMONS.WIKIMEDIA.ORG/WIKI/FILE:P20210211AS-1401_-_50970923622.JPG

need to be revisited. While we may want to laud the Fuller Court for this specific case, not everything they did was so wonderful. For instance, in 1901 they decided a number of situations that became known as the "Insular Cases". Without going into too much detail, these cases decided how the Territories of the United States—such as Puerto Rico—should be treated and that only "some" parts of the Constitution applied there, and that several rights were "fundamental" while others were not. Which are which? That is still fought over in the 2020s, but it allows people who are born in a Territory like American Samoa to be called "nationals" instead of "citizens" and the rights of citizenship and free movement refused to them.

Further, in 1908 this nearly identical group (one Associate Justice had been replaced) voted 7 to 2—the same as they did in *Jacobson v. Massachusetts*—in favor of a racist law with **BEREA COLLEGE V. KENTUCKY, 211 U.S. 45**[71]. In this case, the Supreme Court affirmed the idea that a State could pass a law requiring the separation of races and could compel private institutions to enact said policy. Further, through the Court's opinion, they expanded the idea of "separate but equal" and led the way for decades of suffering under Jim Crow and decades more of dealing with the generation-spanning repercussions. What is one of those repercussions? People of color are less likely to trust the government in general and especially when it comes to law, medicine, and authority. Further, due to the loss of generational wealth going all the way back to slavery, they are more likely not to be able to take the necessary time off from work or have as easy access to vaccination clinics. In early July 2021, the Kaiser Family Foundation found in an **ANALYSIS OF CDC DATA**[72]:

---

[71] HTTPS://SUPREME.JUSTIA.COM/CASES/FEDERAL/US/211/45/
[72] HTTPS://WWW.KFF.ORG/CORONAVIRUS-COVID-19/ISSUE-BRIEF/LATEST-DATA-ON-COVID-19-VACCINATIONS-RACE-ETHNICITY/

> [T]HE PERCENT OF WHITE PEOPLE WHO HAVE RECEIVED AT LEAST ONE COVID-19 VACCINE DOSE (47%) WAS ROUGHLY 1.4 TIMES HIGHER THAN THE RATE FOR BLACK PEOPLE (34%)...

The terrible decision in *Berea College v. Kentucky* directly caused at least some of the COVID-19 vaccine hesitancy in the Black Community. Thankfully, the rulings in *Berea College v. Kentucky* were overturned by **BROWN V. BOARD OF EDUCATION OF TOPEKA, 347 U.S. 483**[73] in 1954, as they should have been. Unfortunately, as seen in these statistics, the damage was done. In the end, the point really is this: let us not pretend for a moment that what the Fuller Court decided over a century ago is a panacea of good intentions that we are forever bound to.

Was *Jacobson* decided correctly and *Berea College* decided incorrectly? Were both poorly reasoned opinions? Should President Biden or another future President choose to pursue this path, he stands the potential of overturning over 115 years of affirmed State power around public health. Is that risk worth it? What chaos could ensue should the Supreme Court throw out this authority? *Jacobson v. Massachusetts* has been hardly challenged in all of this time. Should the Supreme Court sitting in the early 2020s be the one that hears that contest?

That leaves the President with one last move. Just before the case would be heard before the Supreme Court, he could cancel his Executive Order, throw away all

---

[73] HTTPS://SUPREME.JUSTIA.COM/CASES/FEDERAL/US/347/483/

outstanding fines, refund all fees that had been collected, and pardon anyone who had been jailed. In that way, there would be no order to argue and there would be no harm that could be claimed by anyone. The point would be moot and the Supreme Court would be forced to dismiss the case on a technicality. Again, the idea is to get as many people vaccinated as possible, not to punish them for not doing so. If all of these actions got even 10% more of total population vaccinated, then it would have totally been worth it!

» THE PLAN COMES TOGETHER

Could President Joe Biden or some future President use a stick to compel hesitant people to get the COVID-19 or some other necessary vaccine? The answer appears to be "yes, sort of", but with a very particular set of circumstances and a lot of risk. However, if he:

- Signed an Executive Order instructing HHS and CDC to use their authority under Section 361 of PHSA to mandate the vaccine;

- Referenced *Jacobson v. Massachusetts* as "stare decisis" reasoning;

- Made sure there were noted exceptions in his order for things like deeply held religious beliefs and health-related reasonings;

- Instructed HHS and CDC to use Section 368 of the PHSA to fine and/or jail people who refuse to be vaccinated;

- Fended off a preliminary injunction and delayed as long as possible any court proceedings using all legal tactics and tricks available;

- Used the time it took the case to work through the court system to coerce as many people as possible into getting vaccinated; and

- Canceled his Executive Order, refunded all fees collected, annulled any fines not collected, and released and expunged the records of anyone arrested shortly before the case would be heard by the Supreme Court—thus making the case moot;

Then yes, it certainly seems plausible to mandate any pandemic-attacking vaccine while also minimizing all potential legal and governmental hazards. Yet the other perils for anything from political fallout to pockets of armed rebellion are very real. Only the President himself can answer if those gambles are worth it.

A Tyrannosaurus rex sculpture outside Boston's Museum of Science on May 31, 2021 wearing a face mask and a Band-Aid indicating a COVID-19 vaccine has been administered. Photo and description by **WHOISJOHNGALT**[74], **CC BY-SA 4.0**[75], *via Wikimedia Commons.*

---

[74] HTTPS://COMMONS.WIKIMEDIA.ORG/WIKI/FILE:TYRANNOSAURUS_REX_SCULPTURE_WITH_MASK_AND_BAND-AID.JPG
[75] HTTPS://CREATIVECOMMONS.ORG/LICENSES/BY-SA/4.0

Yelling Fire in a Vaccination Clinic

Religious freedoms do not trump the rest of the Constitution

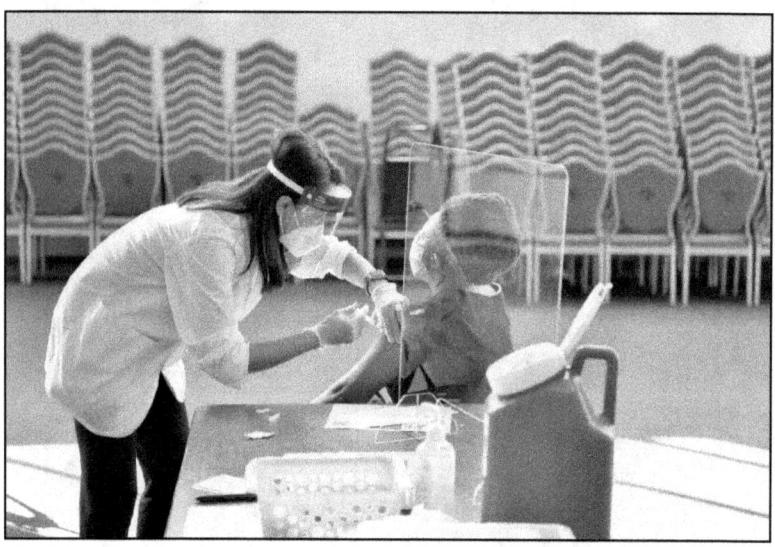

A COVID-19 vaccination site at New Shiloh Baptist Church in Baltimore, MD on March 6, 2021. Photo and description by **MDGovPics**[76], **CC BY 2.0**[77], via Wikimedia Commons.

---

[76] HTTPS://COMMONS.WIKIMEDIA.ORG/WIKI/FILE:PS1_7933.JPG
[77] HTTPS://CREATIVECOMMONS.ORG/LICENSES/BY/2.0

» Key Points

- *Even though every major religion supported getting the COVID-19 vaccine, a noticeable number of people attempted to use religious excuses to opt-out of vaccine mandates.*

- *All rights and responsibilities in the Constitution and the laws that support it have limits for the betterment and safety of society as a whole.*

- *The religious protections of the First Amendment to the Constitution are not a panacea that gives people the ability to do anything they want.*

> **THIS CONSTITUTION, AND THE LAWS OF THE UNITED STATES WHICH SHALL BE MADE IN PURSUANCE THEREOF... SHALL BE THE SUPREME LAW OF THE LAND...**
>
> *CONSTITUTION OF THE UNITED STATES OF AMERICA*
> *ARTICLE 6, CLAUSE 2 (PARTIAL)*

Coming in to summer 2021, mandates for the COVID-19 vaccine began popping up around the United States. Some came directly from employers and schools, others through executive and/or legislative government action. Certain ones focused in on particular groups like health care workers while others applied to all equally across the board, so long as they were part of the assemblage of people the vaccine had been approved for. On September 9, 2021, President Joe Biden finally ran out of patience and **ANNOUNCED THE LARGEST EXPANSION OF COVID-19 VACCINE MANDATES**[78] to date. Seemingly, those mandates would have applied to over 100 million Americans, which amounted to nearly 2/3rds of workers in the United States.

Yet among all these mandates—aside from a few rare specific circumstances—there were exemption allowances for those who are medically unable to take the vaccine or for those having ardent religious beliefs.

---

[78] HTTPS://WWW.CNN.COM/2021/09/09/POLITICS/JOE-BIDEN-COVID-SPEECH/INDEX.HTML

*Protesters, including Proud Boys, targeted a local Pizza Place & Music Club on August 15, 2021 because of their COVID-19 policies. One of the protesters attacked photographers at the location outside of Columbus, OH. Photo and description by **BECKER1999** FROM **GROVE CITY, OH**[79], CC BY 2.0[80], via Wikimedia Commons.*

The latter situation caused an interesting phenomenon. Despite no major religion prohibiting vaccines—and leaders of all major religions actively encouraged it and saying it was people's God-given duty to take the vaccine to protect themselves and others—there was a not insignificant number of people who attempted to go down that route. Even religions like Christian Scientists that scorn almost all modern medicine do not have a vaccine prohibition, just a general tenant not to use them unless it is necessary. What people were claiming as a "religious" belief was more a "political" one, and most places

---

[79] HTTPS://COMMONS.WIKIMEDIA.ORG/WIKI/FILE:ANTI_VAX-MASK_PROTEST_%28WORTHINGTON,_OH-_08.14.21%29_IMG_3893_%2851379802877%29.JPG
[80] HTTPS://CREATIVECOMMONS.ORG/LICENSES/BY/2.0

required some type of essay from the objector plus testimony from a religious leader to be included with an application for an exemption.

However, not everywhere found all of this paperwork worthwhile. According the **Providence Journal**[81], as of September 2, 2021 about 1,080 students —roughly 5% of the student body—at the *University of Rhode Island* (URI) requested an absolution from the school's COVID-19 vaccine requirement, the majority on religious grounds. URI's form did not require any declaration, reasoning, or justifications; all that was necessary was checking a box. Further, University of Washington Professor Doug Opel **told NBCNews**[82] that he did not believe it was a good use of resources to test religious sincerity since those opting out would only amount to a small percentage of the population. If URI was a test case study of his theory, the numbers were on his side. While 5% may seem significant, the opposite side means 95% of the people took the jab either willingly or begrudgingly.

In other words: mandates work.

» Deep Down Inside

Nevertheless, whether those claiming religious exemptions held beliefs that were sincere and true or not is actually irrelevant. Beliefs are just unprovable feelings that people act upon. If we want to go with the full spirit of the 1st Amendment to the Constitution—that **"Congress shall make no law respecting an establishment of religion, or prohibiting the free**

---

[81] HTTPS://WWW.PROVIDENCEJOURNAL.COM/STORY/NEWS/LOCAL/2021/09/02/HUNDREDS-URI-STUDENTS-HAVE-OBTAINED-RELIGIOUS-VACCINE-EXEMPTIONS/5684055001/
[82] HTTPS://WWW.NBCNEWS.COM/NEWS/US-NEWS/RELIGIOUS-EXEMPTIONS-VACCINE-MANDATES-COULD-TEST-SINCERELY-HELD-BELIEFS-N1278514

exercise thereof"—then we should just accept whatever people say are their religious tenants. It is not the job of the Federal or State Government nor an employer or school to tell someone whether their beliefs are real or not. But that does not mean their creeds and dogma supersede everything else.

While the 1st Amendment does not allow for the establishment of a religion or the suppression of one, that privilege is not superior to all other rights, responsibilities, and requirements of the Constitution and the laws created to support it. Everything in the Constitution and the Amendments (and thus the laws birthed by them) has equal weight; all parts are as important as this one small clause. And there are limits on the freedom of religion just as there are limits on any and all parts of the Constitution.

For instance, the next line after religion says that Congress cannot make a law **"*abridging the freedom of speech"***, but of course there are parameters around this. While this chapter's title makes an allusion to not being able to yell fire in a crowded theater[83], that is actually not a good example because it is not a real law. What is real law is speech that incites hatred or calls for violence, that leads to dangerous situations, or is blatantly false—mostly through civil action like libel and slander as opposed to legal action. The point is that there are confines when it comes down to the rights in the same Amendment.

Naturally, it is not as if it ends there. Where the 2nd Amendment has been interpreted to mean every person has the right to firearms, even a State as heavily a

---

[83] The actual words in Justice Oliver Wendell Holmes' opinion in Schenck v. United States is "falsely shouting fire in a theatre and causing a panic..."

proponent of gun-rights as Texas has laws on the books that do not allow convicted felons or intellectually disabled people to possess them; nor do they permit them inside bars or anywhere that makes 51% or more of their revenue from alcohol. In a similar vein: despite the fact that the 15th, 19th, 24th, and 26th Amendments all expanded the right to vote to more people (race, gender, poll tax, and age, respectively), almost all States do not allow incarcerated people to vote and many place restrictions on those same people from being able to vote once released until "all restitution has been made".

"Rally Against Gun Control" in Minnesota on April 28, 2018. Photo by **FIBONACCI BLUE**[84], **CC BY 2.0**[85], via Wikimedia Commons.

---

[84] HTTPS://COMMONS.WIKIMEDIA.ORG/WIKI/FILE:GUN_RIGHTS_RALLY_%22COME_AND_TAKE_IT%22_FLAG_AT_THE_MINNESOTA_STATE_CAPITOL.JPG
[85] HTTPS://CREATIVECOMMONS.ORG/LICENSES/BY/2.0

Each of these limitations and many more have been upheld by the courts at all levels of the government. The bottom line is this: a right to practice the beliefs of your choice are not an all-encompassing panacea that gives you unlimited powers to do anything and everything you would ever want. There are bounds, and plenty already exist today as laws to protect the interests of the State, the country, and the rest of society.

» LIMIT BREAK

Religion is tempered by many different acts across the country. As an example, Jewish law calls for a body to be returned to the earth simply and without any type of adornment or preservation that slows the body from returning to dust. Traditionally, this has meant putting a body in a type of sac made out of natural fibers so that it can quickly and easily decay. However, this runs afoul of almost all State laws, including in Massachusetts whereas of 2021 people of Jewish descent represent over 4% of the population. According to the **MASSACHUSETTS' GOVERNMENT WEBSITE**[86]:

> **M.G.L. CHAPTER 114, SECTION 44A, REQUIRES A BODY TO BE PLACED IN A "SUITABLE RECEPTACLE"... THE BODY SHOULD BE PLACED IN A RIGID CONTAINER LINED WITH PLASTIC SHEETING TO PREVENT LEAKAGE OF BODY FLUIDS... MOST CEMETERIES REQUIRE THAT THE CONTAINER BE PLACED INSIDE A CONCRETE GRAVE LINER TO PREVENT THE GROUND FROM SUBSIDING.**

---

[86] HTTPS://WWW.MASS.GOV/GUIDES/ISSUES-TO-CONSIDER-IN-PREPARING-FOR-DISPOSITION-OF-DECEDENTS#-BURIALS-

Placing a body inside a casket with a plastic liner and then putting that into a concrete grave liner is about as far as one can get from Jewish law. But the State has made its interest known for environmental reasons, as well as the protection of those handling the bodies. While there is a religious credence, one that is sincerely held and backed up by thousands of years of history, the other rights based in the Constitution and Law win out here. In the eyes of the country, it is not considered an undue burden.

In another Commonwealth down the coast, a different religious minority must also conform to the law against their greater beliefs. Pennsylvania has very detailed laws on what turn signals and break lights look like on vehicles and what type of conveyances are required to have them. Among the text, horse-drawn carriages that go on main roads and highways must have an electronic, colored turn signal system. This means that the Amish must use electricity when bringing their buggies out past their villages.

The Amish community is known for eschewing most modern conveniences, including electricity. A high-level view of their belief structures is that anything that leads to the creation of leisure time must be avoided as their days should be spent either working or in prayer. Having modern electrical amenities would get in the way of that for the most part. While there are variations between each community, some electrical use does happen, although usually not provided through the central grid. When it comes to their transport, though, they do not have a choice. This also means they need batteries of some kind to power their turn signals, something they cannot produce within their own walls. So once again, a State interest in safety and a Constitutional responsibility on maintaining Postal Roads has created a situation where religious beliefs have been subdued and subsided.

*Amish buggy in Lancaster County, PA. Note that the reflectors and orange triangle are concessions to Pennsylvania traffic laws. Photo and description by **AD MESKENS**[87], **CC BY-SA 3.0**[88], via Wikimedia Commons.*

We could go on with these examples forever. Many religions, including native ones of the southwest, use hallucinatory substances in ceremonies. Those ingredients have been banned from consumption and that is enforced. There are religions that call for marrying off girls as soon as they reach puberty, but almost all States do not allow child marriages. Connecticut passed a law requiring employers to accept whatever Sabbath day an employee said they needed, but the Supreme Court held that this created an establishment preference of religion and made an undue burden on secular purposes. Bob Jones University claimed that they had sincerely held religious beliefs against interracial relationships and could use that in their admittance decisions. Instead, their bigotry cost them their tax-exempt status.

---

[87] HTTPS://COMMONS.WIKIMEDIA.ORG/WIKI/FILE:TRADITIONAL_AMISH_BUGGY.JPG
[88] HTTPS://CREATIVECOMMONS.ORG/LICENSES/BY-SA/3.0

» It's My Life

Of particular note for our purposes, the Supreme Court has upheld again and again the right to mandate vaccines against any and all objections. This applies to all public and private institutions. The enforcement mechanisms are simply not enough of an undue burden on those who claim any type of religious exemption. Once again, **AS PREVIOUSLY DISCUSSED**, the setback of President Biden's OSHA-enforced mandate was a technical one, not one on mandates in general. The mandate on healthcare workers was allowed to remain as written.

While the government cannot physically force a person to have something put into their bodies against their will, it is well within their powers over commerce to disallow those people from participating in the rest of society. Whether during the COVID-19 pandemic or some other future event, those objectors are free to go on believing whatever it is they claim is their real and true faith; they just are not guaranteed to be able to maintain a job, go into a store/restaurant/stadium, get on any mode of transport with other people, receive treatment at a private medical facility, or avoid surcharges on their insurance because of that belief.

If religion trumped all other concerns, then anyone could claim any extreme view. For instance, there are religions and groups that exist today—such as particular sects of Bedouins—that do not believe in property rights and land ownership the way we in general implement it in America. If we allowed convictions to be superior to these laws then someone could just pitch a tent in your backyard and say that their religion and belief structure allows it.

The same could be said about someone who works in a kitchen but considers it is against God's glory to wash their hands after going to the bathroom. Or another person could say that clothing blocks what God created in his own image and that we must return to how Adam and Eve lived before eating the fruit of knowledge. Should we allow these principles, as well?

Associated Press: "Texas man strips at meeting to make point on masks". HTTPS://YOUTU.BE/F9D8OHPK1MK

No, we have laws that protect people, property, society, the environment, the government, and all other concerns despite whatever an individual's or group's beliefs may be, no matter how big that group is or how loud their voices are. Religious freedom does and should have confines, just as all other freedoms do. There is a delicate balancing act among all the many contradictory parts of the Constitution and law; but at the end of the day, it all comes down to this simple equation:

NO RELIGIOUS BELIEF SUPERSEDES MY RIGHT TO LIVE.

My Family is Underground

How does a life defined by death affect the course of history?

Bones inside the ossuary below the Cemetery Church of All Saints in Sedlec, Czech Republic. The ossuary is estimated to contain skeletons of between 40,000 and 70,000 people. Photo and description by **JAN KAMENÍČEK**[89], **CC BY-SA 3.0**[90], via Wikimedia Commons.

---

[89] HTTPS://COMMONS.WIKIMEDIA.ORG/WIKI/FILE:OSSUARY_IN_SEDLEC.JPG
[90] HTTPS://CREATIVECOMMONS.ORG/LICENSES/BY-SA/3.0

» Key Points

- *Because so many family members died before I was even born, entire branches of my family tree and their history were completely lost to me.*

- *Throughout my life, the rate of death has only accelerated to the point where there are more people underground than there are those walking on it.*

- *Death has taken many other forms, including of the self due to dementia, of relationships due to estrangement, and of connection due to disappearance.*

THEY STARTED TO DIE BEFORE I BORN...

When I was a small child, I had one grandmother—my mother's mother. Even now I can distinctly remember being bewildered when I started to learn that other people had two sets of grandparents. Though I understood well enough that I was missing a grandfather, the thought that there should be an entirely different pair for my father was beyond my comprehension. Much like how my family has a peculiar way of making french toast, my perception from birth became locked into this fundamental idea, one that shaped my reality until I was old enough to understand what happened to my lost family.

A view inside St. Louis Cemetery №3 in New Orleans, LA on March 6, 2020. Photo by J.P. Prag.

Both of my father's parents and my mother's father died within 16 months of my progenitors getting married, which was 8 years before I was born. My father was a reserved, private man himself and getting any information on our family history out of him was nearly impossible. Where my father was introspective, his brother was gregarious. Yet he would not provide any details on their parents or the generations that preceded them, either. My father used silence and his brother used humor and misdirection, but the results were the same. Everything I know about my paternal history comes from snippets of conversation, research on genealogy sites, and conjecture—at best.

Their deaths deprived me of a legacy. Perhaps that legacy was horrific and filled with undesirable traits, but at least it would have been mine! The loss of my mother's father had a similar effect that I have only learned about in the past few months prior to this writing. You see, my maternal grandmother grew up spoiled and—from what I can understand—her future husband came from the other side of the tracks. On his side of the tracks they ate roasted eggplant while on her side they had never even heard of such a proletariat vegetable. From what I was able to glean, it did not appear that my maternal grandmother's parents were particularly happy with the match. After he died, it would seem that they forced a cutoff with his entire family, depriving my mother and then me and my brother of access to an entire tributary.

I am aware of this because I made contact with a large number of my maternal grandfather's family, who for decades I did not know existed. From genetically close cousins to people flung around the world—thanks to DNA matches and family trees we have found each other. Through these connections I learned about an entire

Romanian branch of my family that had never even been hinted at. Scores of them have lived and died without me having the slightest inkling that they were out there. How much family did I lose just because a couple of ancestors looked down their noses at some other ones? How much has been lost to me because of one death?

» Karma Incarnate

Sadly, I see the potential for history to repeat itself. If my partner and I had children today, they would grow up almost exactly as I have. Where my partner's mother is alive and well and we see her regularly, my mother died 12 years ago. She had been sick for years with a rare blood disorder that made her red blood cell count drop like a rock. This left her lethargic and sedentary, which in turn eventually led to her death. My father called me when it happened, and I was thankfully working locally so I could get to their house. But I got there too quickly and walked right through the front door and into her corpse.

My father is currently among the living dead. He has advanced Parkinson's related dementia which has robbed him of almost everything he was. The shell that he is now is unrecognizable to the person he was before. We have had many close calls over the past couple of years, including with COVID-19. While he is resilient and I have seen him bounce back from some of the worst situations you can imagine, his luck cannot hold out forever. And even if it did, I would not want to expose my children and father to each other. It would only be painful for all of them. While he is technically alive, I have already mourned his loss, too.

A slightly different situation exists with my partner's father. He is also technically alive and doing well as far as we know. Still, she has almost no association with him, which means neither do I, nor would our children. It is a very different type of death here, the death of a relationship. We would intentionally keep him out of our children's lives, if he even tried to be a part of them. Thus, our children would grow up with just their maternal grandmother to count on, the same as me.

Maple Grove Cemetery in Townshend, VT on June 19, 2021. Photo by Caroline Prag, used royalty free with permission.

» Closing Doors

In actuality, though, I did have more than my maternal grandmother. Both of her parents—my great-grandparents—were still alive when I was born, but were as distant from me as a set of octogenarians and a toddler can get. It was not to last, anyway.

> **When I was barely 7 years old, I saw my first dead body.**

My great-grandfather's passing is the first death I can remember. In Jewish custom, caskets are closed for the funeral and bodies are buried as quickly after demise as allowed, preferably within a day or two, and definitely without any preservation methods aside from refrigeration. But what has also become custom—at least in North America—is for close family to visit the body ahead of the funeral officially starting and see the person before the casket is permanently shut. Thus, I got my first introduction to real death through someone I knew well and at a very young age.

Just over two years later, his wife joined him in the ground. Another two years after that was a great uncle on my father's side. And another, and another, and so on and so forth and *"so it goes"* for my entire life. Sometimes there were several in a year, other times we could go a few years without anyone dying. There were occasions when there was almost no one available to remember a life, like when my mother's brother died and was buried near Christmas Day. In latter incidents, the whole gang (what was left of it) was there and we laughed about how we only ever saw each other at funerals. Of course, it was unfortunately true.

St. Louis Cemetery №1 in on April 6, 2014. Photo by J.P. Prag.

With each death, another part of the family history shut its door to never reveal the truth of what happened. There was a time I showed up at my father's house for a surprise visit and found him returning home in a suit. When I inquired about what had happened, he told me of another person who had died and that he was just coming from the funeral. Death had reached the point where it was so common it did not even merit a mention.

Yet death had a way of taking not just the ones it was after, but those associated with them. After my cousin—who was also my godmother—lost both of her parents, she and the rest of her immediate family literally left the country and were not heard from again. That branch has now been sawed off from me.

Because of the death of my mother earlier, as my grandmother grew older and sicker I started to take care of her. Despite her protestations, my partner and I insisted she would be at our wedding no matter what. Always getting her way, she died just a few weeks before the ceremony. I told my then-boss that I needed to take time off of work to take care of everything, manage all the arrangements, and also clean out her place (all while finishing preparations for my own wedding). He was unsympathetic and harshly asked, "Don't you have some cousins or something that can help with that?"

Kinneret Cemetery near the shores of the Sea of Galilee in northern Israel. Photo by J.P. Prag on January 17, 2007.

"No," I forlornly told him, "almost everyone is dead, not here, or incapable of support. I am all that is left."

He did not understand what it means to lose almost everyone so only a handful of family members remained;

and even among those they were either far flung or frail themselves. It was also around then that my father started to take a turn for the worse, too. Thus, as a relatively young, newly married person I was taking care of generations of people; a heavy burden. Almost an entire generation in between had died off and it has left me—going on for over five years at the time of this writing—with being the only support mechanism available.

While my father trudges on, others have fallen by the wayside that I have not even told him about. What would be the point? My grandmother's brother died on New Year's Day 2020. He had been suffering for years with Alzheimer's related dementia and made quite a scene at his sister's funeral. That incident was a peek at my father's future; as was the loss of my aunt who also had dementia and was killed by COVID-19 a year later.

> **AS IF BECKONED BY THESE VERY WORDS, ON THE DAY THIS WAS ORIGINALLY COMPLETED I RECEIVED A CALL FROM MY COUSIN THAT HER MOTHER—WHO I HAD LAST SEEN AT HER HUSBAND'S FUNERAL—HAD DIED, TOO.**
>
> **RELENTLESS...**

Death has been part of my life and informed everything I have ever done or ever will. I would not say I am numb to it, nor would I say I accept it—especially for myself, my partner, and our remaining family. But death and I have come to an informal understanding with each other, a détente of sorts. Though I know death will win in the end, I can still go on living.

EULOGY FOR MY DAD

Alan Prag: April 24, 1947 to November 20, 2021

Alan Prag at the wedding of Doug and Kelly Prag on April 2, 2011. Photo cropped and edited by J.P. Prag

Thank you to everyone who is here today, to everyone who cannot be here and is holding us in their thoughts, and to everyone else who has been taken from us over the years. My dad, Alan, joins those souls today after a long battle with Parkinson's. It is a disease that first robbed him of his physical control, then his mental, and finally his life. Even though we have been preparing for this day for years, it still takes me by surprise. The one thing my father was—the one thing that you could call his defining characteristic—was resilient.

This is a man who could and did survive everything. Many decades ago, he fell asleep behind the wheel of his car and flipped over several times. He walked away without a scratch. A forklift dropped its load on him, and he only had a plate and a few screws in his ankle to show for it. His longtime job was eliminated, and he changed careers the next day. He lost both of his parents at a young age, just after he and my mom Rochelle married. Life went on, and they thankfully decided to have my brother Doug and me. When my mom died just over 12 years ago after battling her own long-term illness, he kept on living because—as he said—that is just what you do. Even with these, his last days, he held on far longer than any medical expert projected he could. If he was going to leave us, it was going to be on his timeline and according to his terms.

We've had plenty of scares over the years, for sure, but he always found a way to bounce back. Earlier this year, he was diagnosed with COVID-19 just a day before he was supposed to get his first vaccination shot. At the same time, my Aunt Cindy—who was in similar physical and mental health straits—also caught COVID. She did not make it, but my Dad somehow came out in better shape on the other side, giving us a few more months. At her funeral, my cousin Marci said something during the eulogy that touched me deeply and resonated with everything I was going through, too. In so many words, she explained that she had already mourned the loss of her mother because the person she knew was long gone. What remained behind was a vessel, just an echo of the human being that used to be.

As such, I choose not to remember the remnants of the person I saw over the past couple of years. Instead, I choose to remember the man who placated a precocious child with his ever-expanding overelaborate bedtime routine. I recall Monday nights, sitting together as I pretended to do my homework and we watched wrestling together. I hear him fruitlessly trying to dress down the dogs because they dared to need to go outside again, yet allowing them to jump up on the couch and lick him all over his face. I smell the garden he planted and tended, even though our yard received no sun. I admire him for convincing the plow guy to clear out his driveway not for a fee, but with a trade in kind for a hooded sweatshirt. I watch him beam with delight as he described some bargain he had hunted down, whether he needed the item or not. I feel a day half the temperature of today where he would be standing outside at the flea market trying to sell another pair of diabetic socks. And where did those diabetic socks come from? Why, a potato farm in Alabama, of course. How did my father ever find a potato farm in Alabama that was also a socks distributer? This was his magic!

These were among his many secrets. My Dad had an amazing capacity to hide almost everything from everyone who knew him. Even under the influence of heavy prescription drugs and a degenerative brain disorder, when I probed him whether he wanted to tell me anything about his own parents, he still had the wherewithal to say, "No, I don't think so." He was private, he liked to be on his own, and he didn't have a great need for the rest of the world. Without my mother, his antisocial behavior was allowed to run a little wild... or rather mild. I know he was difficult with his friends, and cannot express my appreciation enough for those who realized that you just had to show up unannounced and tell him that you were taking him to dinner. Trying to plan anything was a recipe for disaster.

And try we all did! He loved sports, especially basketball, but trying to convince him to go to a game was impossible. Whether it was sports, classic car auctions, town board meetings, parades, or even fireworks, there was only one place he wanted to watch them from: his seat on the right side of the couch. A visit with him was more often than not ordering some pizza and sitting in front of the TV. He would complain about having seen the same episode of NCIS hundreds of times, but that would not inspire him to search out something different. The creation of ION Television was both his greatest godsend and his worst enticement. Yet just a few weeks ago he told me that it was good when family visits, even if they just sit there for a half hour and say nothing. Apparently, he cherished those moments of silence.

A couple of years ago when things started to turn but it looked like he could still live an independent life, we asked him what he really wanted, what would make him content. After much prodding, he definitively said, "If I can have a bed to sleep in, some half-decent food brought to me, and a TV to watch, I'll be happy." And it would have, truly, if he was given the chance. Sure, he still would have found something to complain about, but that was also one of his favorite activities. And despite all those complaints, he never wanted to give up; he always worked to persevere.

That perseverance; that ethic that if you want something, you are the one who has to work for it; that you are responsible for yourself—these are the ideals he helped instill in my brother and me. It is also what we looked for in our spouses Kelly and Caroline. Was he the Dad who was going to be there for all our soccer games? No. Was he the Dad who gave us the freedom to make our own mistakes but helped pick us up when we went astray? Absolutely. Was he the husband who was going to surprise my Mom with a romantic gesture? No. Was he the husband who was going to deal with all of the day-to-day minutia of a marriage and be a supporting partner in that way? Once again, yes. Was he the type of guy who was going to forcefully rise up the rungs of the corporate ladder, putting his stamp on the company? No. Was he the type of guy you could depend upon, who was loyal, and knew the specific types of shoes and sandals that sold at every unique storefront? Indeed, these were the skills he brought to the table.

My Dad was not a person looking to make waves, but only wanting to ride them out. He would never have wanted to be a burden on anyone, never would have wanted to be dependent on any other person for anything. His passing, in so many ways, is a relief to him. He is independent and free again. Now he can go back to all of his idiosyncrasies, and never have to explain why he does them to any of us.

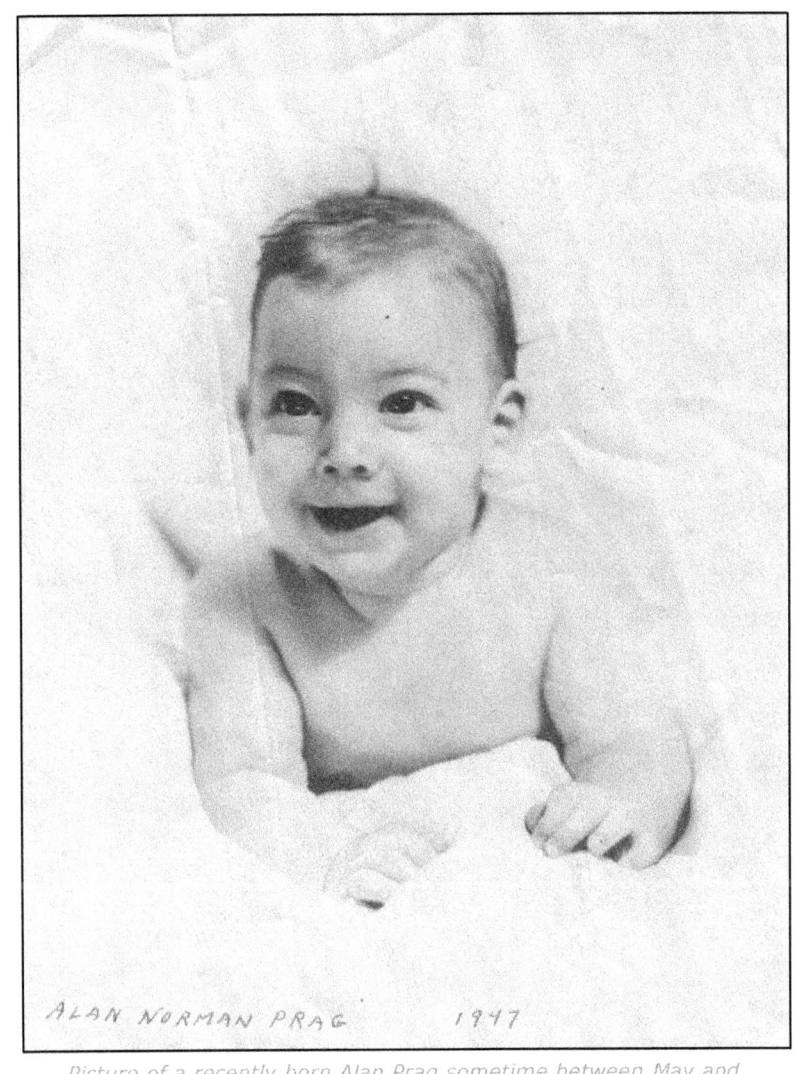

Picture of a recently born Alan Prag sometime between May and December 1947 by an unknown photographer.

PART 3: SCIENCE AND CONSEQUENCES

ENVIRONMENTALISM: WORST CASE SCENARIO

Is it a problem if we are completely wrong about Global Climate Change?

Photo by **JOHN CAMERON**[91] on **UNSPLASH**

---

[91] HTTPS://UNSPLASH.COM/@JOHN_CAMERON

» Key Points

- *Trying to teach environmentalism to those opposed to believing there is a crisis is a fruitless and wasteful pursuit.*

- *Instead of emphasizing what needs to be removed, we should be focusing on what gains there are to be made.*

- *We should appeal to the basest, self-serving instincts of human beings to make sure they understand the personal benefits of saving the world.*

IS THE EARTH WARMING AT AN UNPRECEDENTED RATE? ARE HUMANS CAUSING THIS CHANGE THROUGH THEIR ACTIONS?

IT DOES NOT MATTER.

For those who do not believe that Global Climate Change is real or acknowledge that it is happening but do not believe humans have a material impact, there is no compelling narrative that will spur them into immediate action. The facts, figures, and scientific consensus are never going to make a dent in their perceptions. Yes, there are a few exceptions, but on a mass scale it is a fruitless argument. Frankly, it is the wrong approach.

Of course, we should still continue to educate others on the dangers of human-caused Global Climate Change and work towards a more conscientious future. However, that is a multi-generational project of changing human behavior and does not answer the question of "**what can we do now?**" In order to answer that, the conversation needs to be completely reversed. Let us pretend for a moment that the Earth is a stable system and no action is needed to reverse the ongoing trends. Then the questions simply become:

- If we still do all of the environmental projects, what is the worst that can potentially happen?

- What do we objectively gain by doing these projects anyway?

- Are we really in danger of losing anything? And if we are, is what we are replacing it with better anyway?

» CLEAN AIR, WATER, AND GROUND

Walking down the street, you see a plastic bag is fluttering, entangled in a tree. Further on, a storm drain has become completely clogged with wrappers from a local fast-food restaurant. Your walk takes you down to the water and you see someone has actually thrown a whole shopping cart in, where it will now lay forever.

Smog settles over Los Angeles, CA on December 28, 2017. Photo by J.P. Prag

This is the world we live in. Trash is everywhere and it makes the very ground we walk on disgusting. Forget everything about the impact on animals and plant life; you are free to be selfish here. Who wants to walk through refuse? It is an assault on our senses—unless you are Oscar the Grouch. Cleaning up all of this mess would beautify the world we inhabit. And candidly, beauty increases the value of a space. That is not an esoteric thought, either, but a literal truth in real estate. Property values go down proportionately to the amount of pollution nearby and the general state of an area. Cleaning up around a parcel makes it more desirable to be lived in, which in turn can be a personal benefit.

Of course, this does not just apply to what we can see, but what we inhale. Smog settles over cities, industrial parks, highways, and everywhere that the combustion of fossil and other fuels happen. Smog unambiguously makes it difficult to breathe and—again speaking to our baser instincts—looks gross. In places like Mexico City, the situation got so bad that in the early 1990s private companies started installing "oxygen booths", phone booth-like contraptions to get a few minutes of clean air. Removing particulate matter from the air does nothing less than make it easier to respire.

As with the land and air, the rivers, lakes, waterways, and seas can all benefit. While it may cost businesses more money to maintain protections against runoff and for underground water, it is cheaper for people to have access to potable H_2O nearby. Further, freshwater is the most important resource in the world for every purpose imaginable—from drinking to farming, from fracking to nuclear power, from cleaning to building. We need as much of it as we can get and doing everything to ensure our limited supplies are readily and easily available benefits all groups, no matter their intentions.

» INDEPENDENCE & NATIONAL SECURITY

When it comes to water in particular, though, it is a security issue. While places like the United States may have enough freshwater for a population greater than the over 330 million living in the country in the 2020s, that is not the case everywhere in the world. Freshwater scarcity has already led to skirmishes and wars. Even if someone does not believe that a warming world is making water less available, an overpopulated one certainly is. As populations grow around the planet, they need additional sources of water, which in turn leads to more trouble.

But what about closer to home? For simplicity's sake, let us focus on the United States' perspective. In the U.S.A. a bigger issue is energy usage. Great strides have already been made in efficiency and these continue to expand with each year. Efficiency means less energy usage, which in turn means less costs to do an action. There is no downside to continuing to innovate and enforce more efficient use of energy as waste is truly money lost.

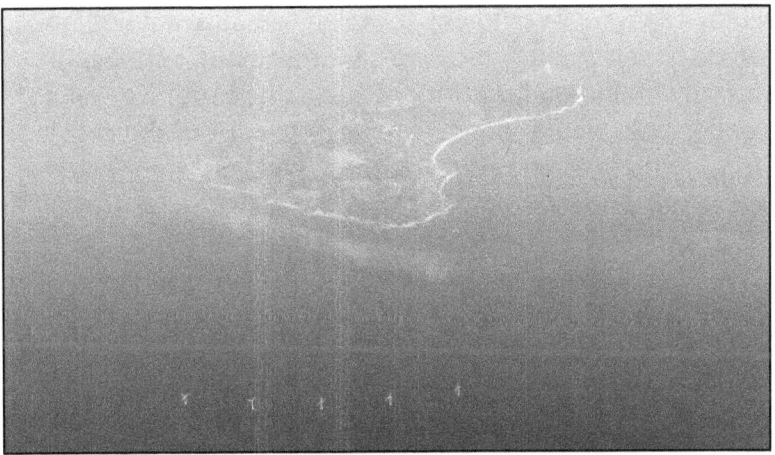

The first offshore wind-farm in the United States near the coast of Block Island (New Shoreham), Rhode Island on August 6, 2018. Photo by J.P. Prag.

The United States in the 2020s still produces the majority of its energy by burning fossil fuels and similar substances. Despite strong production at home, a vast amount of this petrol comes from foreign sources. In other words, we have made ourselves dependent upon outside countries and multi-national corporations, which is a security threat. It has been seen many times when there are issues with the delivery system—whether intentional or not—destruction, loss, and death have followed. Why would we want to be intertwined with others when we can do it all on our own? Why open ourselves up to that unnecessary risk?

Even something like shale oil is highly dependent on a foreign country (namely: Canada). Thus beyond cleaning up our air for the self-serving reasons above, we can also move to completely renewable energy sources for nationalistic reasons. What is a better American story than innovating with our own technology and creating an infrastructure and distribution system that is ruggedly independent? Why should any American be beholden to some foreign government (or even the faraway Federal or State government) when we can utilize our own local resources and do it better? At the same time, we will no longer be sending money overseas (or out of the region) to regimes that do not support us, our values, or our more natural allies.

The United States is a place of extensive resources. We can control nature and harness the sun, wind, waters, movements of the earth, and even the slightest fluctuation of temperatures. At the end of the day, an American destiny can be demonstrated by taming Gaia herself and bending her to our will.[92]

» JOBS AND INFRASTRUCTURE

In order to move away from a greenhouse gas dependent society, a lot must be developed. Solar panels and fields, windmills and their farms, hydrogen liquefaction systems and pipelines, geothermal machines and the vehicles to move them—everything must be built, installed,

---

[92] Note this is intentional misogyny.

maintained, and replaced over time. Modernizing our infrastructure is not a one-time activity, though; it will be an ongoing effort that creates permanent jobs in manufacturing, transportation, maintenance, technology, support, and more.

Photo by **NOAA**[93] on **UNSPLASH**

A "Green Economy" is a misnomer. There is no difference between electricity being produced by coal and it being produced by a windmill or a paddle-wheel. In either situation, it is still plain electricity (electrons free-flowing through conductors) that is used to power all of our modern conveniences. A "Green Economy" takes absolutely nothing away. Instead, it is just a simple replacement. In other words, there is no separate and different "Green Economy". As the saying goes:

---

[93] HTTPS://UNSPLASH.COM/@NOAA

[It's t]he Economy, stupid.

James Carville, 1992
Political strategist to Bill Clinton

While a "Green Economy" may sound like something is being lost, an "Economy" for people is simply about gains. Here, the semantics do truly matter and are getting in the way of making progress. Instead of focusing on what will be lost or removed, the answer is thinking about all that can be added. We are just swapping out one old technology for a new one, something natural in our capitalist system. Would we try to save cassettes and VHS a from CDs and DVDs? And in turn, would we avoid using streaming services to protect CDs and DVDs? No, the American ideal is to encourage further advancement and replace the old with new and better. The "average person" will not lose a thing.

» Life as Normal

As a matter of fact, the "average person" will not notice a difference at all. Everyday life, the tools we use, the entertainment we enjoy, the places we go—none of this will change. Someone does not need to be "aware" and "know" about climate science in order to profit from it. Are you one of the few people who understands how the device you may be reading this on works? What percentage of the population can replace a sink faucet? How many people even know how a simple desk fan functions? Knowledge of scientific principles and applications is not a requirement to take advantage of and benefit from a technology.

Outside Biosphere 2—one the most unique environmental experiments in human history—located in Oracle, Arizona on December 30, 2013. Photo by J.P. Prag.

That is the real message to walk away with here. Having a cleaner environment does not cost anything for the everyday Joe and Jill Schmoe. On the contrary, over time those cleaner streets, air, and waterways will—at a minimum—provide the most personal kind of benefits. Technologies get cheaper as they get more widely spread and dispersed through economies of scale. Because of this, in the long run home-brewed solutions mixed with efficiencies mixed with a shinier world will result in lower costs, thus more dollars that could be spent on something else or saved for another day.

DOES IT MATTER IF WE CLEAN UP THE WORLD FOR PURELY SELFISH REASONS?

ABSOLUTELY NOT.

Anyone wanting to teach a "lesson" about humanity's impact on the world should swallow their pride and realize that they are taking the wrong approach. You can be "right" and argue all day long and get nowhere, or you can forget about all that and shift the paradigm to get the necessary results to save the Earth. Appeal to the basest instincts and the worst stereotypical characteristics expected of members of the human race. Let them know they will lose absolutely nothing and focus on everything they will gain. Their creature comforts are not under threat; there will be jobs aplenty; they will have more money; the world will be less gross everywhere they go; and wherever they live will be free of interference from outsiders.

Even if nearly every scientist and environmentalist is completely wrong, it makes no difference. Implementing their plans will—in a worst-case scenario—personally benefit you in every way.

The sun gently sets into the Pacific Ocean outside San Diego, CA on December 29, 2017. Photo by J.P. Prag.

THE VEGAN EXTINCTION

Everything has unintended consequences

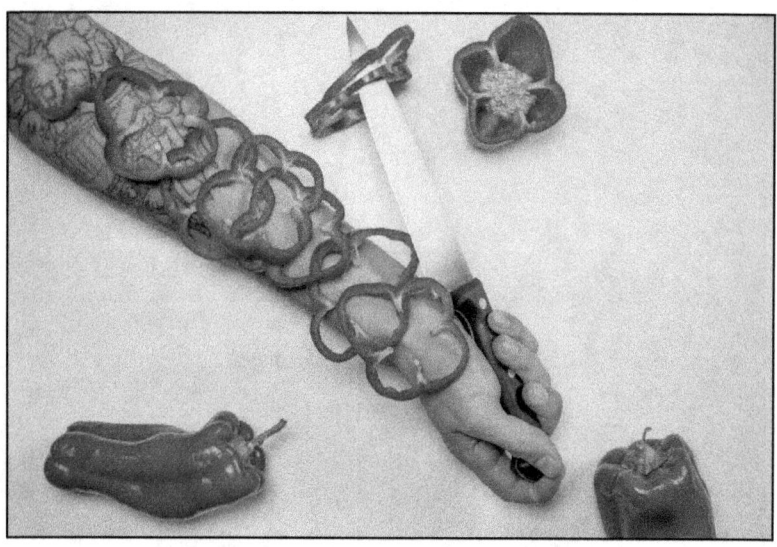

*Photo by **Angelique Emonet**[94] on **Unsplash***

---

[94] HTTPS://UNSPLASH.COM/@ANGELIQUE_EMONET

» Key Points

- *Today it is possible for the world to become completely plant-based; and it is already heading in that direction for reasons of economics.*

- *Despite that, it does not mean all problems related to animal husbandry will be immediately resolved, nor that new issues will not be created.*

- *To prepare for the future, we have to be honest about the real impact of our actions in order to plan and act accordingly.*

> [T]HE GREATEST HARM CAN RESULT FROM THE BEST INTENTIONS. IT SOUNDS [LIKE] A PARADOX, BUT KINDNESS AND GOOD INTENTIONS CAN BE AN INSIDIOUS PATH TO DESTRUCTION... [IT] CAN CAUSE ANYTHING FROM DISCOMFORT, TO DISASTER, TO DEATH.
>
> STONE OF TEARS, CHAPTER 63, BY TERRY GOODKIND

Imagine a world where we have been able to solve all food insecurity; cure a large amount of our environmental issues; free up ground, water, and other similar resources for either human use or returning to nature; and have ended pain and suffering for billions of creatures a year. This is a reality that is not only possible in our land of make-believe, but readily available with current technologies and techniques. We have all of the means necessary, just not the willpower to make it happen. Yet given time and incentives, even this lack in spirit may be overcome.

This is a utopia foreseen by communities like those committed to *veganism*—an overall pan-belief that covers various viewpoints that can be best summed up as the removal of animal products from human consumption. Now, there are plenty of arguments over what is an "animal product" and what is "consumption". For instance, is keeping a dog as a pet an issue? We are not here to resolve these subtle nuances, though, so that debate can continue outside of these pages.

Instead, let us pretend that the world has for the most

part converted to a *plant-based lifestyle*. This term is more encompassing as it describes what people are doing: using plants for sustenance and survival. The impacts would be immediately obvious as animal agriculture is the second largest contributor to global climate change just after burning fossil fuels. This comes from the greenhouse gasses chattel animals release; the land and water they use; and what is necessary to process, transport, and store animal products. Growing plants simply uses less of everything for a higher caloric, macrobiotic, and useful material result.

*Photo by **VIDAR SMITS**[95] on **UNSPLASH***

It all sounds wonderful, right? Maybe not for you personally as you may really love the flavor of raw beef, but as a general concept? Still, that does not mean it is not without unintended consequences. Like any utopia, it comes at a very personal cost, one that must be acknowledged. One cannot demand this future without

---

[95] HTTPS://UNSPLASH.COM/@VIDARSMITS

accepting what else is going to happen because of it, especially those things that are not so directly connected.

To be clear, this is not an argument against a plant-based world because of what might happen to specific jobs or industries or any such thing; nor the way particular bodies may react to the diet. Further, this is also not an argument for a plant-based world for all the reasons listed above. This is just asking everyone—even those who believe they are fighting for a better future—to be honest about what the impact of their actions may actually be.

» WALKING INTO SPIDERWEBS

Around 9,000 to 10,000 years ago, humans began adding new animals into their stationary agrarian lifestyle. Where dogs have been with humans for perhaps 30,000 years and sheep and goats go back about 11,000 years, it was during this time that the wild auroch branched off to become the common domesticated cow. Today, there is not a wild auroch left anywhere in the world, with the last ones possibly seen in the early 17th century. Meanwhile, in the early 2020s, there are about 1 billion cattle in the world, or about 1 cow for every 8 people.

Cows have changed everything about humans, including for the majority's ability to tolerate lactose into adulthood—most interestingly the lactose of other animals, something no other creature can do. But the act of raising cows to produce milk is not exactly profitable nowadays or good for the environment. That is part of the reason why companies like **PERFECT DAY**[96] and **BIOMILK**[97] are developing processes to make "real" milk without daily cow involvement (although through wildly different

---

[96] HTTPS://PERFECTDAYFOODS.COM/
[97] HTTPS://WWW.BIOMILK.COM/

methods). Meanwhile, companies like **IMPOSSIBLE FOODS**[98] have worked tirelessly to mimic meat in every way, including creating a plant-based heme to replicate the blood found in slaughtered flesh. Other companies are looking to grow meat directly from cultured cells; so in reality the protein is animal, just without the "breeding a live beast" part.

Photo by **ROBERT BYE**[99] on **UNSPLASH**

Whatever technology or mix of technologies wins out in the end is irrelevant. What matters the most is that at economies of scale these products will be less expensive to produce than the animal-based commodities they are designed to supplant. This is the inflection point where corporations transition to sources not derived from live animals, but from any and all of these other methods. The process is already well underway with major investors like Tyson and Coca-Cola involved. Besides, for decades now soy and corn proteins have been mixed into all kinds of

---

[98] HTTPS://IMPOSSIBLEFOODS.COM/PRODUCTS/BURGER
[99] HTTPS://UNSPLASH.COM/@ROBERTBYE

"100% pure meat" products. Companies are interested in keeping costs down so long as quality is at least the same or imperceptibly changed.

The average consumer has no idea where their milk and meat are truly sourced from and what it is made out of, so swapping in an exact replica product will not make a difference, especially if it is not advertised as such. And when that happens, there will be less and less need for our domesticated cattle. Sure, there will always be connoisseurs who will pay hundreds or thousands of dollars for rare flanks, but the vast majority of consumers will move on to the affordable products that are no different than anything they have today. Unfortunately for cows, that means there will be less of a need for them to exist at all, especially at their relative expense.

As already noted, the wild auroch ancestor of today's cows is completely extinct, as are all cousin species. While earlier breeds of escaped cows were able to become feral—such as the ones from the late 18th century in Hawai'i that have evolved to be a smaller size with long legs like sheep—most of today's breeds cannot survive without human intervention. Humans have bread them to be so large that in many cases artificial insemination is the only way they can reproduce. Let loose into the wild, almost all the cows would be dead in just one generation (not to mention the havoc they would cause being an invasive species). In other words, veganism will yield a genocide for cowkind.

Cows are not alone in this, though. Most fowl—especially turkeys and chickens—have been bred to have breasts so big that they cannot mate. And since we are now countless generations in with artificial insemination, they may not even know how. Unlike cows, there are still wild versions of these animals, but the domesticated lines are mostly incapable of breeding with them and therefore their bloodlines would die out. Most of our domesticated food, labor, and companion animals stand no chance in the wild, whether they have brethren or not.

Photo by *IVA RAJOVIĆ*[100] on *UNSPLASH*

Additionally, there are impacts up and down the food chain. Insects like mosquitos, fleas, ticks, and biting flies are often specialized to target specific animals. If those animals do not exist, then the insect population that depends upon them will also crash. Of course, then there are animals (and even some plants) that feed on those insects. Without their major food source, whole colonies of animals like bats may die out. Since bat guano is a potent resource for plants, that in turn may limit their growth which impacts animals that are dependent upon them. Thus the whole entangled food web must be completely realigned.

---

[100] HTTPS://UNSPLASH.COM/@EKLEKTIKUM

Again, this is not an argument against going down the road of retiring animals from human service. However, we have to be honest that it is not an ideal situation and it will not immediately solve all of our woes without causing new ones. Humans and our domesticated animals are not separate from the environment; we are just as much a part of all of these cycles as anything in the "natural world". When we make major changes like this, the impacts are far and wide, and usually out of our control.

We must be honest about what is about to happen so that we can plan and mitigate. The (feral) horse is out of the stable[101] and this changeover is already underway. Yet animals are only part of the equation that must be considered.

» And all I Wanted Was the Simple Things

> **When all greenhouse gas emissions from food are taken into account, rice emits more greenhouse gases per calorie than wheat or corn but less than fruits, vegetables, legumes, or any animal sources.**
>
> "Should We Eat Less Rice?[102]" by Evelyn Lamb[103] for *Scientific American* on August 21, 2019

---

[101] There is no such thing as a wild horse, that species is also extinct.
[102] HTTPS://BLOGS.SCIENTIFICAMERICAN.COM/ROOTS-OF-UNITY/SHOULD-WE-EAT-LESS-RICE/
[103] HTTPS://WWW.SCIENTIFICAMERICAN.COM/AUTHOR/EVELYN-LAMB/

Animals may be one of the largest producers of greenhouse gases, but removing them from the equation does not make those gasses just disappear. The predominant method of growing rice (in open, wet paddies), in particular, is a potent producer of methane—which has far more short-term impact than carbon dioxide when it comes to global climate change. Whether we eat more whole plants or use plants as feeder stock for other downstream products, the result is the same: we must grow the calories.

Photo by **NICK FEWINGS**[104] on **UNSPLASH**

Experiments in the 2020s are ongoing to grow rice with drip irrigation to limit this issue, but even in the best case it will not *eliminate* the emissions. Nor will the other considerations that must be made with all plants. Some—especially popular crops like almonds and avocados—take a disproportionate amount of fresh water. According to

---

[104] HTTPS://UNSPLASH.COM/@JANNERBOY62

ERIC HOLTHAUS OF THE SLATE[105], in 2014 and 2015 almond growing used up around 10% of California's agricultural water supply. Even with higher water use, in the context of the output of calories and nutrients, these crops are still more efficient than animals. Even so, that does not mean they are 100% more efficient! Water use may be less with plants, but it is still a huge amount that must be removed from nature for human use (or withheld from direct human consumption to grow plants). We must not pretend that we are getting all of that water back.

This is true for all resources necessary for plants. Animals take up a lot of land, but so do plants. Less land, yes, but still significantly more than nothing. We might be creative with rooftops, vertical spaces, indoor hydroponics, and many other potentialities, but everything is still a limited supply. Honesty is required in order to tackle the issues with being completely plant-based, not just believing it is going to resolve all the problems we have right now.

Beyond all of that, we create a new danger in massive mono-culture. Frankly, we have very little diversity in our plant stocks already and there is no reason to believe this would not be the case if plants were a larger percentage of the human diet. If anything, the issue would be exacerbated to the point where a blight in a single crop could cause a worldwide starvation event. As stated early on, economics will be the largest driver of the changeover to a plant-based society. At the same time, economics will drive the creation of cheaper, faster, and bigger plants to continue to push down cost. Those developed seeds (most likely genetically modified, at that) will be sold around the globe and further push out native and diverse species.

---

[105] HTTPS://SLATE.COM/BUSINESS/2015/04/ALMONDS-IN-CALIFORNIA-THEY-USE-UP-A-LOT-OF-WATER-BUT-THEY-DESERVE-A-PLACE-IN-CALIFORNIAS-FUTURE.HTML

Still, it does not even end there. While we may be able to mitigate a disaster related to growing, plants do not solve our other epidemics.

*A tree pangolin on January 1, 2009. Photo by **VALERIUS TYGART**[106], CC BY-SA 3.0[107], via Wikimedia Commons.*

» Don't Tell Me 'Cause it Hurts

Zoonotic diseases—those that originate in animals, especially intensely farmed animals—have always been a problem, but that issue has only grown with further expansion of global meat eating and the farming necessary to support it. Even COVID-19 most likely has a zoonotic source, whether that be bats or pangolins or some other intermediary. Seemingly, moving away from regular interaction with other animals and not having waste runoff should help limit and perhaps end viral and bacterial epidemics related to them.

---

[106] HTTPS://COMMONS.WIKIMEDIA.ORG/WIKI/FILE:TREE_PANGOLIN.JPG
[107] HTTPS://CREATIVECOMMONS.ORG/LICENSES/BY-SA/3.0

Nevertheless, growing plants often uses pesticides and other chemicals, which may have adverse effects on the health of all living beings. Runoff from farms—including from simple things like nitrogen added to the soil to help feed plants and inspire growth—can cause downstream environmental impacts that hurt and kill not just humans, but wildlife at large. Beyond that, to protect plants from the aforementioned blights, it seems likely that farmers would implement similar techniques they use with animals, thus the equivalent of the overuse of antibiotics.

Yet all of these issues are still not the epidemic we must be most concerned with.

Even with COVID-19 contributing to over 520,000 excess deaths in the United States in 2020 and at least another 467,000 in 2021 **ACCORDING TO PRELIMINARY STATISTICS**[108], heart disease remains the number one killer of Americans. What is the top contributor to heart disease? None other than the obesity epidemic that is sweeping America and many other nations. At no point in history have calories been so cheap and accessible, yet nutrition so lacking.

And frankly, a plant-based lifestyle does nothing to solve this. A person could eat nothing but french fries and frosted cake and still be a technical vegan. Food manufacturers are not going to stop adding excess sugar to their products. On the contrary, it is more likely to be used along with fats in order to make sure flavor profiles are closer to meat. Being made of plants does not make a food automatically healthier. There is no such thing as an organic cookie tree.

---

[108] HTTPS://JAMANETWORK.COM/JOURNALS/JAMA/FULLARTICLE/2778361
HTTPS://USAFACTS.ORG/ARTICLES/COVID-EXCESS-DEATHS-CAUSES-2021/

Photo by **SIGMUND**[109] *on* **UNSPLASH**

Changing behavior to eating more whole, unprocessed foods would be a multi-generational affair and may be a complete failure anyway due to what people expect their food to taste like and be able to do. As discussed at the onset, in order to get people to switch away from meats, the replacement products must be a near one-for-one match. But in order to be that, they must be nearly as unhealthy—and in some cases even more so. Further, from a worldwide logistics perspective: processing, genetically modifying, and using chemicals is actually the better, safer, and more economical route to making sure all people have equal access to food. Mitigating blight conditions can be as simple as processing and storing excess product until it is needed. In other words, better for us is not necessarily the best solution to the other difficulties related to feeding nearly 8 billion people.

---

[109] HTTPS://UNSPLASH.COM/@SIGMUND

» Take This Pink Ribbon Off My Eyes

Plants are not going to cure the world of all of the woes of animal husbandry. While there are many beneficial impacts to completely removing animal products from the world, it is not a panacea solution without its own drawbacks. Let us be clear: these deterrents should not be enough to dissuade humanity from ultimately pursuing this path, nor are the issues presented insurmountable themselves. But that is the overall point: we must acknowledge all of the real consequences of these actions. Ignoring them or pretending they do not exist does us no favors. If we can think through the real impacts and concede where these changes to society make no impact, then we can face those facets head-on and provide a more accurate and accountable solution. Otherwise, we are just lying to ourselves and setting ourselves up for the next failure in the attempt to mend everything with quick fixes.

*An array of thoroughly enjoyed selections from **Sweet Soulfood: NOLA Vegan Cuisine**[110] in New Orleans, LA on March 6, 2020. Just because it is plant-based, it does not mean it still cannot be the same type of heavy foods loved by the masses. Photo by J.P. Prag.*

---

[110] HTTPS://WWW.SWEETVEGANSOULFOOD.COM/

FORGET MARS, LET'S COLONIZE VENUS

Earth's sister planet has much more to offer

Approximate relative sizes of the terrestrial planets, from left to right: Mercury, Venus, Earth and Mars. Credit: **MERCURY IMAGE: NASA/JHUAPL | VENUS IMAGE: NASA/JPL-CALTECH | EARTH IMAGE: NASA/APOLLO 17 CREW | MARS IMAGE: ESA/MPS/UPD/LAM/IAA/RSSD/INTA/UPM/DASP/IDA**[111], Public domain, via Wikimedia Commons.

---

[111] HTTPS://COMMONS.WIKIMEDIA.ORG/WIKI/FILE:TERRESTRIAL_PLANET_SIZES2.JPG

» Key Points

- *The most Earth-like place in the Solar System is actually floating above the clouds in the skies of Venus.*

- *With a gravity near that of Earth, an induced magnetic field for protection against cosmic radiation, and the ability to create a perfect perpetual summer environment, Venus is much more appealing than Mars.*

- *There are far more opportunities to make the transit between Earth and Venus than Earth and Mars, and being closer on average greatly reduces the time it will take to send messages and data between worlds.*

Finally, the culmination of your three-and-half month journey is within sight. The long period of weightlessness in the microgravity between planets has left you weaker and your body will need months more of physical therapy to return to what it once was—if you can ever really get it back there. Some calcium loss from your bones is bound to be permanent, and the onboard shielding against radiation was hardly perfect. Though it is not the same as Earth, the gravity here is about 90% the same as what you left behind and you cannot tell the difference. Yet you needed to escape the pull of your home planet in order to start over. That yellow dot in the sky beckoned you with the love and beauty for which she was named.

And now you have entered her crushing embrace. Before you appears the city of Aestas, named for the Roman goddess that is the personification of Summer. Here, floating in the skies of Venus, it will always be just that one season. The warmth in your heart is nothing compared to the extreme temperatures just beyond your protective bubble. Should you ever try to leave this sheltering womb, it would be an irrelevant exercise figuring out which specific factor killed you first. Still, you feel safe and more at home than you ever did back on Earth. You, and many others—perhaps one day millions of others—have set about to colonize and create the world of your dreams.

You have become... Venusian...

*Artist's rendering of a NASA Cloud City on Venus. Image and description by **NASA**[112], Public domain, via Wikimedia Commons.*

» REDISCOVERING A CLASSIC

The story Aestas—derogatorily nicknamed the "Yellow Balloon" by those who believe it is a waste of time to colonize Venus rather than spend those resources fixing the Earth—**WILL CONTINUE ANOTHER DAY**[113]. Here on the worldline in spacetime that we are on, we are a long way from even returning to Venus in any meaningful way. On June 2, 2021, **NASA ANNOUNCED**[114] that for the first time since the 1989 to 1994 Magellan mission that the United States would be returning to our sister planet. A little over a week later, the European Space Agency (ESA) **ALSO ANNOUNCED**[115] their plans to head back to Venus.

---

[112] HTTPS://COMMONS.WIKIMEDIA.ORG/WIKI/FILE:NASA_CLOUD_CITY_ON_VENUS.JPG
[113] HTTPS://WWW.JPPRAG.COM/UPCOMING
[114] HTTPS://WWW.NASA.GOV/PRESS-RELEASE/NASA-SELECTS-2-MISSIONS-TO-STUDY-LOST-HABITABLE-WORLD-OF-VENUS
[115] HTTPS://PHYS.ORG/NEWS/2021-06-VENUS-HOTTER-3RD-ROBOTIC-EXPLORER.HTML

However, NASA's mission is scheduled to blast off sometime between 2028 and 2030 and the ESA's mission is poised for the early 2030s. If everything remains on schedule, it will be at least a decade before we see any data from these enterprises. Judging by the **JAMES WEB SPACE TELESCOPE**[116] (announced in 1996, scheduled for launch in 2007, finally left the planet on Christmas Day 2021), the projected timelines may be optimistic.

Thankfully, these are not the only chances to observe the hottest terrestrial object in our solar system. Throughout mid-August 2021 both the ESA's Solar Orbiter and the joint ESA / Japan Aerospace Exploration Agency (JAXA) craft BepiColombo quickly flew by on their unrelated primary missions. JAXA actually already has a probe named Akatsuki in orbit, which has been there since 2015. It replaced the ESA's Venus Express that wrapped up its core operations in 2014. Even though the Americans have been negligent, others have tried to pick up the slack.

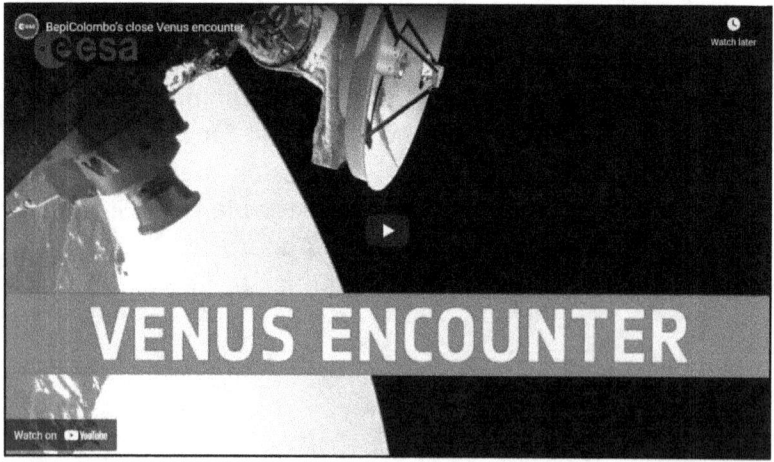

The ESA released a video of images taken by BepiColombo as it flew by Venus starting on August 10, 2021. **HTTPS://YOUTU.BE/B4SKGFQGUGQ**

---

[116] HTTPS://EN.WIKIPEDIA.ORG/WIKI/JAMES_WEBB_SPACE_TELESCOPE

The reason the United States has spent so little energy on Venus is because of their near singular focus on Mars, especially with the concern of one day sending humans and even colonizing the red planet. And sure, Mars does have a lot going for it, but it is nothing compared to the potential for Venus. As stated in part by Gareth Dorrian and Ian Whittaker of Nottingham Trent University in **The Daily Galaxy on October 16, 2018**[117]:

> **As surprising as it may seem, the upper atmosphere of Venus is the most Earth-like location in the solar system.**

» A Place to Lay my Head

That deep emphasis on Mars comes from one simple fact: we can walk on the surface. While Mars has a very thin atmosphere and provides virtually no protection against cosmic radiation, with proper equipment humans could leave their underground dwellings and walk around outside for a few hours. Still, the majority of any future colonist's life would be spent under the regolith because that is the only place on Mars that is relatively safe for people, animals, and plants. And frankly, if humans are just going to live bottom-side with limited trips up top, we already have a planet where that is available to us and it is far less resource intensive to get there. Should we just need more space for people, digging into the bedrock here on Earth and creating outposts on the ocean floor

---

[117] https://dailygalaxy.com/2018/10/could-it-harbor-life-the-upper-atmosphere-of-venus-is-the-most-earth-like-location-in-the-solar-system/

are technologically feasible today.

*Artist impression of a Mars settlement with cutaway view. Image and description by **NASA AMES RESEARCH CENTER**[118], Public domain, via Wikimedia Commons.*

Of course, that is not the only goal of going to Mars; some imagine terraforming it, turning it into a second Earth. Unfortunately, even if such a thing would be possible in the future, Mars is not ideal in this regard. At roughly 38% the gravity of Earth, the human and other Earth-based organisms would not react well in the long term. We are designed for the gravity of our home planet and even a few days in space leaves permanent scars. A lifetime in such an environment may yield health conditions we have not even considered. Meanwhile, as noted above, Venus has a gravity almost the same as Earth, coming in at roughly 90% of it.

---

[118] HTTPS://COMMONS.WIKIMEDIA.ORG/WIKI/FILE:CONCEPT_MARS_COLONY.JPG

Gravity is important for more than just human health, though. Being of a smaller mass, Mars literally cannot hold on to an atmosphere, especially one that would reach the minimal comfort levels for humans (think of the top of a Tibetan mountain). That means there would be an effort to constantly replenish the atmosphere, all while also carrying around portable oxygen. And even if we could keep it up from a ground-level perspective, solar winds from the sun and the rest of the universe would continually strip it away from above, much as what happened to Mars billions of years ago.

Again, because of its relatively smaller size, any rotating liquid metal core that Mars may have had has long since cooled off and seized up. That means it has almost no magnetic field to speak of, which in turn means it has limited protections against the solar winds. The auroras we see on Earth are an indication of the strength of our magnetic field as it captures dangerous solar particles and removes them from directly hitting us and stripping away our own ozone. Our magnetic field is far more important than the atmosphere, in that respect. If you want to see what a body in Earth's position and with a similar composition looks like without one, peer no further than the moon overhead. The dead world above us started with all of the same building blocks, but like Mars lost any magnetic field and potential atmosphere, essentially killing it.

Now, there is a **NASA PROPOSAL FOR GENERATING AN ARTIFICIAL MAGNETIC FIELD**[119] that could protect a whole planet. Again, though, we may be a long way off from successfully doing this. And at the same time, there is an ethical question if we have a right to terraform an entire

---

[119] HTTPS://WWW.HOU.USRA.EDU/MEETINGS/V2050/PDF/8250.PDF

planet. Creating a limited human habitation area is one thing; transforming an entire planet destroys the scientific experiments that could be conducted there under natural conditions. Further, we have not explored the entirety of Mars, not even a fraction of 1% in any significant detail. There is still the potential for life there, and if we change the planet to suit our needs we could be committing genocide on a planetary scale. This is something humans have done over and over again to every environment we have visited on our home planet, so perhaps it would be better to leave this one alone, at least for now?

*Telluric planets size comparison. From left to right, back row: Earth and Venus, front row: Mars and Mercury. Image and description by LSMPASCAL[120], **CC BY-SA 3.0**[121], via Wikimedia Commons.*

Where, then, does Venus stand in comparison to this? Although Venus is nearly the same size as Earth, some catastrophe in its past caused it to start spinning in the opposite direction of all other planets (save Uranus, which is completely tipped over on its side but would be

---

[120] HTTPS://COMMONS.WIKIMEDIA.ORG/WIKI/FILE:TELLURIC_PLANETS_SIZE_COMPARISON.JPG
[121] HTTPS://CREATIVECOMMONS.ORG/LICENSES/BY-SA/3.0

spinning in the same direction if it was not). And whatever it was—possibly another planet hitting it on its way out of the solar system—made it so Venus is spinning so slowly in the "wrong" direction that a day on the planet (~243 Earth days) is longer than a full rotation around the Sun (~225 Earth days). This is far too slow to generate a magnetic field of its own the way Earth does.

However, thanks to the aforementioned ESA mission **WE HAVE LEARNED**[122] that Venus appears to have an "induced magnetic field". Without getting too deep into it, this means Venus—without any modification—can provide the protections from dangerous solar radiation that we need to survive. Unfortunately, while that does mean we are safe from one component, Venus' atmosphere and runaway greenhouse gas effect has created a hellish environment where it is on average 465°C (869°F), which would melt lead—not to mention you—instantly. Not that you could even get to the surface since the pressure is 93 times that of the face of the Earth.

But that brings us back to Aestas. That pressure and temperature is true of the surface, but it is not accurate when describing the upper atmosphere. Were we to fill a balloon full of Earth-like air at a pressure that is livable for humans, it would float like a dirigible. At those heights, the temperature outside the balloon would be around 65–80°C (149–176°F). While still too hot to handle, it is certainly within the range of current refrigeration technology to cool the interior. Or rather—as refrigeration actually works—condensing hot humidity and pushing it back outside, leaving the interior cooler.

---

[122] HTTPS://SCI.ESA.INT/WEB/VENUS-EXPRESS/-/50246-A-MAGNETIC-SURPRISE-FOR-VENUS-EXPRESS

PROJECT HAVOK[123] *was a NASA study on how to explore and live on Venus. The project was closed without implementing any of the ideas, but they are all still viable.* HTTPS://YOUTU.BE/0AZ7DEWG68A

Now, being a floating city, Aestas would not have to stand still. Instead of being dependent upon the slow and retrograde natural rotation of the planet, the city could literally propel back and forth across the terminus line, creating the illusion of sunrises and sunsets. Sure, the sun would appear to be about 50% bigger compared to Earth, but on Mars it would seem 33% smaller. Also, although Mars is close to the rotation of Earth, a sol (day) there is about 24 hours, 39 minutes, and 35 seconds long. Those extra 39 minutes and 35 seconds may not seem like a lot, but if you try to live in that cycle your entire circadian rhythm would be thrown off. After just a single Earth-year, you will have added an additional 10 Earth-days trying to internalize that extra time. Meanwhile, with Aestas moving freely in the upper atmosphere of Venus, it could be set up to have the same 24 hour-ish cycle we have on Earth.

The other thing to consider is the actual orbit of the

---

[123] HTTPS://SACD.LARC.NASA.GOV/SMAB/HAVOC/

planets and their tilt. Earth has two things going for it that create the seasons we have. First is the fact the Earth is tilted on its axis, right now at about 24°. As we orbit the sun, one hemisphere of the Earth is ever so slightly closer to our nearest star while the other is further away, creating Summer and Winter, respectively. However, Summer and Winter in the northern and southern hemispheres are not created equal as Earth actually has an elliptical orbit. In January Earth is closer to the sun than in June, generating an imbalance in how extreme on the hot/cold scale seasons can get. It is where the landmasses and waters are now that makes that difference much less apparent.

Mars—while having a similar 25° tilt—has an orbit that is much more elliptical and extreme than that. A Martian trip around the sun is about twice as long as Earth to begin with, but with its eccentric path the season lengths are all over the place. In the northern hemisphere, the seasons would last:

- **Winter:** 154 sols
- **Spring:** 194 sols
- **Summer:** 178 sols
- **Autumn:** 142 sols

Now imagine trying to convince Earth plants to adapt to that type of cycle or to store enough food for the long periods without being able to grow. Here it is worth mentioning that the Martian regolith would be highly toxic to Earth plants, even when mixed with Earth soil. As such, no matter where we go, we would have to make our own soil or grow hydroponically until we could make soil. Therefore, with Mars we are again just underground and growing plants in controlled labs. Having land available would not provide any advantage at all.

> TO FURTHER CEMENT THIS POINT, ON AUGUST 18, 2021, A STUDY OUT OF WAGENINGEN UNIVERSITY AND RESEARCH AND THE REACTOR INSTITUTE DELFT[124] SHOWED THE IMPACT OF GAMMA RADIATION ON GROWING PLANTS. THE PAPER FOCUSED SPECIFICALLY ON THE LEVELS SEEN ON THE SURFACE OF MARS (ALMOST 17 TIMES THAT OF EARTH DUE TO THE LACK OF A MAGNETIC FIELD AND THICK ATMOSPHERE) USING GREENHOUSE TECHNOLOGY. IN THE END, THE SCIENTISTS CONCLUDED THAT THE ONLY SAFE LOCATION TO GROW PLANTS ON MARS WOULD BE BENEATH THE SURFACE, ONCE AGAIN SHOWING THE FRUITLESSNESS OF HAVING THE VAST MARTIAN LANDSCAPE AVAILABLE.

Meanwhile on Venus, the planet has a tilt of just below 3° and an orbit that is almost a perfect circle. That means, for all intents and purposes, it would always be one season on Venus. Since the environmental controls of Aestas would determine the overall temperature, that season could easily just be early Summer all the time. As a result, the plants could be grown out in the open areas of the colony instead of inside white-walled rooms, using actual sunlight instead of grow-lamps.

At the end of the day, living in the floating city of Aestas on Venus would feel in the literal gravity-based sense very much like being on Earth, except an ideal one with a

---

[124] HTTPS://WWW.UNIVERSETODAY.COM/152232/GREENHOUSES-PROBABLY-WONT-WORK-ON-MARS-BECAUSE-OF-COSMIC-RADIATION-EVEN-THE-PLANTS-WILL-HAVE-TO-LIVE-UNDERGROUND/

never-ending Summer and predictability we cannot begin to offer on our homeworld.

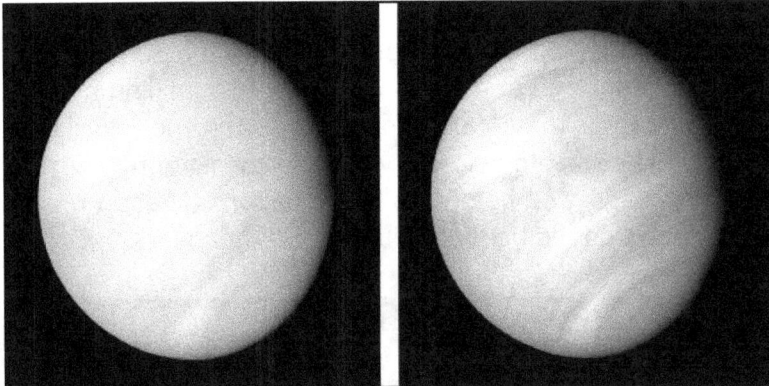

As it sped away from Venus, NASA's Mariner 10 spacecraft captured this view of the planet. Both images have been reprocessed from the original data using modern software, with a contrast enhancement applied to the right image. Composite image and description by **NASA/JPL-CALTECH**[125], Public domain, via Wikimedia Commons.

» E.T. Needs to Phone Home

Lastly—though in many ways of first import—there is the question of logistics. When it comes to Mars, the closest our two planets get (which is around when we would want to attempt a transfer) comes once every 25–26 months. Yet, because of that same highly elliptical orbit, "closest" has a fairly wide range. In July 2018, Mars made its truly nearest approach at 57.6 million km (35.7 million miles), a feat that will not be repeated until September 2035. Meanwhile, in between, around February 2027 this closest point will be 101 million km (63 million miles) away, nearly double what was seen in 2018.

Venus' closest approach comes in around 39.8 million km (24.7 million miles), which most recently happened in

---

[125] HTTPS://COMMONS.WIKIMEDIA.ORG/WIKI/FILE:PIA23791-VENUS-REALANDENHANCEDCONTRASTVIEWS-20200608.JPG

January 2022. Even missing a window like this, though, is not as big of a deal because these inferior conjunctions happen every 19 months or so and generally fall in the 42–43 million km range (26–27 million miles). As an example, the next pass in August 2023 will actually be a rather distant one at 43.2 million km (26.8 million miles), but still nearer than Mars can ever get. In other words, Venus will always be closer, will have consistently shorter distance trips, and has many more opportunities to move people and goods between our worlds than Mars.

A side-by-side comparison of the sizes of Venus and Earth. Photo by ESO/Y. BELETSKY[126], CC BY 4.0[127] via Wikimedia Commons.

Without diving into the painful math of orbital mechanics, it is fair to note that the energy and time necessary to get into Venusian orbit is not that much less than Martian, almost to the point of being negligible. In many ways, it is easier to go outbound in the solar system than to go inbound. That, though, is with today's technology and infrastructure. Future situations may change these equations greatly, but we will not speculate here.

---

[126] HTTPS://COMMONS.WIKIMEDIA.ORG/WIKI/FILE:MERCURY,_VENUS_AND_THE_MOON_ALIGN.JPG
[127] HTTPS://CREATIVECOMMONS.ORG/LICENSES/BY/4.0

Instead, let us again focus in on that distance measurement. The finite speed within the universe is limited to that of light, so any communication tool we use will also be at most that velocity. Assuming we can send data at near the speed of light (which we already do on Earth with fiber-optics), then Venus is again going to be the hands-down winner on keeping up with our far-flung cousins. Looking at how fast light moves between our worlds:

	To/From Mars	To/From Venus
Shortest	193 Seconds	133 Seconds
	3 Minutes | 13 Seconds	2 Minutes | 13 Seconds
Longest	1337 Seconds	869 Seconds
	22 Minutes | 17 Seconds	14 Minutes | 29 Seconds
Average	762 Seconds	227 Seconds
	12 minutes | 42 seconds	3 Minutes | 47 Seconds

Table showing the time it takes light to travel to/from Earth from/to Mars and Venus.

Since Venus will be closer more often on average than Mars, there are far more opportunities for faster communication, hence the average time being less than 4 minutes instead nearly 13 minutes. While that is certainly not real time (and you have to double it for two-way communication), it is very comfortable lengths for a text/messenger style conversation. And communication will be critical when we are talking about the isolation and separation of building a colony on a whole new world.

No matter which way it is sliced, Venus is the superior destination when it comes to being the launching point for humanity's propagation to the stars, at least in comparison to Mars. Not that we should abandon scientific research of Mars, nor should we give up sending astronauts there for study—but when it comes to building a new home, there is nowhere else quite like above the yellow skies of Venus.

*A conjunction of Mercury and Venus, aligned above the Moon, as seen from the Paranal Observatory. Photo and description by **ESO/Y. Beletsky**[128], **CC BY 4.0**[129], via Wikimedia Commons.*

---

[128] HTTPS://COMMONS.WIKIMEDIA.ORG/WIKI/FILE:MERCURY,_VENUS_AND_THE_MOON_ALIGN.JPG
[129] HTTPS://CREATIVECOMMONS.ORG/LICENSES/BY/4.0

PART 4: AMENDING THE FUTURE

Complete Overhaul: Electing the President of the United States

Ending the Electoral College is not nearly enough

President Donald Trump shakes hands with Barack Obama during the Presidential Inauguration at the U.S. Capitol Building, Washington, D.C., on January 20, 2017. Photo and description by **U.S. Marine Corps Lance Cpl. Cristian L. Ricardo**[130], Public domain, via Wikimedia Commons.

---

[130] HTTPS://COMMONS.WIKIMEDIA.ORG/WIKI/FILE:BARACK_OBAMA,_DONALD_TRUMP,_JOE_BIDEN_AT_INAUGURATION_01-20-17_%28CROPPED%29.JPG

» Key Points

- *The Democratic and Republican Parties have intentionally created a feeling of hopelessness among voters in order to manipulate the results of elections, especially for President of the United States.*

- *Eliminating the Electoral College is only the start; it must be replaced with a system that combines ranked choice with negative votes in order to tabulate the actual will of the people.*

- *Unless election timeframes are extended and results are withheld for at least a week after polls close, then there is the potential for people to feel they still have no voice and instead choose to stay home.*

MAYBE DONALD TRUMP IS RIGHT...

Of course, by all measures and statistics he did not win the Presidential election in November 2020, nor was it particularly close. Actual, true, and verified President of the United States Joe Biden won with 81.2 million members of the populace, which translated into 306 votes of the type that matters when electing the leader of the free world. This is in comparison to Mr. Trump's 74.2 million supporters yielding 232 votes. But perhaps—just perhaps—we actually do not know the real will of all the American people, especially since so many have remained silent. Or more accurately: since so many of them remained home.

Although the 2020 Presidential election had a "massive" turnout by all modern standards, only 62% of the voting age population (VAP) bothered or were allowed to cast a ballot. Further, how many people voted was not evenly distributed across the land. In a key battleground State like Wisconsin the VAP was over 72% while predetermined locations like Oklahoma and New York saw far fewer people make an effort—a VAP of 52% and 56%, respectively. If you live in a State that is just going to support a single Party for President (whether you wholeheartedly back or despise that Party) and the patterns make it unlikely your vote will make an impact, then you are more apt not to show up at all.

*President George H. W. Bush and wife Barbara Bush with former Presidents and their wives (Gerald and Betty Ford, Ronald and Nancy Reagan, Richard and Pat Nixon) at the opening of the Nixon Library on July 19, 1990. Photo and description by the **GEORGE BUSH PRESIDENTIAL LIBRARY AND MUSEUM**[131], Public domain, via Wikimedia Commons.*

Because of that, there is a big question mark on what the other 38% of the country who did not or could not vote thought about either of these candidates or their lesser-known competitors. And frankly, even among those who did vote, it is an open question if they all cast their ballots with their hearts. The cynical and autocratic approach of the Republican and Democratic Parties to create "winner takes all" islands has resulted in a type of voter suppression among the citizenry, one that is based in a

---

[131]

HTTPS://COMMONS.WIKIMEDIA.ORG/WIKI/FILE:PRESIDENT_GEORGE_H._W._BUSH_AND_FIRST_LADY_BARBARA_BUSH_WITH_FORMER_PRESIDENTS_AND_FIRST_LADIES.JPG

hopelessness that the Parties try to manipulate and control.

As an understatement, this is a huge problem that is contributing to the destruction of Democracy.

Unfortunately, that is just the tip of the iceberg when it comes to voter suppression. For instance, there are sets of people like those living in the Territories who have always been completely excluded from ever having a say. We could spend hours going through all of the marginalized groups and how they have been systematically and intentionally separated from their vote, but there is no need to delve into that now. What this is all coming down to is the most undemocratic, horribly designed, and antithesis of the American experiment we still have left in the Constitution:

THE ELECTORAL COLLEGE

Just knowing that in 2020 its very existence automatically excluded 3.6 million people who lived in the Territories from having a voice and potentially discouraged another 80 million from voting should be enough to prove that this system is as broken today as it was in 1788. I will not mince words: the only reasons to support the Electoral College are because it is self-serving and gives outstripped power in places that would not naturally have it. It is not a "fair" system that was created to make sure cities did not dominate rural areas. On the contrary, it was a compromise between those that wanted a direct vote for President and Vice President and those that wanted Congress to decide who should run the nation. Much like other compromises in the Constitution—namely that slavery could exist in certain areas and that slaves would be counted as 3/5^{ths} a person for representation and taxation purposes—it is far past time to end this archaic travesty of justice.

President Bush and his wife are joined by former Presidents Carter, Ford, Nixon, and Regan with their spouses and Mrs. Johnson at the dedication of the Reagan Presidential Library on November 4, 1991. Photo and description by SERIES: GEORGE H. W. BUSH PRESIDENTIAL PHOTOGRAPHS, 1/20/1989–1/20/1993 COLLECTION: RECORDS OF THE WHITE HOUSE PHOTOGRAPH OFFICE, 1/20/1989–1/20/1993[132], Public domain, via Wikimedia Commons.

More crucial than just terminating the Electoral College, though, is making sure the people of the United States are a part of the election process. They will not feel that way unless their voices are truly being heard, starting with the highest office in the land. And the only way that

---

[132]

HTTPS://COMMONS.WIKIMEDIA.ORG/WIKI/FILE:PRESIDENT_GEORGE_H._W._BUSH_AND_BARBARA_BUSH_POSE_WITH_THE_FORMER_PRESIDENTS_AND_FIRST_LADIES.JPG

is going to happen is with a specific set of **Amendments to the Constitution**.

» FIRST THE PERSON…

Where else would we begin amending the Constitution but right at the top:

> THE PRESIDENT AND VICE PRESIDENT OF THE UNITED STATES SHALL BE DIRECTLY ELECTED BY THE PEOPLE OF ALL STATES AND TERRITORIES HERE WITHIN.

The Constitution does not have to be complicated, but a single sentence saying all people have a say in selecting the President and Vice President is enough!

Actually, though, it is not nearly enough. The method by which to elect the President and Vice President is a different story entirely that must be fully flushed out. Just saying that people should be able to vote for the President and Vice President directly does not actually resolve the core issue because that could just mean directing the Electoral College to vote for the popular winner. This is what has been going on through the date of this release in 2022 with the "**National Popular Vote Interstate Compact**" in which States pledge that all of their Electors will go to the popular winner across the nation, but only should the number of States in the compact meet or exceed the number of Electors required to select the President. While a noble goal, it is still a sidestepping of the Constitution and leaves all the same problems of excluding people. Additionally, there are many other issues that also suppress turnout, all of which we will get to forthwith. For now, we also need to focus on widening the playing field:

> **THE PRESIDENT AND VICE PRESIDENT SHALL RUN TOGETHER ON A SINGLE TICKET AND THERE SHALL BE NO CRITERIA FOR A PRESIDENT OR VICE PRESIDENT TO APPEAR ON THE BALLOTS SAVE FOR MEETING THE CRITERIA FOR EACH POSITION AS STATED IN THE CONSTITUTION.**

The 12th Amendment to the Constitution attempted to fix errors in how the President the Vice President were elected so that they could not end up being from different political ideologies again. However, it still maintained them as separate positions instead of a single ticket, leaving the potential for disaster. While Political Parties were not imagined by the writers of the Constitution (even though they were already in many different camps of thought), it is a *de facto* part of human existence that must be accepted.

Yet even though creating groups is a natural expression of Homo Sapien[133] behavior, many States control which Political Parties and candidates can even appear on the ballot. These States can decide to restrict anyone they want for capricious reasons. There is absolutely no reason to exclude any duo from running for President and Vice President save the conditions as laid out by the

---

[133] The author is aware that "Sapiens" is singular and the "S" should not be dropped due to its Latin root. However, since language is free to evolve like species do, the author has chosen to make this evolutionary leap in the name of sounding better here and everywhere in this book.

Constitution (and even some of those are suspect, but we will leave them all be for the time being).

*President Clinton and First Lady Hillary Rodham Clinton attending the funeral of President Richard Nixon in Yorba Linda, California. Former Presidents Bush, Reagan, Carter and Ford with First Ladies: Barbara Bush, Nancy Reagan, Rosalynn Carter and Betty Ford are present on April 27, 1994. Photo and description by **WHITE HOUSE PHOTOGRAPH OFFICE BARBARA KINNEY**[134], Public domain, via Wikimedia Commons.*

Now, with so many people on the ballot, how are voters to make their selection? Theoretically, the Political Party is irrelevant as anyone could run. Perhaps Political Parties would still conduct primaries and make decisions about how many of their people will appear on the final ticket, but that will be up to them. If someone wants to run and meets the criteria, they should be on the ballot everywhere without exception. Does that mean hundreds of pairings could be on the ballot? Absolutely! Why should choice be limited?

---

[134] HTTPS://COMMONS.WIKIMEDIA.ORG/WIKI/FILE:PRESIDENTS_AT_THE_FUNERAL_OF_PRESIDENT_RICHARD_NIXON.JPG

But how do we work through the noise of so much variety? Well, we will take a cue from the 12th Amendment again. The way it is set up now is that if no candidate receives an absolute majority (i.e., greater than 50%) of the Electoral College votes then the top 3 candidates will be sent to the House of Representatives to decide which one should be President. Instead, we can replace that with an instant runoff:

> **ELIGIBLE VOTERS OF THE STATES AND TERRITORIES SHALL RANK THEIR TOP THREE CHOICES FOR PRESIDENT AND VICE PRESIDENT AND SHALL ALSO BE GRANTED A SINGLE VOTE AGAINST A CHOICE FOR PRESIDENT AND VICE PRESIDENT.**

Some States and other countries have a system requiring an absolute majority, otherwise there is a runoff race. In the 2016 Presidential Election, Hillary Clinton had 48% of the popular vote and Donald Trump had 46%. Now, again, we cannot know what the 113 million people who did not or could not vote in that election would have done (far less eligible voters took part in the 2016 election than 2020), so we should assume for now this result reflects the overall desires of the nation. That said, if we extended the "absolute majority" rule with the popular vote, we would end up in the exact same situation.

Libertarian candidate Gary Johnson had 3% of the vote, Green Party candidate Jill Stein had 1%, and everyone else had another 1% combined. If we wanted a runoff vote with the top 3 people, it is possible Mrs. Clinton could have picked up another 2–3%, but it is just as likely that Mr. Johnson would have scooped up enough to still not elect her, creating a stalemate.

President-elect Obama with former Presidents Bush (41), Carter and Clinton and current President Bush in the Dining Room of the West Wing at the White House on January 7, 2009. Photo and description by **Pete Souza**[135], ***CC BY 3.0***[136], *via Wikimedia Commons.*

Meanwhile, the expense and time of putting on another election would have been astronomical. Let us not forget that the election was in November and the President assumes office in January. That means a runoff election would have needed to happen somewhere between Thanksgiving and the winter holidays—and could still have resulted in no clear winner. The aforementioned places that do runoff races have dealt with this exact issue and it has resulted in unfilled positions for months on end. That

---

[135] HTTPS://COMMONS.WIKIMEDIA.ORG/WIKI/FILE:PRESIDENT-ELECT_OBAMA_WITH_FORMER_PRESIDENTS_BUSH_%2841%29,_CARTER_AND_CLINTON_AND_CURRENT_PRESIDENT_BUSH_IN_THE_DINING_ROOM_OF_THE_WEST_WING_AT_THE_WHITE_HOUSE_ON_JAN._7,_2009.JPG
[136] HTTPS://CREATIVECOMMONS.ORG/LICENSES/BY/3.0

is not acceptable for the President of the United States.

Instead, we can eliminate the guessing game by asking a different question: if your first pick for President cannot be elected, who is your second choice? Who is your third choice? With this, we already have the runoff election completed because we can assign a point value to each of these choices. Also, sometimes people do not have a clear idea of who they want to vote for, but they do know who they *do not* want as President. That should be reflected in the vote, too, as an allowance for a negative vote.

> **A VALUE SHALL BE ADDED TO EACH VOTE SUCH THAT THE FIRST CHOICE GETS THREE POINTS, THE SECOND CHOICE GETS TWO POINTS, AND THE THIRD CHOICE GETS ONE POINT. FURTHERMORE, THE VOTE AGAINST SHALL SUBTRACT TWO POINTS. THE CANDIDATES THAT RECEIVE THE NET HIGHEST NUMBER OF POINTS SHALL BE THE PRESIDENT AND VICE PRESIDENT OF THE UNITED STATES.**

Here we lay it out simply: your first choice gets 3 points, your second choice gets 2, and your third choice gets 1. Further, the voters could use their voice to have a candidate lose 2 points. This would not completely negate someone's first choice vote but would partially remove it while allowing other points to accumulate. Whichever candidate duo has the most net points is the winner as the points would already reflect the main, backup, and tertiary will of the people, along with the one they most strongly do not want.

Let us play this out with some real-world examples using various assumptions:

- Every candidate that received a popular vote was the first choice and would get 3 points for that.

- 90% of Democrats and Republicans would use their negative vote on the opposing Party, as would 40% of all other voters.

- Roughly 1% of votes cast by all other parties would be used against every Third Party and Independent.

- 5% to 10% of every group would use their second and third choices for major parties or third parties, depending on relative political alignment.

This could be modeled forever using a ton of other assumptions, but the idea is to get an impression of where this might fall out. For the 2016 Presidential election the results would have been:

	Party	Electoral College	Popular Vote	Net Point Vote
Donald Trump	Republican	57%	46%	39%
Hillary Clinton	Democratic	42%	48%	43%
Gary Johnson	Libertarian	0%	3%	10%
Jill Stein	Green	0%	1%	7%
All Other	Many	1%	1%	2%

As can be surmised, Hillary Clinton would have won the election based on net points, just not by the same expanse as the popular vote—though the margin would be wider. More so, while they would not get closer to winning in this particular contest, the Third Parties would have received a lot more attention and net points so that it would be more likely they would be recognized in the future. It is worth noting that both Republicans and Democrats engaged in fear mongering during this election by saying a Third Party vote would be a waste or—worse—that it would help their opponent get elected. This is just the oligopoly talking to maintain its power and has nothing to do with reality.

That type of rhetoric impacted the results of the 2020 election and had an immediate downward effect on all Third Parties. Putting that election through the same model produced these results:

	Party	Electoral College	Popular Vote	Net Point Vote
Joe Biden	Democratic	57%	51%	48%
Donald Trump	Republican	43%	47%	39%
Jo Jorgensen	Libertarian	0%	1%	6%
Howie Hawkins	Green	0%	<1%	5%
All Other	Many	0%	<1%	<1%

The outcome is the same with Joe Biden winning the election, though with a much higher spread. Still, with millions upon millions of eligible people not voting, millions more not allowed to vote, and who knows how many people scared out of voting for who they wanted for fear of the candidate they least liked being elected, it is impossible to say how altered these number would have turned out. It does not necessarily mean the result would have been different or that a Third Party would have won, but perhaps the gaps would not be so large. Maybe a significant number of people would have voted for Third Parties first, Major Parties Second, and used their negative vote for the other Major Party? We cannot tell until we make the change and allow it to happen.

That is also why the popular vote of today is not even a good measure of the will of the people. We do not really know what voters would do, whether they cast a ballot or not. We can take assumptions like above, do projections, and run models to find probable outcomes; but none are real until such a time that we can get more people involved in the voting process.

The Negative Vote is incredibly important in this scheme because it frees people to vote for who they want. Giving people full control and meaning to their selection is the truly virtuous thing to do in a representative democracy. As mentioned earlier, though, a lot more needs to be done to get everyone involved and engaged.

» ... THEN THE PROCESS

The horrors of the **Electoral College** are one thing; the election process itself is another massive problem.

Per the Constitution, Congress controls when the election is and—as surprising as this sounds—there is no recommendation to change that. You may be among the people who complain that the actual day is stuck in a 19th century mentality of market days, when agrarians would be available to vote. Or you might be among the others who point out that almost all other western representative democracies have their elections on a holiday or a weekend. Of course, all of these views are true, correct, and righteous!

But so are the people who say that elections that are on a holiday or weekend would disproportionately eliminate poorer Americans who work Saturdays, Sundays, and "off hours" at a far higher rate than more well-to-do citizens.

One way or another, some group of people is going to be negatively impacted by a single day election. Therefore, the problem is not the day, but the timeframe in which the election happens. We need to build on our current laws with an Amendment to get more people involved, starting with the "when" and "for how long" components:

> **ELECTIONS FOR SENATORS, REPRESENTATIVES, AND THE PRESIDENT AND VICE PRESIDENT SHALL START AT LEAST THREE WEEKS BEFORE THE DAY CHOSEN BY CONGRESS FOR HOLDING ELECTIONS.**

Elections being held on one day is truly the issue at hand because it limits the options for people voting in person, remotely, or by proxy. Instead, elections should happen for at least 3 weeks before whatever day is chosen as the "official" election day. Based on the current system, this would put elections starting in mid-October and would go through several weekends.

> **THE ELECTION TIMEFRAME MAY BE EXTENDED BY LAW BUT SHALL NOT BE SHORTENED FOR ANY REASON.**

Further, this Amendment would allow Congress—or any other local municipality—to expand the timeframe even more. Thus, if it makes sense to vote for two months, then that is what will happen; just at a minimum there should be three weeks. One of the issues in the past has always been pegging government functions to the behaviors and customs of the current age, but those do change over the decades and centuries. Flexibility is key, but so is meeting people where they are instead of trying to confine them to the Government's expectations:

> **ELECTION POLLING MUST BE MADE AVAILABLE WHEN AND HOW IT IS MOST CONVENIENT FOR THE PEOPLE OF THE UNITED STATES AND INCLUDE HOURS AND DAYS IN WHICH THE MAJORITY DO NOT MAKE LABOR.**

Here, the Amendment has stated that polling stations must be made available at a time that is "most convenient", in particular that it is when "the majority do not make labor". In other words, we are talking about "off-hours".

To answer when that is and how to implement it will always be a rolling equation. If Congress sets polling stations to be open between 12pm and 8pm every weekday and 10am and 4pm on the weekend, then it should cover the vast majority of Americans without as much interference in the workday, at least the workday as defined today. Potentially, Congress or a local polling authority could also alternate days with different hours to allow more plasticity for varied groups of people. Either way, these days and times could be easily and regularly revisited as the habits of society changed, or challenged in court when legislatures and executives refuse to act. The important thing is the options of having voting available and within decent timeframes to get as many people involved as conveniently as possible.

*President Donald J. Trump and First Lady Melania Trump, joined by former President Barack Obama and First Lady Michelle Obama, former President Bill Clinton and First Lady Hillary Clinton and former President Jimmy Carter and First Lady Rosalynn Carter, watch as the casket of former President George H. W. Bush departs the funeral service on December 5, 2018. Photo and description by **ANDREA HANKS**[137], Public domain, via Wikimedia Commons.*

For those who scoff at the cost of doing all this, my questions for you are:

- *What should the government spend money on that is more important than having an active, engaged, and represented populace?*

- *What is the point of having a government at all if it is not spending its funding on the people who are the true rulers of this country?*

---

[137] HTTPS://COMMONS.WIKIMEDIA.ORG/WIKI/FILE:PRESIDENTS_AT_BUSH_FUNERAL.JPG

However, having such a long timeframe can cause a backlash effect if results are made available too soon. Just releasing preliminary numbers before all absentee ballots were counted in the 2020 election has brought us endless conspiracy theories, including from the former President himself. Since the elections are in early November and the President is not sworn in until January 20th, what is the rush to get the results out the door? The only reason is because we are part of a society that demands instantaneous satisfaction and information. Patience is a lost concept in a world where every bit of media is available by saying a few words to an Artificial Intelligence living inside of a hockey puck.

We need to end any potential look of impropriety to bring trust completely back into the election procedure. It does not matter if the concerns of some people are based on a complete fabrication; we want all citizens to believe and know that election results are true and just. The only way we are going to do that is by Amending the Constitution to decelerate the process:

> **THE GOVERNING BODY OF EACH ELECTION—FEDERAL OR OTHERWISE—SHALL MAINTAIN THE SECRECY OF BALLOT RESULTS UNTIL AT LEAST SEVEN FULL DAYS HAVE PASSED FROM THE DAY OF ELECTION. THIS TIMEFRAME MAY BE EXTENDED BY LAW OR IN ORDER TO HAVE THE APPROPRIATE TIME TO VERIFY THE RESULTS, BUT SHALL NOT BE SHORTENED FOR ANY REASON.**

One of the reasons why a State like Hawai'i has such low

voter turnout (52% VAP in 2020) is because the election is already decided in the middle of their voting day. While another contributing factor is certainly the "my vote does not matter" impact of having an area solidly with one Political Party, the other is the time-zone differential of the elections. Hawai'i is six hours behind the East Coast of the United States and as the years have gone on news outlets have been declaring winners of elections within seconds or minutes of polls closing. If the President is already decided before you get a chance to go vote after work, why would you even bother to do so?

Photo by **TOBI OLUREMI**[138] on **UNSPLASH**. Read and watch more about the story of this location at HTTPS://ABC11.COM/VIDEO/5579369/

This plays out all over the country and even within States. Releasing even tentative polling results discourages people from going out and voting because there is a feeling of uselessness. While there is nothing that can be done to stop the press and other pundits from making projections, the government does not and should not be

---

[138] HTTPS://UNSPLASH.COM/@_OLUSION_

part of the process. Additionally, trying to get out election night results puts undo strain on workers that can create mistakes. The method of counting votes should be slow, deliberate, and careful such that by the time the official results are given they are 100% accurate, or as close to that as humanly possible.

Joe Biden (L) and Donald Trump (R). Description and composite photo by JOE BIDEN: GAGE SKIDMORE FROM PEORIA, AZ, UNITED STATES OF AMERICA (SOURCE: JOE BIDEN); USER:TDKR CHICAGO 101 (CLIPPING) DONALD TRUMP: SHEALAH CRAIGHEAD (SOURCE: WHITE HOUSE) COMBINATION: KRASSOTKIN[139], CC BY-SA 2.0[140], via Wikimedia Commons.

To be fair and safe, ballots should be protected for a detailed count, re-count, and verification. And there may be times to extend this process, such as in incredibly close races or if absentee ballots have been delayed—for

---

[139] HTTPS://COMMONS.WIKIMEDIA.ORG/WIKI/FILE:JOE_BIDEN_AND_DONALD_TRUMP.JPG
[140] HTTPS://CREATIVECOMMONS.ORG/LICENSES/BY-SA/2.0

instance, when troops are deployed in a war zone during a global pandemic. Every vote should have a reasonable chance, and every voter should have the feeling that their voice matters, especially because it would be truer with these Amendments than it is today.

But what can be done to make sure the results are not leaked? There is only one thing we can do:

> **NO MEMBER OF THE GOVERNING BODY OF EACH ELECTION MAY SHARE RESULTS OR ESTIMATES OF THE ELECTIONS DURING THIS TIMEFRAME UNDER PENALTY OF TREASON.**

Doing anything to undermine the election, even the simple act of releasing polling information early, is an attack upon America because it discourages participation. In other words, it is **treason**. Finally, this level of scrutiny should be extended to all layers of government, ensuring that this same amount of care would be equally applied to the local sheriff race as to that of President of the United States of America.

How to Stop Voter Suppression... Permanently

Hundreds bills to restrict voter access have and continue to be introduced

Photo by **Elliott Stallion**[141] on **Unsplash**

---

[141] HTTPS://UNSPLASH.COM/@EAGLEBOOBS

» **KEY POINTS**

- *In order to maintain power, a certain Political Party has attempted to restrict access to the ballot box because the fewer people who vote, the better they do. These efforts have happened mostly in the State legislatures that they control, but there are efforts to move to a national level.*

- *The only way to stop this and permanently bolster voter access is with a set of Constitution Amendments.*

- *Beyond just making it more convenient to cast a ballot and eliminate various methods of suppression, the people of the United States need an actual right to vote that they sorely lack today—and a compulsion to do so to go along with that right.*

While the changes made to voting in the **PREVIOUS CHAPTER** are a good beginning, they are not nearly enough to truly end both intentional systematic voter suppression and unintended repression caused by the flaws in our system and society. As a start, something similar as was done with the President and Vice President would have to be done with the House of Representatives. The Senate is a slightly different story since it is supposed to controlled by the States, but the idea would be same. Both of these will be discussed in the **NEXT CHAPTER**. For now, though, there is a much bigger issue that we have yet to address.

Since the election of Democrats Joe Biden as President of the United States and **RAPHAEL WARNOCK AND JON OSSOFF AS SENATORS FROM GEORGIA**[142] in a runoff election, the Republican Party has been in a scramble. Despite the massive amount of gerrymandering to have a higher proportion of control than their numbers would normally allow, the trends continue to move away from the Republican Party's favor. Areas that were Republican strongholds are becoming competitive; areas that were competitive are becoming Democratic strongholds. Demographics have been changing at a rapid pace, even during the COVID-19 pandemic.

In order to reverse these losses, the Republican Party has two avenues. The first is a grassroots movement to find more voters and attract them to support their cause either by demonstrating the superiority of the Republican platform or by changing the platform to get disinterested people involved. They are going about this with the latter by becoming more populist and **MOVING AWAY FROM POSITIONS THAT WOULD BE CONSIDERED SACROSANCT TO A**

---

[142] HTTPS://WWW.NPR.ORG/2021/02/06/964614820/HOW-DEMOCRATS-FOUND-THOUSANDS-OF-NEW-VOTERS-AND-FLIPPED-GEORGIAS-SENATE-SEATS

REPUBLICAN OF JUST A DECADE AGO. Standing by a long-held belief and letting the chips fall where they may is not the policy of the modern Republican Party.

*Photo by **OBI ONYEADOR**[143] on **UNSPLASH***

---

[143] HTTPS://UNSPLASH.COM/@THENEWMALCOLM

Still, drumming up support from new and reluctant voters will take time and will not guarantee victory in the short term. Unfortunately, the Political Parties in the United States only care about one thing: getting more votes than their opponents (Democrats are no different in this regard). The margins of victory around the country are razor thin in these competitive races. Thus, if their opponents are getting ever so slightly more votes than they are and they cannot find enough people to vote, the logical solution is to get less people to vote in general, especially people most likely to vote for their opponents.

In order to accomplish this, within three months of Joe Biden being sworn in as President, **REPUBLICANS IN 43 STATES HAD PROPOSED OVER 250 BILLS**[144] to restrict access to the ballot box. Since that time, there have only been more of these propositions, with many of them passing through their legislatures and being signed into law by their Governors. These acts take many forms—from limiting the ability to get a mail-in-ballot to restricting the availability of polling stations. In response, Cinde Weatherby of the League of Women Voters Texas noted:

> **IF YOU CAN NAME AN IMPROVEMENT, THERE'S A BILL THAT'S BEEN FILED TO TRY AND ELIMINATE IT.**

To be fair, there are efforts to fight these restrictions. For instance, on March 5, 2021 I received an email from Representative David Cicilline (D-RI) that stated in part:

---

[144] HTTPS://WWW.NBCNEWS.COM/POLITICS/ELECTIONS/TEXAS-GOP-LAUNCHES-AVALANCHE-BILLS-CURTAIL-VOTING-N1260747

> EARLIER THIS WEEK, THE HOUSE PASSED THE FOR THE PEOPLE ACT (H.R.1), A SWEEPING REFORM PACKAGE THAT RETURNS POWER IN WASHINGTON TO THE AMERICAN PEOPLE... THIS LANDMARK LEGISLATION WILL FIX WHAT IS BROKEN IN OUR DEMOCRACY. IT EXPANDS ACCESS TO THE BALLOT, REDUCES THE CORRUPTING INFLUENCE OF CORPORATE MONEY IN POLITICAL CAMPAIGNS, AND RESTORES ETHICS AND INTEGRITY IN GOVERNMENT. I'M ESPECIALLY PLEASED THAT IT INCLUDES MY PROPOSALS TO MAKE IT EASIER TO VOTE, REQUIRE GREATER TRANSPARENCY FROM PRESIDENTIAL CANDIDATES, AND LIMIT THE INFLUENCE OF CORPORATIONS OVER OUR GOVERNMENT.

You can listen to Representative Cicilline's speech on the House floor here:

HTTPS://YOUTU.BE/DVS8ZTPGRE4

As noble as the ideals of this legislation are, they are simply not enough as there will be a continual tension between it and the States attempting to limit access to certain people's voices. If this act somehow passes in the Senate (it will not with **CURRENT FILIBUSTER RULES AND NO REPUBLICAN SUPPORT**[145]), it will most likely face lawsuits that will attempt to overthrow the provisions. The problem comes back to one simple truth:

YOU DO NOT HAVE A RIGHT TO VOTE.

Sure, Amendments to the Constitution say that your right to vote cannot be restricted due to race (15th), sex (19th), failure to pay a poll or any other tax (24th), or being over 18 years old (26th)—the **CONSTITUTION DOES NOT EXPLICITLY GIVE THE PEOPLE THE RIGHT TO VOTE**[146]. We will not get into the history of why that is here, but the ability for people to vote pretty much comes from the **10th Amendment** that notes that any power the Federal Government does not claim as its own belongs to the States. Over the past couple of centuries and as recently as the 2020 election, the Supreme Court has held up again and again that voting is a power vested in the States in part because it is not a power vested in the Federal Government.

As such, there is no choice of the matter. In order to avoid someone taking away our access to voting, we first

---

[145] HTTPS://WWW.TIMESUNION.COM/NEWS/ARTICLE/FOR-THE-PEOPLE-ACT-PASSES-HOUSE-HEADS-TO-SENATE-16007457.PHP
[146] HTTPS://THECONVERSATION.COM/THE-RIGHT-TO-VOTE-IS-NOT-IN-THE-CONSTITUTION-144531

need to have a right to vote! And the only way we can have a right to vote is if we have a set of Constitutional Amendments so that voting is included within the sphere of control of the Federal Government.

Photo by JANINE ROBINSON[147] on UNSPLASH

» GAINING THE RIGHT TO VOTE

There are several key elements that are used to stop people from voting, not the least of which is getting and staying registered. Therefore, that is the most logical place to begin Amending the Constitution:

---

[147] HTTPS://UNSPLASH.COM/@JANINEKROB

> **ALL ELIGIBLE VOTERS OF THE UNITED STATES SHALL BE AUTOMATICALLY REGISTERED TO VOTE AND BE PROVIDED ALL NECESSARY MATERIALS AND INFORMATION IN ORDER TO GIVE THEIR VOTE.**

Why does anyone need to register to vote at all? There is nothing in the Constitution that says voter access should be restricted; quite the contrary, as previously noted the **15th, 19th, 24th, and 26th Amendments** all deal with removing restrictions on voting in one form or another. The **24th Amendment, Clause 1** in particular states:

> **THE RIGHT OF CITIZENS OF THE UNITED STATES TO VOTE IN ANY PRIMARY OR OTHER ELECTION FOR PRESIDENT OR VICE PRESIDENT, FOR ELECTORS FOR PRESIDENT OR VICE PRESIDENT, OR FOR SENATOR OR REPRESENTATIVE IN CONGRESS, SHALL NOT BE DENIED OR ABRIDGED BY THE UNITED STATES OR ANY STATE BY REASON OF FAILURE TO PAY ANY POLL TAX OR OTHER TAX.**

It could be (and has been) argued that registering to vote is yet another type of tax. Tax does not have to be money, but it can be time or meeting criteria that States set up. There are active lawsuits that deal with States setting up restrictions for voter registration, for purging voter rolls, and for other forms of refusing to allow people to vote due to so-called discrepancies. Voting should not be abridged in any way and the Constitution already does not give any leeway in this. Now, this Amendment would codify that certainty and not just sustain it implicitly.

Photo by **ARNAUD JAEGERS**[148] on **UNSPLASH**

The easier it is to register, the higher the turnout. Looking at the Voting Age Population (VAP) turnout percentages for 2016, the eight States with the highest values all had same day voter registration (Maine, Minnesota, New Hampshire, Wisconsin, Iowa, Colorado, Vermont, and Michigan). Among all the States with same day voter registration, the VAP was just over 56% compared to 54% of those States without. If we exclude California and Hawai'i—two of the three lowest VAP States (Texas being the other) because of reasons of their geography and lack of competition—that value jumps to almost 62%. Those numbers are clear: the easier it is to register and vote without restriction, the higher turnout is. It is so clear that since the 2016 election, four more States had added

---

[148] HTTPS://UNSPLASH.COM/@AJAEGERS

the same option in time for the 2020 election.

In order to be an informed voter, the government often prints out materials to explain particular items or what is being voted on—in other words, a voter's handbook. All of this should be readily available to the people. That is not the only material that should be provided, though. One of the best ways to understand what is going to be on the ballot is to *have the ballot*, and as such the following Amendment should be added:

ALL ELIGIBLE VOTERS OF THE UNITED STATES SHALL BE PROVIDED A BALLOT AT THE COMMENCEMENT OF THE ELECTION TIMEFRAME. THIS BALLOT SHALL BE ABLE TO BE SUBMITTED BY ALL METHODS AS HAVE BEEN MADE AVAILABLE BY LAW DURING THE ELECTION TIMEFRAME.

There are not a lot of examples in the United States, but the three States that do have automatic mail ballot voting (Colorado, Oregon, and Washington) have a combined VAP of over 61% compared to the rest of the States with about 54%. It should be noted that Colorado also has same day registration and is a "battleground" State, so it is hitting all the right checkboxes. Additionally, another 19 States have laws that allow counties or other municipalities to have entirely vote-by-mail elections if they so choose. Altogether, the data is probably not enough to base a statistical analysis on, especially since that is not the complete point of this Amendment.

States like Colorado do not just force everyone to vote by mail. While the ballots are sent out to all eligible voters, the voters can then mail it back, drop it off at a designated polling box, or vote in person at a polling station. That is what the second part of this Amendment is talking about. Today, the ways to vote might consist of by mail, by a drop-box, early in person at a designated location, or directly at the polling stations. In the future, though, maybe elections via the Internet will be safe and secure. Perhaps there is another method we have not quite figured out how to implement yet that would be easier and more accurate. In any case, all methods should be made available for the people to vote.

Photo by *JENNIFER GRIFFIN*[149] on *UNSPLASH*

Therefore, sending out the mail ballot ahead of time could be considered just another piece of election material. In the (at least) 3-week timeframe that voting would happen, voters could use any of the methods available to them, not just the mail ballot itself—which then could just be informational in that case. It will give voters the

---

[149] HTTPS://UNSPLASH.COM/@DOTJPG

opportunity to be informed and no room to complain that every opportunity was not granted to get their vote in.

That said, there is one last measure that can be used to increase turnout and participation.

> **ALL ELIGIBLE VOTERS WITHIN THE UNITED STATES ARE REQUIRED TO VOTE IN FEDERAL ELECTIONS UNLESS UNABLE TO PHYSICALLY OR MENTALLY DO SO OR HAVE BEEN GRANTED AN EXCEPTION BY LAW. CONGRESS SHALL LAY A LEVY ON THOSE WHO FAIL TO SUBMIT BALLOTS WITHOUT MEETING AN EXCEPTION.**

You did not think you were going to get away without having a responsibility in all of this, did you? Yes, for all of this and the prior chapter the onus has fallen on the government to change, but that does not mean there are not civic duties for the people.

Compulsory voting would be impossible in the United States right now because it would violate the 1st Amendment. One could easily argue that forcing a person to vote could be considered a type of speech that someone may not want to give. Because of that, an Amendment would be needed to make it part of the Constitution in order to have equal weight.

Others think of compulsory elections like those used in North Korea. Yes, everyone must "vote", but there is only one item to vote on and the answer is "Yes" no matter what, so it is not a real democracy. However, countries closer to our own like Australia, Belgium, Brazil, and plenty of others do have a compulsory system and see voter turnout rates in the 90% or above range. One of the key difference makers is the fine for those who fail to vote. Many countries that have compulsory voting do not have a fine or do not enforce it, and the rates of participation are noticeably lower.

Some may fear the idea of an uneducated or uninterested class of people being involved in the voting process who would not otherwise participate. Studies show, however, that because of the compulsion, interest in the political process and desire to have one's views be heard *increases*. And yes, the correlation exists that those who are more disadvantaged are less likely to vote and thus perpetuate the cycle. Just giving people the ability to have their voice be heard is one step, but it is another entirely to fuse their voice to the chorus.

There are exceptions, of course, that must be accounted for. Being in a physical state where voting is impossible or having a mental debilitation could be reasons for exclusion. Others may have religious reasons for not voting, or there are laws that restrict certain classes of people (think people in prison). As such, Congress would be allowed to create and maintain that list of exceptions.

Plus, nothing is stopping someone from returning their ballot blank or filling it in with nonsense. Nothing is stopping people from doing that now! There were over 763,000 write-in votes for President in 2016, and a large number of votes were for fictional characters like Mickey Mouse and Elmer Fudd, or non-humans like the deceased gorilla Harambe. At the time of this writing, only limited details have been released for the 2020 election, but you can expect more of the same. What we do know for sure is that there were far fewer write-ins and "none of the above" selections, coming in just under 174,000 votes combined.

Studies have shown that while disengaged people may start off with more comedy or protest votes, over time they tend to vote for "real" candidates. Consider the reason for many of these choices—even among the limited constituents—as a response to living in an area where their vote makes no impact on the outcome. The 2020 election was felt as more consequential and as a result the engagement levels increased, as did the picking of specific candidates.

Of course, there will always be jokers, anti-establishment types, and general protesters, but that is their right. Should we find that compulsory voting in the field is not as effective as hoped, Congress could always lower the fine to $0 and therefore there would be no compulsion mechanism. That is one of the reasons for allowing Congress to control the rate as opposed to building it into the Constitution.

The government has a responsibility to the people of the United States; but how can the government be responsible if the people do not fulfill their duty to it? And the duty of the people is to vote.

The Washington Monument stands over the National Mall in Washington, D.C. on December 31, 2019. Photo by J.P. Prag.

Fix Congress? No, Demolish It!

Amending the Constitution is the only way to make Congress be the people's house

We the People queue up to visit the United States Capitol Building in Washington, D.C. where Congress meets and has many of its offices. Photo by J.P. Prag on December 28, 2019.

» **KEY POINTS**

- *Congress cannot represent the will of the people because the Constitution is irreparably flawed. Only by Amending the Constitution can we better the Legislative Branch for everyone.*

- *The House of Representatives needs to be changed from a "winner takes all" system using voting districts to one with a proportional mix for all the varied political views in America.*

- *While the Senate needs to remain a State check on Federal power, that does not mean each State should have equal power no matter its size and/or population.*

CONGRESS IS NOT THE WILL OF THE PEOPLE.

There are many ways to divvy the American populous up. However, no matter which way you do Congress does not align to the unique mix of people in this country. Whether it is age, gender/sexual identity, race, religion/religiosity, age, education, earnings, net worth, or any other superfluous factor—the members of Congress are as far from the mean as could be. Even something as simple as political alignment completely misses the mark!

	House	Senate	Total Congress	2018 House Election Results	People of the U.S.A.
Democrat	54%	45%	52%	53%	31%
Republican	46%	52%	47%	44%	28%
Independent / Other	0%	2%	0%	3%	39%
Vacant / No Answer	0%	1%	0%	0%	2%

The majority of people in America do not align to any political party. Yet, as shown in this table from 2019, Congress is completely dominated by the oligopoly of just two parties.

We could go much deeper into specific policy beliefs, desires for the direction of the country, and other socio/economic/physical differences, but that is unnecessary. The point is just to show that no matter which way you slice it, Congress is not in line with those they are supposed to stand for. If the will, setup, and diversity of the people is not reflected in the government, then how can the government give back to the people what is needed?

The United States Capitol Building in Washington, D.C. is filled with art and symbolism that attempt to create a uniquely American mythos while borrowing heavily from other cultures. This example was photographed on December 28, 2019 by J.P. Prag.

To be clear, much of this is not Congress's fault. Members of Congress should not feel shame or be diminished because they happen to be part of group that is severely over-represented. Being more educated, making a fair wage, following your beliefs, expressing your culture and ethnicity—these are all things that should be pursued by those who desire it. In a way, Congress is as much of a victim as the citizenry because if there are no representatives to express other views, how can these incumbents possibly respond? If it is not part of their life experience and there is no one in Congress to express another perspective, how would they know?

There is a systematic issue here. No amount of law, policy, redistricting, quota filling, or any other *"bubble gum and masking tape"* method can change the current situation. All of those solutions can make slight tweaks but will still leave at least half of America without someone to speak on their behalf. The Legislature of the United States of America is broken at its core because of the compromises that were made to get 13 former colonies to agree to join and stay in a single federalist union. We have had over 230 years to experience the consequences firsthand.

Even if Congress functioned perfectly, the parties worked together, and legislation passed regularly, they would still have no incentive to fix these glaring holes. Instead, our Representatives and Senators benefit from a broken system that keeps them indefinitely employed, well paid, and with a modicum of power. No, in order to fix these base concerns, we need to Amend the Constitution and bring Congress back under **WE THE PEOPLE**.

» WHOSE HOUSE?

Though the Founders wanted to avoid political parties, it is just not in human nature. Homo Sapiens will create groups no matter what, and we must accept that it is always going to be this way in order to move on. While the purpose of a Political Party is to group together like-minded people into a single force, the two main parties in the United States are so large that there is no way they can cover the many nuanced and various viewpoints of the American people. One of the biggest lies these parties tell is that there are "two sides to every issue". In reality, most concerns have a rainbow of different perspectives and approaches, and others have almost universal agreement.

A replica of the Library of Congress at the United States Botanical Garden in Washington, D.C. on December 28, 2019. Photo by J.P. Prag.

If we want the House of Representatives to be a reflection of the people's will at the Federal level, we must Amend the Constitution to make it so:

THE HOUSE OF REPRESENTATIVES SHALL BE COMPOSED OF MEMBERS CHOSEN EVERY FOURTH YEAR ON THE EVEN YEARS OPPOSITE ELECTIONS FOR PRESIDENT AND VICE PRESIDENT BY THE PEOPLE OF THE SEVERAL STATES AND TERRITORIES.

THE PEOPLE OF THE UNITED STATES AND ITS TERRITORIES SHALL VOTE FOR THE POLITICAL PARTIES DIRECTLY.

Today, the entire House of Representatives is re-elected every two years. Because of this cycle and the focus on individual races, most Representatives spend a majority of their time campaigning and fundraising instead of governing. Therefore, let us first aim to smooth out the schedule and make it every four years instead; as well as time those elections to be opposite the ones for the Executive Branch. That will give the people a voice during the middle of a President's term and they will have a say about what their priorities are: do they want more legislators in line with the President to push forward the Executive agenda, or do they want to rein the office in? And this would for the first time include the 4.4 million people who live in the Territories[150]—people who have no voice in Congress at all right now.

They are not the only ones who have never had a voice in Congress, though. As noted above, our current "Winner Takes All" system is not getting us anywhere near the breakdown of the American populace by any factor. Many other western-style democracies elect their legislature by Political Party and not by individuals that cover specific oddly-shaped slices of the country. The House of Representatives should follow a similar methodology in order to align to the will of the people. In other words, it will not be a zero-sum game of winning and losing, but a distribution game by the intent of the people. This would bring further engagement of the citizenry because people would have actual representation no matter where they live and what their beliefs are.

Here, let us return to the political affiliation chart from the top of this chapter, but with some modifications. If we extrapolate a few assumptions, we can see a couple of different scenarios in how a straight party election would

---

[150] Note that for our purposes, the District of Columbia is being considered a 'Territory' even though technically it is a 'Federal District', something quite distinct.

result in a very different distribution in the House of Representatives:

- **Both Scenarios:** 95% of Democrats and Republicans vote for their preferred party, 2% of Democrats and Republicans vote for the other party, 3% of Democrats and Republicans vote for Third Parties, and all Unknowns vote for Third Parties.

- **Scenario 1 [Independents Lean to Major Parties]:** 40% of Independents vote Republican, 40% of Independents vote Democrat, 20% of Independents vote for Third Parties.

- **Scenario 2 [Independents Lean to Third Parties]:** 20% of Independents vote Republican, 20% of Independents vote Democrat, 60% of Independents vote for Third Parties.

In this, we get two potentialities where Scenario 1 is most Independents lean either Democrat or Republican and Scenario 2 where a small majority of Independents lean Third Party. This results in a striking re-alignment of the House of Representatives:

	House	2018 House Election Results	People of the U.S.A.	Scenario 1	Scenario 2
Democrat	54%	53%	31%	46%	38%
Republican	46%	44%	28%	43%	35%
Independent / Other	0%	3%	39%	12%	27%
Vacant / No Answer	0%	0%	2%	0%	0%

Even in Scenario 1, neither the Democrats nor the Republicans would have been able to take single Party control of the House. In order to pass legislation, they would have to work with others! This is the utmost critical element of this process: breaking up the oligopoly of the two major Political Parties and getting more competition and diversity. Instead of extremists on either the left or the right being able to control the agenda for as long as they are in charge, discussion and deals among many parties with particular needs would be necessary.

> **THE NUMBER OF MEMBERS OF THE HOUSE OF REPRESENTATIVES SHALL BE NO LESS THAN ONE HUNDRED. THE MEMBERS SHALL BE DETERMINED BY TAKING THE NUMBER OF VOTES FOR A POLITICAL PARTY AND DIVIDING AMONG TOTAL VOTES TO GET A PROPORTIONAL VOTE. THOSE ATTAINING AT LEAST ONE PERCENT OF THE VOTE SHALL RECEIVE A SEAT AND SHALL RECEIVE AN ADDITIONAL SEAT FOR EACH PERCENTAGE POINT ABOVE THAT. PARTIAL PERCENTAGES SHALL ALWAYS BE ROUNDED UP TO THE NEXT HIGHEST FULL NUMBER. WITH THE NUMBER OF SEATS BY EACH PARTY SET, THE MEMBERS SHALL BE FILLED BY THE LISTS PROVIDED BY THE POLITICAL PARTIES.**
>
> **POLITICAL PARTIES SHALL CREATE LISTS OF ONE HUNDRED PERSONS IN ORDER OF PREFERENCE TO BE CONSIDERED FOR MEMBERSHIP.**

Just to clear this up, there are currently 435 members of the House of Representatives as that is what Congress decided it should be, not because it is mandated anywhere in the Constitution. As such, let us go through a couple of situations to see how this new math could result in different mixes:

- If one party receives 99.00...1% or higher of the vote, they would receive 100 Seats, which would be the absolute minimum. Since no other Party would have passed the 1% threshold, they would be alone in the House of Representatives; thus showing why a list of 100 people is necessary as it is the maximum number of potential Members that a Party can receive.

- If 99 Parties receive 1.00...1% of the vote, then all other Parties cannot reach the 1% threshold. Since all percentages are rounded up to the nearest whole number, each of the 99 Parties would receive 2 Seats. In this situation, the House of Representatives would have a maximum of 198 Members.

Elephants and Donkeys are not the only animals on Capitol Hill. A squirrel ponders the future of the federal government outside the United States Capitol Building in Washington, D.C. on December 28, 2019. Photo by J.P. Prag.

Both of these conditions are highly unlikely to happen. In the 2018 election, no third party made the 1% threshold by themselves so that election would have ended up with 55 Democrats and 46 Republicans. However, Third Parties receive so few votes because of various methods of suppression, not the least of which are gerrymandered districts. Since there is not good enough data on Third Parties, if we go back to Scenarios 1 and 2 from before we could have ended up with any of these other situations (and many in between):

Democrats	Republicans	Other Parties	Total Members
46	43	12	**101**
38	36	28	**102**
46	43	24	**113**
38	36	56	**130**

The last situation is particularly interesting in that it makes all Other Parties the largest party by Members. While none individually would be the largest Party, by design it gives them an outstripped power so that the larger Parties could not run roughshod over them and dismiss their claims. In other words, it is a check within the House of Representative to make sure those in the minority are still heard and must be worked with.

> **THE GOVERNMENT OF THE UNITED STATES AND THE GOVERNMENTS OF THE STATES AND TERRITORIES SHALL PROVIDE NO SUPPORT TO POLITICAL PARTIES FOR DETERMINING THEIR LISTS AND THE POLITICAL PARTIES ARE SOLELY RESPONSIBLE FOR DETERMINING THE METHOD OF DEVELOPING THEIR LISTS. NOR SHALL THE GOVERNMENT OF THE UNITED STATES NOR THE GOVERNMENTS OF THE STATES AND TERRITORIES PROVIDE ANY OTHER TYPE OF SUPPORT OR RESOURCES FOR INTERNAL POLITICAL PARTY DECISIONS.**
>
> **THERE SHALL BE NO CRITERIA FOR A POLITICAL PARTY TO APPEAR ON THE BALLOTS SAVE PRODUCING THE LIST OF CANDIDATES, THOUGH THE LIST MUST BE LIMITED TO THOSE PEOPLE WHO MEET THE CRITERIA FOR THE HOUSE OF REPRESENTATIVES AS WRITTEN IN THE CONSTITUTION.**

Part of the issue with the Democratic/Republican oligopoly is that they have created rules that have the Federal, State, and local governments spending time, money, and resources on what should be internal Party responsibility. In particular, the fact that Primaries are conducted as if they are part of the election system and that the government should support them is completely the antithesis to equal protections.

Why should the government spend any time and resources on helping a Political Party decide who is going to run in their spots for an election? That is purely a Party responsibility, and as such this clause makes it clear that there is a separation of roles between the government and those running to be in it. The act of coming up with a list of candidates and putting them in order of preference is a methodology that the Parties must decide themselves. If they need to go through a Primary process, it is up to them to create a voting system and pay for that with internal funds. Neither the United States government nor the governments of States, Territories, Counties, Cities, or any other division should have a responsibility for determining how an—essentially—nonprofit organization makes management decisions.

Further, in order to fully remove the Government from being involved with Political Parties, all criteria for what a "Political Party" is needs to be eliminated. One of the major issues for Third Parties like Libertarians, Greens, and others is that they must go State-by-State and meet criteria that may be impossible unless they were already on a ballot. And even after they pass those criteria, they can still be capriciously removed and have to go through the whole process all over again.

WHEN VACANCIES HAPPEN IN THE REPRESENTATION THE PARTIES ELECTED SHALL FILL THOSE VACANCIES FROM THE NEXT ELIGIBLE AND AVAILABLE NAMES ON THEIR LISTS.

Finally, instead of expensive new elections in an area and a long time without some people having representation, a stability is created. With the pre-defined Lists, the next people in line are already there if for any reason a replacement is needed.

» More than Mittens

As set up today, the Senate makes absolutely no sense. Every State has two Senators no matter if there are more sheep than people or the amount of land is bigger than ten other States combined. Meanwhile, the largest Territories that are physically and population wise bigger than half the rest of the country have no say whatsoever. It is an incredibly imbalanced solution to a real concern.

Looking across the Tidal Basin from the Ohio Drive Bridge towards the Washington Monument in Washington, D.C. on December 31, 2019. Photo by J.P. Prag.

The genuine issue that the Senate tries to resolve is that the States need to be a check on the power of the Federal Government so that the latter does not become too authoritative and trample on their rights. While this was the gravest concern in the late 18th century, this is still a logical—though not as pronounced—consideration even today. In order to balance out the will of the Federal Government, there must be a counter. However, the counter needs to be fair to all constituents within it.

> **THE SENATE OF THE UNITED STATES SHALL BE COMPOSED OF AT LEAST TWO SENATORS FROM EACH STATE AND TERRITORY WITH PERMANENT POPULATION, ELECTED BY THE PEOPLE THEREOF, FOR FOUR YEARS ON THE EVEN YEARS OPPOSITE ELECTIONS FOR PRESIDENT AND VICE PRESIDENT.**

The first change is the relative number of Senators by saying that each State and Territory must have at a minimum two. Once again, Territories are included so that the millions of people living in those places and the thousands of square miles are not excluded. However, unlike the House of Representatives' Amendments, there is an important distinction in Territories that have a permanent population since there are several more that do not have any people at all. These places do not need special attention because there is no real citizenry to represent and the Federal Government already manages the land.

Beyond the structure, much like the House of Representatives, the Senate would be elected every four years in totality and once again on the even years opposite the Executive Branch. This would ensure that the entire Legislature is renewed during the term of the President and serve as a check on or expansion of power as defined by the will of the people. Using this method would make each 2-year election cycle incredibly important because either it would be for the President/Vice President or all Congressional positions would be filled at once.

Only a select few Congresspeople have offices in the United States Capitol Building in Washington, D.C. while the rest must work from offsite buildings. Here we see the entrance to Speaker of the House Nancy Pelosi's office on December 28, 2019. Photo by J.P. Prag.

> **THE TOTAL NUMBER OF SENATORS RECEIVED BY EACH STATE AND TERRITORY SHALL BE ONE SEAT FOR EACH STATE AND ZERO SEATS FOR EACH TERRITORY; PLUS A PROPORTIONAL DISTRIBUTION OF ONE HUNDRED SEATS BASED UPON THE TOTAL POPULATION OF THE STATES AND TERRITORIES; PLUS A PROPORTIONAL DISTRIBUTION OF ONE HUNDRED SEATS BASED UPON THE TOTAL LAND AREA OF THE STATES AND TERRITORIES; SUCH THAT EACH STATE SHALL HAVE NO LESS THAN THREE SENATORS AND EACH TERRITORY SHALL HAVE NO LESS THAN TWO SENATORS.**

Continuing on this path, there would then be a distribution of available Seats. While we have previously condensed the House of Representatives, we have expanded the Senate within certain confines. Where the House of Representatives needed pruning for efficiency, the Senate needs expansion to limit power mongering. The first part is saying that if the location is a "State" it would receive a Seat and if it was a "Territory with Permanent Population", it would not. There are certain rights and responsibilities that come with being a full-fledged State and this is one of those areas where it makes sense to include a distinction to incentivize Territories to become full States.

That is not to say Territories would not receive full representation, though. As the next part lays out, there would be 100 Seats to be distributed by physical area and another 100 Seats to be distributed by population. Given the current layout of the United States, this would result in a total of 250 seats—which would go up slightly by 1 as

Territories became States or a new State were admitted to the Union. Even breaking up California or Texas would have a minimal impact compared to what would happen today (each new State getting two Senators would be replaced with one new Senator and a redistribution of the limited area and population seats).

What you will notice is that this re-imagining of the Senate is rather silent on the method by which the distribution is to happen, and this is intentional. Trying to use straight methods on limited seats always creates exceptions, so therefore it would be up to Congress to determine the necessary formula.

As an example, I have used a method where rounding at a particular point for area worked fine, but left me with one extra Senator for population no matter what I did. In the end, looking at overall population criteria, Indiana had to have one Senator removed. Apologies to Indiana. The result was this:

	Is a State	Area Distribution	Population Distribution	Total Senators
Alabama	1	1	1	3
Alaska	1	17	1	19
American Samoa	0	1	1	2
Arizona	1	3	2	6
Arkansas	1	1	1	3

	Is a State	Area Distribution	Population Distribution	Total Senators
California	1	4	11	16
Colorado	1	2	1	4
Connecticut	1	1	1	3
Delaware	1	1	1	3
District of Columbia	0	1	1	2
Florida	1	1	6	8
Georgia	1	1	3	5
Guam	0	1	1	2
Hawai'i	1	1	1	3
Idaho	1	2	1	4
Illinois	1	1	3	5
Indiana	1	1	1	3
Iowa	1	1	1	3
Kansas	1	2	1	4
Kentucky	1	1	1	3
Louisiana	1	1	1	3

	Is a State	Area Distribution	Population Distribution	Total Senators
Maine	1	1	1	3
Maryland	1	1	1	3
Massachusetts	1	1	2	4
Michigan	1	2	3	6
Minnesota	1	2	1	4
Mississippi	1	1	1	3
Missouri	1	1	1	3
Montana	1	3	1	5
Nebraska	1	2	1	4
Nevada	1	3	1	5
New Hampshire	1	1	1	3
New Jersey	1	1	2	4
New Mexico	1	3	1	5
New York	1	1	5	7
North Carolina	1	1	3	5
North Dakota	1	1	1	3

	Is a State	Area Distribution	Population Distribution	Total Senators
Northern Mariana Islands	0	1	1	2
Ohio	1	1	3	5
Oklahoma	1	1	1	3
Oregon	1	2	1	4
Pennsylvania	1	1	3	5
Puerto Rico	0	1	1	2
Rhode Island	1	1	1	3
South Carolina	1	1	1	3
South Dakota	1	2	1	4
Tennessee	1	1	2	4
Texas	1	7	8	16
U.S. Virgin Islands	0	1	1	2
Utah	1	2	1	4
Vermont	1	1	1	3
Virginia	1	1	2	4
Washington	1	2	2	5

	Is a State	Area Distribution	Population Distribution	Total Senators
West Virginia	1	1	1	3
Wisconsin	1	1	1	3
Wyoming	1	2	1	4

Of the 56 States and Populated Territories, exactly half (28) ended up with 2 or 3 Senators. Among the States and Territories at the top of the charts, Alaska is by far the biggest winner expanding to 19 Senators based almost solely on its massive land area (which might make a case for splitting Alaska up, but that is not a concern for this particular argument). Outside of Alaska, though, the real winners were as expected with California and Texas each receiving 16 Senators—the exact outcome one would surmise for States with such vast amounts of area and populations to go along with them. The next highest States were Florida at 8 Seats and New York at 7 Seats. Though a precipitous drop off, it does reflect fairly the two factors of population and size. From there it continues to drop off so that States with large populations and small sizes (like Massachusetts) share the same number of Senators with those that have small population and large sizes (like South Dakota). None of the Territories escaped their 2-Seat minimum.

Per above, this is just an example and Congress may make other decisions on distribution, but it shows the methodology in play. It makes sure States and Territories that have more land and people in turn have a larger say while also making sure that no area has too little say or blocks of votes. Yes, it is not completely even, nor is it 100% fair; it is just intended to level the playing field without going overboard to create perfection.

> **THE LEGAL BODY OF EACH STATE AND TERRITORY SHALL DETERMINE THE METHOD BY WHICH SENATORS ARE ELECTED.**

Critically different compared to the House of Representatives, though, is that the Senators are selected in a method decided by the States and Territories themselves. Once they know how many Seats they have, the method they choose to fill those positions is up to them save for being elected by the people (already an Amendment). Now, it would be hoped that they would fill them in a distributed manner akin to the House of Representatives, but that is a regional decision that must be up to each locale, as is the right of a State/Territory.

» PUTTING CONGRESS IN A BOX

With these Amendments to the Constitution, we have completely changed the makeup of Congress so that it is more balanced and a closer reflection of the will of the people. Now, getting them to do their jobs once elected... that is a different story.

Inside the Lincoln Memorial in Washington, D.C. on December 31, 2019. Photo by J.P. Prag.

PART-TIME // CITIZEN LEGISLATURE

We need to fire everyone in Congress, cut almost all of their pay and benefits, and take away their toys

Northern elephant seals at Año Nuevo State Park on February 9, 2019. Photo and description by **RHODODENDRITES**[151], **CC BY-SA 4.0**[152], via Wikimedia Commons.

---

[151] HTTPS://COMMONS.WIKIMEDIA.ORG/WIKI/FILE:ELEPHANT_SEALS_AT_ANO_NUEVO_%2891674%29.JPG
[152] HTTPS://CREATIVECOMMONS.ORG/LICENSES/BY-SA/4.0

» **KEY POINTS**

- *Congress is a do-nothing organization because they have unlimited time and resources and are paid handsomely no matter what.*

- *In order to create some urgency and perhaps make Congress more productive, we need a set of Constitutional Amendments to require turnover and make sure Congresspeople have far less of everything.*

- *At the end of the day, we would return Congress to what it was originally conceived as by the Founders: a part-time, citizen legislature.*

PICK YOUR BIG POLITICAL ISSUE...

Is it infrastructure? Or perhaps it is immigration? What about the response to COVID-19? Could it be the latest laws passed by particular States because of the lack of overriding Federal guidance? Are taxes your main concern? What do you think about the current military engagements and disengagements around the world? Does a very specific clause in a massive communication statute bother you to no end?

Whatever it is, just ask yourself: has Congress really done anything about it? Congresspeople are highly paid, work extreme hours, employ a massive support staff, and have near limitless resources to self-fund anything they could ever want to do. Yet despite all that, almost nothing gets done, even when one party has majority control of both chambers. They certainly do not need more time or money to make actual accomplishments, so what is the problem?

The answer is actually that they have too much time and money! There is no urgency because they can waste resources, do nothing, and still get paid more than almost all other Americans. What is their incentive to do a better job and be more efficient and productive? There is none because over the years Congress has turned itself into a monolith of inaction. Should we continue to put up with this intransigence, especially since it will only get worse?

No, a resolution is necessary to align membership in Congress to the position as it was originally envisioned by the Founders: a part-time, citizen legislator. In order to do that, there is a simple, three-step solution:

- Fire everyone;
- Cut hours, pay, and fringe benefits;
- Take away their toys.

And through a set of Constitutional Amendments, this is how it can be done...

» FIRE EVERYONE

One of the reasons that members of Congress do not align to any factor of the populace (age, wealth, belief structures, etcetera) is because people join Congress and for the most part never leave. According to the Congressional Research Service (CRS)—an agency of the Federal Government—in the 116th Congress the average time for members of the House of Representatives was 8.6 years while the Senate was 10.1 years. Average is an interesting statistic, but distribution of total stints in Congress (no matter which chamber) gives a clearer picture:

	House	Senate	Total Congress
New (0)	20%	4%	17%
Regular (1 – 12)	56%	57%	56%
Long (13 to 24)	16%	23%	17%
Ultra-Long (25 to 49)	8%	16%	10%

A table demonstrating that many Congresspeople have been in the legislature for way too long.

Members of both divisions also have a large amount of prior experience in government not only from serving in the other chamber, but also as legislators at the State level, Governors, appointed positions, and more. In other words, the vast majority of the Legislative Branch is filled with long-time employees of one government or another.

*Male northern elephant seal at Año Nuevo State Park on February 9, 2019. Photo and description by **RHODODENDRITES**[153], **CC BY-SA 4.0**[154], via Wikimedia Commons.*

The CRS also has a chart that makes it clear: since the beginning of the first Congress to now, the tenure time in the Legislative Branch has been on a straight upward trajectory. Sure, there are dips and bumps as you go, but overall it has been ranging upwards, most especially post the Civil War. Yet despite that, the CRS refuses to write the obvious conclusion:

---

[153] HTTPS://COMMONS.WIKIMEDIA.ORG/WIKI/FILE:ELEPHANT_SEALS_AT_ANO_NUEVO_%2891593%29.JPG
[154] HTTPS://CREATIVECOMMONS.ORG/LICENSES/BY-SA/4.0

TOO MUCH TIME SERVING IN GOVERNMENT IS THE ANTITHESIS OF A REPRESENTATIVE DEMOCRACY.

Being in Congress creates an inherent bubble around legislators that disconnects them from the actual concerns and opinions of their constituents. There needs to be turnover in order to get current perspectives and knowledge into the Capitol Building. In other words, every member of Congress needs to be forcibly retired at some point. The only way we are going to do that is with an **Amendment to the Constitution**:

> **NO PERSON SHALL BE ELECTED TO THE HOUSE OF REPRESENTATIVES MORE THAN TWICE NOR TO THE SENATE MORE THAN TWICE, AND NOT MORE THAN FOUR TIMES FOR ALL OF CONGRESS. AND NO PERSON WHO HAS HELD A POSITION IN CONGRESS FOR MORE THAN TWO YEARS OF A TERM TO WHICH SOME OTHER PERSON WAS ELECTED SHALL BE ELECTED TO THE HOUSE OF REPRESENTATIVES OR THE SENATE MORE THAN ONCE. BUT THIS CLAUSE SHALL NOT APPLY TO ANY PERSON HOLDING A POSITION IN CONGRESS AT THE TIME OF RATIFICATION UNTIL THE END OF HIS CURRENT TERM.**

Does that sound familiar? It is practically an exact crib (some would say plagiarism) of the 22nd Amendment that limited the President to two terms. Prior to Franklin

Delano Roosevelt, no President had ever served more than two terms. After FDR, it was clear that a rule was needed to force the issue and make sure that no single person could amass that much power and control over America's policy and its future. The progression to ultra-long serving members of Congress has been a much more gradual slide, so it has not hit as many people in the face like FDR did. Besides, Congress was on board with limiting the strength of the President; they are not on board with limiting their own power and earning potential.

*Male northern elephant seal with four pups at Año Nuevo State Park on February 9, 2019. Photo and description by **RHODODENDRITES**[155], **CC BY-SA 4.0**[156], via Wikimedia Commons.*

This Amendment would reduce employment to two terms in each chamber of Congress, but does allow a person to serve in both for up to two terms each. Under today's

---

[155] HTTPS://COMMONS.WIKIMEDIA.ORG/WIKI/FILE:ELEPHANT_SEALS_AT_ANO_NUEVO_%2891617%29.JPG
[156] HTTPS://CREATIVECOMMONS.ORG/LICENSES/BY-SA/4.0

Constitution, that would mean up to 4 years in the House of Representatives and 12 years in the Senate for a total of 16 years. If we included the **set of Amendments from the prior chapter**, that would make the House and the Senate four-year terms each that happen simultaneously. As such, this would mean that a person could serve up to 8 years in each chamber for the same total number of 16 years. Either way, these Amendments could stand on their own or work in conjunction for a more complete solution.

Sixteen years may seem long, but it is only the potential and requires moving between two different chambers and winning in two disparate systems. People may lose their seat and have to come back in later or not at all, so overall the chambers should still end up with a good deal of new blood while allowing a fair amount of long-term people to stay involved. After all, it is reasonable to have both brand-new people and those with experience on a regular basis, but at the same time make sure no one is serving for an entire generation or beyond.

However, as noted, that has not limited how much time these people could spend in any level of government. With former State-level legislators, Governors, Presidents, Judges, appointed positions—there are just too many other nooks and crannies that a person looking to make a career out of politics could sneak into and have the government cover the bill. If a Political Party wants to pay its members for their service, that is the Party's business. That does not mean that the government should be paying for the Party to retain and use its power and influence. Because of that, we need another Amendment to make sure all of the government is safe from the careerists:

No person shall serve more than a combined twenty-five years in total in any elected or appointed position or combination thereof within any part of government, with no differentiation between local, State or Territory, Federal, or Foreign government. But this Clause shall not apply to any person holding an elected or appointed position at the time of ratification until the end of his current term. Additionally, this Clause does not apply to staff and civil servants that support the functions of Government, nor those serving in the military or militia.

This Clause is about limiting the total amount of time that someone can spend working in Government; not just the Federal Government, but all of Government in any role that is not a support staff or public servant position or involved with the military. Those people are employees, but when it comes to elected and appointed positions, they are supposed to be in service. As such, they need to time out so that we do not create despots. Dictators need not be the master of an entire nation, but they can be someone who controls which legislation is available for debate, which organizations get money, or who can participate in the PTA bake sale. We need a function to clear away people who have served for too long—not because they necessarily are bad people or have done anything wrong, but simply because service is supposed to be temporary and we need new and different ideas on a regular basis.

At 25 years, a person could spend 16 years serving in Congress and 8 years serving as President with one year left over. Or a person could spend 12 years as their Town Selectman, 10 years as Mayor, and 3 years as Governor. Or another person could spend all 25 years being a Judge. The possibilities and paths are endless!

Male Northern Elephant Seals fighting for territory and mates on February 2, 2008. Photo and description by "MIKE" MICHAEL L. BAIRD[157], CC BY 2.0[158], via Wikimedia Commons.

Most importantly, it limits (though does not eliminate, other laws would need to do that) a bit of cronyism. For instance, the President could not just appoint someone to a plush government position that has no turnover. That would not be a support or civil servant position, so that person would have to realize that if they wanted to do something else—like be a Senator—they could not stay in that position forever. These rewards would be fewer and further between.

---

[157] HTTPS://COMMONS.WIKIMEDIA.ORG/WIKI/FILE:ELEPHANT_SEALS_FIGHTING.JPG
[158] HTTPS://CREATIVECOMMONS.ORG/LICENSES/BY/2.0

When you lay it out, 25 years is roughly a generation. Someone could be in the public eye and in service to it for all that time, but then another generation can come in. It will not work out perfectly like that because everyone will be on different schedules and experiences, but there would be a constant sweep of new people ready to be in service to our country with fresh ideas and hopeful desires.

» Cut Hours, Pay, and Fringe Benefits

Now, those amendments may bring in fresh blood, but if their experiences are the same as the current members of Congress then there will be no change. Eventually, they will become just like their predecessors. For that, we need to get much deeper into the job description of a Congressperson itself.

Going back in time, it was never the intent of the Founders that membership in Congress would be a full-time job with a massive salary and benefits. As a matter of fact, making a legislature be a part-time job is not uncommon in our country at all. Among the States, 14 explicitly make their legislatures be part-time and another 26 have a system that makes it so legislators cannot earn a full income in their government jobs. Even large (in area and population) States like Texas and Florida have a part-time legislature.

When a State does have a full-time legislature, the compensation costs immediately skyrocket. In those where the legislature spends around half of their time working in the government the average salary is about $19,000 per year. Yet even when the median time spent working in government is around 85% (not even "full-time"), those numbers jump to about $82,000 per year.

And that does not even begin to get into the non-monetary costs of passing unnecessary law and creating over-criminalization since the legislators do not want to look like they are resting on their laurels when they are in session—even if they have nothing to discuss!

Now that we understand the costs (both literally and figuratively) of having a full-time legislature, what can be done? Taking lessons and wordings from State Constitutions that have part-time legislators, we can add an Amendment to the Federal one:

BOTH THE HOUSE OF REPRESENTATIVES AND SENATE SHALL BE LIMITED IN THE NUMBER OF DAYS THEY MAY MEET PER LEGISLATIVE YEAR AND THE NUMBER OF HOURS THEY SHALL MEET IN ANY SINGLE DAY. WHILE EITHER CHAMBER OF CONGRESS IS IN SESSION, EACH SHALL MEET NO MORE THAN THREE DAYS PER CALENDAR WEEK.

Using this logic, Congress would be restricted to 60% of the total number of working days in a fiscal year. This is a start, and we will cut them down further later. For now, though, let us temporarily put aside "time" and move on to "money".

Your run-of-the-mill Congressperson receives $174,000 per year for their services, with additional pay for leadership positions, and not including benefits. True, as of the early 2020s, Congress has forgone their automatic pay raise they assigned themselves since 2010, so their pay has been stagnant for quite some time. Despite this large number being far above the national average, how does it compare to the past?

At Año Nuevo State Park on February 9, 2019. Photo and description by RHODODENDRITES[159], *CC BY-SA 4.0*[160], *via Wikimedia Commons.*

- In 1969, Congresspeople made roughly the equivalent of $296,000 in 2019 dollars. By that measure, one could say Congress has cut their pay nearly in half!

- Yet in 1855 when Congress permanently changed to an annual salary system, they were making about $88,000 in 2019 dollars. In other words, modern Congressional pay is nearly double what it was when they first started using this method.

- Before that, though, in 1815 Congress tested the annual system for the first time and set wages around $25,000 in 2019 dollars.

---

[159] HTTPS://COMMONS.WIKIMEDIA.ORG/WIKI/FILE:ELEPHANT_SEALS_AT_ANO_NUEVO_%2891615%29.JPG
[160] HTTPS://CREATIVECOMMONS.ORG/LICENSES/BY-SA/4.0

- If we go back to 1790 during the first full year of Congress, their pay would have been about $32,000 in 2019 dollars. This equates to $20.83 per hour.

What does this all tell us? Well, it seems like earlier members of Congress had a different idea about what compensation meant than later members. More so, of the 39 delegates who signed the Constitution, 41% were in the first Congress. In other words, the pay scales we see in the late 1700s and early 1800s are in line with what the Founders and writers of the Constitution intended, not what we see today and not even what we saw starting in the mid-1800s.

When looking at that original $20.83 per hour, it looks very similar to Living Wage calculations. The Living Wage, unlike the Minimum Wage, is calculated according to what it really costs to survive in a given area. As such, could we not peg the wages of Congress to the Living Wage? To do this, we would again add an Amendment:

> **DIRECT MONETARY COMPENSATION SHALL BE LIMITED TO AND EQUAL TO THE LIVING WAGE RATE IN THE SEAT OF GOVERNMENT COMMISERATED WITH THE HOURS SCHEDULED BY EACH CHAMBER OF CONGRESS. ADDITIONAL NON-MONETARY COMPENSATION MAY ONLY BE AWARDED AS DESIGNATED IN OTHER PARTS OF THE CONSTITUTION.**

There are many Living Wage calculations and factors that we can go with, but for now let us just assume one that is

$25 per hour. If we just say Congress should only be a 50% part-time job (1,040 hours per year), then their expected salary would be $26,000. Is it not amazing how that comes out almost exactly in line with the 1790 to 1815 numbers? Maybe it should be a bit more, maybe a bit less, but no matter what it is certainly a noteworthy pay cut that would be in line with their diminished schedules. Also, of much import is that "limited to" clause, which means that Congress cannot grant itself other monetary compensation in service to the Government (i.e., getting paid extra to serve on a committee or in leadership).

At Año Nuevo State Park on February 9, 2019. Photo and description by **R**HODODENDRITES[161], ***CC BY-SA 4.0***[162], *via Wikimedia Commons.*

---

[161] HTTPS://COMMONS.WIKIMEDIA.ORG/WIKI/FILE:ELEPHANT_SEALS_AT_ANO_NUEVO_%2891569%29.JPG
[162] HTTPS://CREATIVECOMMONS.ORG/LICENSES/BY-SA/4.0

But what about that "non-monetary compensation" mentioned in the Amendment? We are talking about more than just health insurance here (although we are considering that, too). One of the reasons Congresspeople are paid so much now is because of the high cost of housing in Washington, D.C., which of course is a trap of their own making. If we are going to reduce what Congress is being paid, the cost of being in Congress needs to be covered another way. However, for a part-time job, Congresspeople should not be expected to set up and maintain a residence in the seat of government, only come for a visit from time-to-time. And as the prior Amendment alludes, we will need another one to determine what Congresspeople are entitled to:

> **THE FEDERAL GOVERNMENT SHALL PURCHASE AND MAINTAIN A PROPERTY OR SEVERAL PROPERTIES TO HOUSE ALL MEMBERS OF CONGRESS WHEN THEY VISIT THE SEAT OF GOVERNMENT OF THE UNITED STATES. THE PROPERTY OR PROPERTIES SHALL BE SPARSE AND UTILITARIAN TO ONLY SERVE THE TEMPORARY HOUSING NEEDS OF JUST THE MEMBERS OF CONGRESS WHEN VISITING THE SEAT OF GOVERNMENT. IN ADDITION TO ROOM, THE FEDERAL GOVERNMENT SHALL PROVIDE BOARD, TRANSPORTATION, AND ALL OTHER BASIC NEEDS WHILE MEMBERS OF CONGRESS TRAVEL TO AND FROM AND STAY IN THE SEAT OF GOVERNMENT.**

Congress already has a right to purchase and maintain property via **Article 1, Section 8, Clause 17** of the Constitution, so this is just a minor expansion of those existing powers. Creating what amounts to a government-run hotel for legislators is really no different. However, what we are actually doing is eliminating any excuse for more direct compensation. This is why the Amendment goes into items like "board" (food); "transportation" (the plane, train, taxi, and other automotive costs of getting to and staying in Washington, D.C.); and "other basic needs" (things like the utilities and water to keep the living spaces going, as well as security). With these principal costs covered, Congresspeople should not need that monetary compensation to take care of these necessities themselves.

A southern elephant seal (nicknamed "Momoa" by locals) resting on the Whakatane River estuary. Photo and description by USER:AIR55[163], CC BY-SA 4.0[164], via Wikimedia Commons on January 2, 2019.

Furthermore, since Congresspeople do not need to move to Washington, D.C. they do not need to bring their

---

[163] HTTPS://COMMONS.WIKIMEDIA.ORG/WIKI/FILE:MOMOA_SOUTHERN_ELEPHANT_SEAL_-_WHAKATANE.JPG
[164] HTTPS://CREATIVECOMMONS.ORG/LICENSES/BY-SA/4.0

families with them. That is why this Amendment is specifically about housing just the members of Congress and that the space be sparse and utilitarian. As the Amendment states, this is just to provide a "temporary" location for the Congresspeople, so it does not need much except the basics of any modern hotel room. That is not to say it should be an uncomfortable Soviet-style cement block with a mattress on the floor, but that Congresspeople do not need multi-million-dollar brownstones. If a Congressperson wants to buy something like that with their own money, that is their prerogative; the cost just does not need to be shouldered by the taxpayers in one way or another.

Therefore, if their lodging, food, transportation, energy, and all other basics costs are covered, they do not need much of a salary anyway. All of those non-monetary components do add up to quite a bit of real value, but at least it is being controlled at a Federal level so that individual Congresspeople are not being influenced by either what they can afford or the gifts and discounts given to them by those looking to get something in return.

» TAKE AWAY THEIR TOYS

Beyond the direct costs and timetable of the Congresspeople themselves, there is one other item that comes from being a full-time worker, and that is the apparent need for an oversized staff on the government payroll. As of 2019 there were about 12,000 people directly assigned to the personal staff of the 535 members of Congress. There are specific limits as to how many people can be hired and into what type of positions, but those were all created by laws Congress passed itself. How much money each member gets is also set by a Congressional appropriations committee. Basically, aside from a Presidential veto of the entire budget, Congress has complete control over how much staff and money they assign themselves.

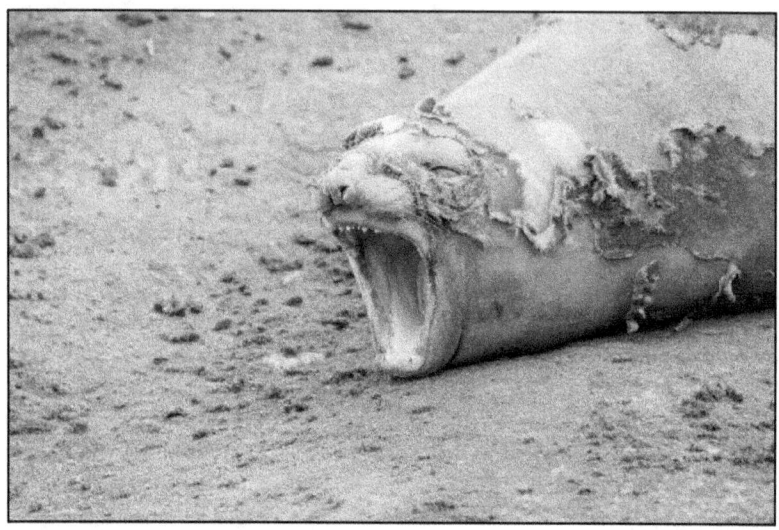

*Southern elephant seal in Hannah Point, Livingston Island, South Shetland Islands on January 18, 2016. Photo and description by Andrew Shiva / Wikipedia / **CC BY-SA 4.0**[165], via Wikimedia Commons.*

As noted before, since legislatures feel pressure to do work when they are in session all the time, then they need more human capital in order to pull that off. These staff people are gathering information, conducting analysis, crafting policy and actual bills, and doing much of the labor required because excess workload has been created. It is a chicken-and-the-egg situation, except we know that there is more work for staff because legislators are making it for themselves by feeling their time needs to be productive.

Meanwhile, the actual Congresspeople spend significant amounts of their time doing non-government activities—

---

[165] HTTPS://CREATIVECOMMONS.ORG/LICENSES/BY-SA/4.0/

mostly fundraising. As such, they need to further offload their work on to others. Congresspeople should be doing all of their own work and research (or at least using Executive Agencies to bring research and analysis to them), and employees of the legislature should be limited to the operational functions needed to run Congress and not personally work for individual legislators on the government dime. Afterall, the legislators were the ones elected to do the job. Why should they be allowed to outsource their workload to an unelected person? By Amendment:

CONGRESS MAY APPROPRIATE FUNDS FOR A STAFF TO COVER THE ORGANIZATIONAL AND FUNCTIONAL NEEDS OF CONGRESS. ORGANIZATIONAL AND FUNCTIONAL STAFF SHALL BE SHARED BY ALL MEMBERS OF CONGRESS EQUALLY. CONGRESS MAY NOT APPROPRIATE FUNDS FOR STAFF ASSIGNED TO INDIVIDUAL MEMBERS OF CONGRESS OR GROUPS OF MEMBERS OF CONGRESS. NO STAFF MEMBER OF THE GOVERNMENT OF THE UNITED STATES MAY BE ASSIGNED TO A SINGLE REPRESENTATIVE OR SENATOR OR ANY GROUP OF REPRESENTATIVES OR SENATORS.

Now we must be clear: there is a need for a support staff. Someone needs to keep the building clean, turn the lights on, run the IT infrastructure, prepare materials, and do all the functions that would make any business run. Government employees are essential to doing the jobs that help everything flow as normal. There are also people that theoretically work for Congress but act in more executive roles like the *Government Accountability*

Office (GAO) and the *Capitol Police*. Altogether, this is not to say that there should not be anyone working for Congress, only that Congresspeople should not have personal staff to do their self-aggrandizing bidding.

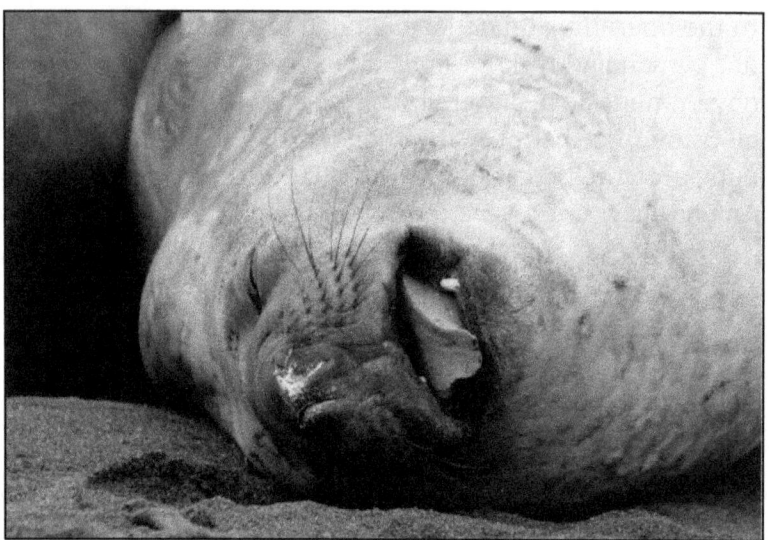

On Macquarie Island on October 28, 2007. Photo and description by BROCKEN INAGLORY[166], *CC BY-SA 3.0*[167], via Wikimedia Commons.

The person who should be responsible for the individual activities of the legislator is the legislator themself. This would also remove the temptation of using support staff for activities outside of running a legislative session (i.e., having them do fundraising activity while taxpayers cover the costs despite the lowly enforced **Hatch Act**). The only assistance Congresspeople need is to make sure they can attend a legislative session. That is the role of the support staff, and this Amendment will help make sure it is nothing more.

---

[166] HTTPS://COMMONS.WIKIMEDIA.ORG/WIKI/FILE:SOUTHERN_ELEPHANT_SEAL_AT_MACQUARIE_ISLAND.JPG
[167] HTTPS://CREATIVECOMMONS.ORG/LICENSES/BY-SA/3.0

How will they, though, decide how the act of legislating happens? Congress currently does not have fixed days and times they must adhere to. As such, legislation can often go to the last minute and beyond. In other words, there is no pressure to get anything done because there are no limits to the amount of time Congress can be forced in session. For this, we must Amend the Constitution and take this power away from them:

> **EACH CHAMBER OF CONGRESS SHALL SET A REGULAR SCHEDULE FOR ITSELF WITH SPECIFIC DAYS AND HOURS IN WHICH ITS MEMBERS SHALL MEET. ONCE SET, THESE DAYS AND TIMES SHALL NOT BE MOVED, CANCELLED, OR EXTENDED UNLESS AN EMERGENCY IS DECLARED BY THE PRESIDENT OF THE UNITED STATES.**

Having this amendment would be the first step to stopping Congress from using time as a weapon. Here, we state that there are certain days and times set up for Congress to meet and those days cannot be modified except in the case of an emergency. In particular, the emergency declaration would have to come from the President, so this is a check on Congress from being able to force a change in schedule on themselves.

The idea of this is that Congress will have regular and expected hours instead of going through endurance tests and other tricks. On the other end, it stops Congress from creating new sessions when no one is available in order to push through legislation. Bills should not be about circumventing the system to make them happen; but should be about closely following the process.

As promised before, in order to keep Congress part-time it is necessary to limit not just the number of days per week, but the number of hours they can work per session and the length of those sessions. This will eliminate the last component of "time as a weapon"—pushing a particular agenda simply by wearing people out by keeping sessions going:

> **ALL SESSIONS MUST BEGIN AFTER SEVEN O'CLOCK IN THE MORNING AND MUST END BEFORE TEN O'CLOCK IN THE EVENING AT THE SEAT OF GOVERNMENT. FURTHERMORE, EACH SESSION SHALL LAST NO LONGER THAN SIX HOURS. GOING BEYOND THIS SCOPE MAY ONLY BE GRANTED IF AN EMERGENCY IS DECLARED BY THE PRESIDENT OF THE UNITED STATES.**

By giving parameters and limiting how often and how long Congress can get together, it will force them to use their time properly, prioritize, vote, and move on to the next item—and cut down their hours further, making them closer to half-time. Some Congresspeople seem to take pride and brag about working on legislation until 3:00 a.m. when they should feel ashamed for procrastinating and not being able to accomplish their work in an acceptable timeframe. And again, only an emergency declaration by the President would be able to expand these sessions.

With their days and hours under control, we can remove their final piece of power: needing to be there in person.

Through the decades, Congress has created a set of rules that say a Representative or Senator must be in the chamber to vote. They generally cannot even vote by proxy or even vote while out in the hallway yet still in the same building. Even if their hologram were projected on the Senate floor, that person could still not vote by current rules. Some allowances were made in the House of Representatives during the COVID-19 Pandemic, but these will most likely be rescinded as the disease retreats. All the Constitution says is that Congress shall assemble at least once a year and that a quorum (that Congress can define) is needed to vote. It says nothing of the where, why, and how a vote is to occur.

Elephant seal colony near San Simeon, California. Photo and description by USER:CILLANXC[168], CC BY-SA 3.0[169], via Wikimedia Commons.

Unfortunately, Congress has chosen to make their lives more complicated than necessary. In the late 1700s and

---

168
HTTPS://COMMONS.WIKIMEDIA.ORG/WIKI/FILE:ELEPHANT_SEAL_COLONY_EDIT.JPG
[169] HTTPS://CREATIVECOMMONS.ORG/LICENSES/BY-SA/3.0

early 1800s, having Congresspeople in a specific location was needed because communication and travel was slow. The day the telegraph was invented was the day this practice should have started to unravel. One of the core issues with the Constitution is that it is hyper-focused within the timeframe it was written. The Founders could not imagine the possibilities we have now, and we may not be able to foresee the possibilities to come.

By refusing to keep up with modern technology, Congress is costing American taxpayers money by forcing Congresspeople to almost always be in Washington, D.C.; and that in turn creates the "costs of doing business". It is a vicious cycle that just keeps repeating itself. With the proper scheduling and technology use at home they should not have to be there in person, at least not all of the time. Of course, then, we need one last Amendment to make that happen:

> **CONGRESS SHALL MAKE ALL METHODS OF DEBATE AND VOTE AVAILABLE TO ITS MEMBERS SUCH THAT MEMBERS NEED NOT BE IN THE SEAT OF GOVERNMENT OR ANY DESIGNATED LOCATION TO PERFORM LEGISLATIVE DUTIES. ALL TECHNOLOGIES AS ARE AVAILABLE SHALL BE ALLOWED AND REQUIRED TO BE USED TO LIMIT THE NEED FOR EACH CHAMBER OF CONGRESS TO MEET IN PERSON. REPRESENTATIVES AND SENATORS MAY RESPOND TO ROLL CALL, DEBATE, CAST VOTES, OR PERFORM ANY LEGISLATIVE DUTY BY ANY LEGAL METHOD AVAILABLE.**

The idea is that a Congressperson can engage in the

process, debate, and vote from any location so that they are not tied to the District of Columbia. For sure, there will be times when they do need and want to get together. However, those times should be fewer and far between. With this remote ability and scheduling control, Congress would actually have the ability to meet more regularly (even during "off hours") instead of taking long, regular breaks to visit their constituents. This way, they would actually live among their own people that they are supposedly representing!

A young elephant seal on September 29, 2010. Photo and description COURTESY OF DR. BRANDON SOUTHALL, NMFS/OPR[170]., Public domain, via Wikimedia Commons.

Again, though, all of that would be up to each chamber to decide what works best. All they would have to do is stay within the limitations of their timetable. And if there is anything the COVID-19 Pandemic has made abundantly

---

[170] HTTPS://COMMONS.WIKIMEDIA.ORG/WIKI/FILE:YOUNG_ELEPHANT_SEAL.JPG

clear is that remote work using tools like Zoom, Teams, and the like is not just possible, it is oftentimes preferable and more productive. There is no reason—with proper security protocols—that Congress could not do the same.

Though we cannot accurately predict the future, perhaps there will be reliable 3D holographic communication, or virtual spaces, or some other method not yet conceived. We simply do not have enough foresight to see what will be available, so we need to leave it open to even better options to come. Unlike our forefathers, we should not bind ourselves and our descendants to the specifics of our particular epoch.

*Elephant Seals in San Simeon, CA on February 3, 2012. Photo and description by **MIKE BAIRD**[171], **CC BY 2.0**[172], via Wikimedia Commons.*

---

[171] HTTPS://COMMONS.WIKIMEDIA.ORG/WIKI/FILE:NORTHERN_ELEPHANT_SEAL_COMBATS.JPG
[172] HTTPS://CREATIVECOMMONS.ORG/LICENSES/BY/2.0

ENDING THE TYRANNY OF MITCH MCCONNELL

Or Nancy Pelosi, or Kevin McCarthy, or Chuck Schumer

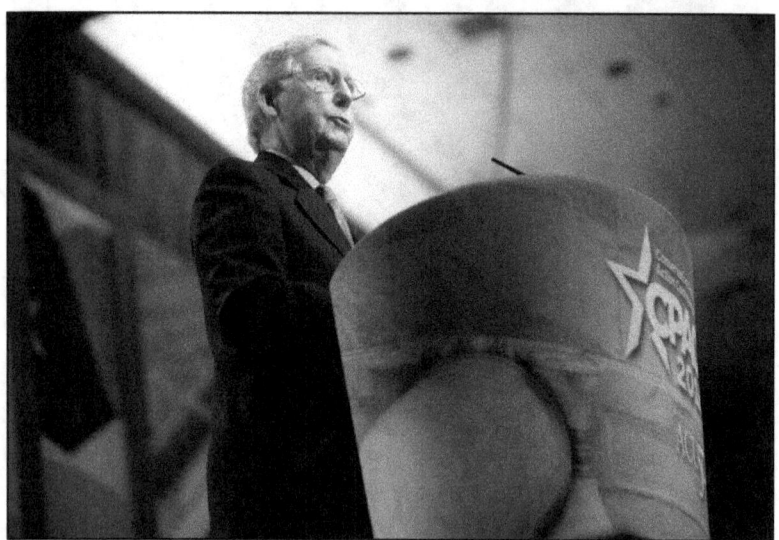

Senator Mitch McConnell (R) of Kentucky speaking at the 2014 Conservative Political Action Conference (CPAC) in National Harbor, MD. Photo and description by **GAGE SKIDMORE**[173], **CC BY-SA 2.0**[174], via Wikimedia Commons.

---

[173] HTTPS://COMMONS.WIKIMEDIA.ORG/WIKI/FILE:MITCH_MCCONNELL_-_12988147624.JPG
[174] HTTPS://CREATIVECOMMONS.ORG/LICENSES/BY-SA/2.0

» **KEY POINTS**

- *Certain members of Congress over time have given themselves an un-Constitutional unchecked power to control the entire legislative process.*

- *All of that power has eroded cooperation, debate, collaboration, compromise, civil discourse, and the general functionality of the federal government.*

- *The only way to remove that power is to amend the Constitution, enforce a legislative methodology, and severely punish those who try to circumvent the rules for personal or Party gain.*

> I DON'T THINK EITHER PARTY IF IT CONTROLLED, IF IT WERE DIFFERENT FROM THE PRESIDENT, WOULD CONFIRM A SUPREME COURT NOMINEE IN THE MIDDLE OF AN ELECTION. WHAT WAS DIFFERENT IN 2020 WAS WE WERE OF THE SAME PARTY AS THE PRESIDENT.
>
> *SENATOR MITCH MCCONNELL (R-KY) ON THE HUGH HEWITT SHOW[175] ON JUNE 14, 2021 DISCUSSING WHAT HE WOULD DO IF THERE WERE A SUPREME COURT VACANCY IN 2024—AND POTENTIALLY 2023—AND THE REPUBLICAN PARTY HELD A MAJORITY IN THE SENATE.*

When Supreme Court Justice Anthony Scalia died in 2016, President Barack Obama did his Constitutional duty by presenting a nominee to the Senate in Merrick Garland. The Senate's job was simple: interview and vet the candidate then cast a yay or nay vote. That is all there is to it! Instead, Senate Majority Leader Mitch McConnell decided to block the candidate from even getting a chance to talk to Congress, never mind voting for or against him. Then, after President Donald Trump took office, he in turn nominated Neil Gorsuch and McConnell immediately took up the nomination. When it became apparent he was not going to have the minimal votes required to instate Gorsuch, McConnell then changed the rules to push the nominee through with a simple majority.

Finally, in May 2019 McConnell told various groups he would completely ignore his own reasoning for not

---

[175] HTTPS://HUGHHEWITT.COM/SENATE-GOP-LEADER-MITCH-MCCONNELL-ON-PRESIDENT-BIDEN-JUDICIAL-NOMINEES-A-NEW-JCPOA/

bringing Obama's nominee to the floor (Supreme Court nominees should not be considered in a Presidential election year) if a Supreme Court position became available in an election year of President Trump. This, of course, came to pass with the death of Justice Ruth Bader Ginsburg on September 18, 2020. At that point, not only was it truly within the election "season", but millions of absentee ballots had already been cast. Justice Amy Coney Barrett was confirmed just 8 days before the official election day—an election in which Republicans indisputably lost both the White House and the Senate.

*President Donald Trump and Supreme Court Associate Justice Clarence Thomas listened as Amy Coney Barrett delivered remarks during her swearing-in ceremony as Associate Justice on October 26, 2020. Official White House Photo and description by Andrea Hanks, **THE WHITE HOUSE FROM WASHINGTON, DC**[176], Public domain, via Wikimedia Commons.*

Those actions were done with the malicious intent of personal Party gain and had nothing to do with just

---

[176] HTTPS://COMMONS.WIKIMEDIA.ORG/WIKI/FILE:THE_SWEARING-IN_CEREMONY_OF_THE_HONORABLE_AMY_CONEY_BARRETT_%2850547408481%29.JPG

fulfilling the roles and responsibilities as laid out by the Constitution. And based upon the quote above and the rest of the interview, McConnell is already prepared to do the exact same and even more in the future. Not taking up legislation within a required timeframe, ignoring the Executive Branch's ability to bring an item to the Senate Floor, pushing bills through below an acceptable threshold, and capriciously changing rules in order to create a loophole around the intent of the Constitution—these are all in the McConnell playbook.

> **WHILE THESE ACTS MAY BE UNSCRUPULOUS, UNETHICAL, CONTEMPTIBLE, ANTI-DEMOCRATIC, AND ANTI-AMERICAN, THEY ARE NOT AGAINST THE CONSTITUTION!**

Reading the Constitution as written, McConnell has done no wrong. He has worked within the framework of the law and manipulated it to his favor. Those like McConnell—whether Republican, Democrat, or otherwise—would also be within their rights to do exactly the same thing or something similar. Many have promised to do so, and others already have done so in the past. For example, in 2014 the Senate was controlled by Democrats while the House of Representatives was in the hands of Republicans. By July 2014, the latter were complaining loudly to the press about the over 300 bills the House had passed but the Senate had not taken up under the tutelage of Majority Leader Harry Reid (D-NV), building a "legislative graveyard" of his own.

And they were exactly right! Sure, those bills stood

almost no chance to pass the Senate and—even if they did—would surely have been vetoed by President Obama. But that is not the job of the leaders of these chambers; the job of Congresspeople is *only* to fashion and vote on bills, not to use legislative tools to avoid doing what they are Constitutionally obligated to do. Most certainly, their job is not to create never ending gridlock.

Outside the United States Capitol Building in Washington, D.C. where Congress meets and theoretically creates law. Photo by J.P. Prag on December 28, 2019.

Actions like these are not in the interests of the people of the United States; they are designed to benefit a single Party's power. Now, a Party may be doing what it thinks is best for all people, but unfortunately Congress is not a representation of the will of the people. We have discussed that in the previous two chapters, so for now let us focus on how to make the legislature we have function with a modicum of normalcy and efficiency.

» SQUARE PEGS AND ROUND HOLES

There is no doubt that Congress has become broken from the simple fact that so little legislation gets through;

there is more time spent on using the made-up rules of Congress as weapons and technicalities than on organization and process; and that the items that do pass often are going through only on Party lines or a thin margin with the other Party involved. With few to no individually minded Congresspeople thinking of their constituents instead of their own Party politics, we are in an era of stall and go-go-go that ebbs only as one Party receives a small level of control of both chambers of Congress and the Presidency.

This is no way to govern.

The Constitution of the United States does not lay out any specific processes about how the House of Representatives and the Senate should work. Instead, it explicitly leaves those decisions up to the individual chambers. All of the rules, procedures, and methods of passing a law are all made up and could be thrown away at any time. Yet, all those measures not only continue to exist, they have become endemic tools and weapons to be used for political purposes instead of the function as laid out by the Constitution: to pass laws.

THE ONLY THING STOPPING CONGRESS FROM FIXING INEQUITIES IN HOW IT IS SET UP IS CONGRESS ITSELF.

While some may want to nitpick over slight adjustments within the existing framework, it is truly past time to consider the indifference of the Constitution to be a detriment. Further ways of skirting the letter of the law continue to be implemented despite the chilling effects on democracy. To end the tyranny of one person or a few select people having such vast controls, Congress needs Constitutionally enforced Amendments to act in benefit of the nation and not in benefit of individual members or their Parties.

» Amending a Day in Congress

We the people have a problem where a handful of individuals—and often just two—have a monopoly control over the country that was never granted to them and power over other legislators that are supposed to be their equals. It does not matter if a Representative is 25 years old and just elected or has been serving for 50 years, they are 100% equal in the eyes of the Constitution. As such, we need to add some Amendments in order to rip back what never should have taken root in the first place and make sure Congress can function nominally:

> **The Speaker of the House of Representatives and the President or President Pro Tempore of the Senate shall be responsible for scheduling all debate and voting of their respective chambers.**

While the positions of Speaker of the House and President/President Pro Tempore of the Senate are laid out in the Constitution, there is nothing that states what those responsibilities include. This Clause is focused on giving them a very specific responsibility: setting the agenda and calendar for debate and voting. Notice as well, that it is the President of the Senate (the Vice President of the United States) or the President Pro

Tempore that are setting the agenda in the upper chamber and not the "Majority Leader". Being that the Majority Leader is not a recognized position, we should work within the framework of the Constitution to grant responsibility to an existing position.

> **ANY LEGISLATION PROPOSED BY INDIVIDUAL MEMBERS OF EACH CHAMBER SHOULD BE CONSIDERED FOR SCHEDULE AND VOTING BY THE LEADERS OF THE RESPECTIVE CHAMBERS. THE LEADER OF THE CHAMBER MAY REFUSE TO ADD THE LEGISLATION TO THE SCHEDULE, HOWEVER IF THE LEGISLATION IS SPONSORED BY TEN PERCENT OR MORE OF THE CHAMBER IT MUST BE ADDED TO THE SCHEDULE WITHIN THIRTY DAYS OF PRESENTING THE REQUIRED SPONSORSHIP TO THE LEADER OF THE CHAMBER.**

Looking along the Reflecting Pool in the National Mall in Washington, D.C. on December 31, 2019. Photo by J.P. Prag.

Basically, this is a codification of how an item is going to come up for vote. The leader of each chamber should act as a gatekeeper because someone needs to be operations manager. But at the end of the day, they are subordinate to the will of all other legislators. The first part of this Clause makes it so anyone can present an item to the leader and the leader can just add it to the agenda with no questions asked. However, given there is a possibility for extreme fringe views to make it into a chamber, the leaders would have a filter mechanism to control what could ultimately just be a waste of time. This, in turn, could be overwritten with a small minority, making sure that power is kept in check.

THE VICE PRESIDENT OF THE UNITED STATES—AS PRESIDENT OF THE SENATE—MAY PROPOSE LEGISLATION THAT MUST BE ADDED TO THE SCHEDULE AND VOTED ON WITHIN THIRTY DAYS.

While it is an odd bit of the Constitution that the Vice President of the United States is the President of the Senate, there is a reason for this. Recall that with our three-part government that we always want to make sure one branch will not have complete power over the others and that each is constantly kept in check by the other two. This power of the Vice President is a check by the Executive Branch on the Legislative Branch by making sure the legislature takes into consideration the concerns of the Executives. Much like minority representation in the prior Clause, this one gives executive representation in the law-making process.

Something similar will have to be done with the Judicial Branch, but we will discuss that in the next chapter. For the moment, the focus must be on what happens to legislation within Congress, no matter its genesis.

> **ANY LEGISLATION THAT SHALL PASS THROUGH EITHER CHAMBER OF CONGRESS MUST BE SCHEDULED AND VOTED ON BY THE OTHER CHAMBER WITHIN TEN DAYS.**

Now we move into the process whereby neither the leaders nor the majority Party of an individual chamber of Congress could stop legislation from moving through the next step. While earlier we established the responsibility of setting the schedules, here we taper that power further by making it clear that there is a responsibility to call a vote on something that has passed. In this way, this clause will remove the un-Constitutional power that the Speaker of the House and the Majority Leader of the Senate have bestowed upon themselves and level the playing field between each chamber. No matter what, then, a piece of legislation must be heard in the other chamber and voted upon.

> **ALL LEGISLATION MUST CONSIST OF SINGLE CLAUSES DIRECTLY RELATED TO THE SAME SUBJECT AT HAND. EACH CLAUSE AND AMENDMENT MUST BE PASSED SEPARATELY IN ITS OWN APPROVAL PROCESS.**

Just as this subchapter has been written in individual clauses, so, too, must Congress write their bills. Then, it is not voting on a bill in totality if there is just one part that is objectionable. Instead, each component would be open for debate, voting, and sending to the President for signature or veto. As written, this would also give the President line-item veto power since each clause would be presented individually and therefore would require specific sign-off on each one.

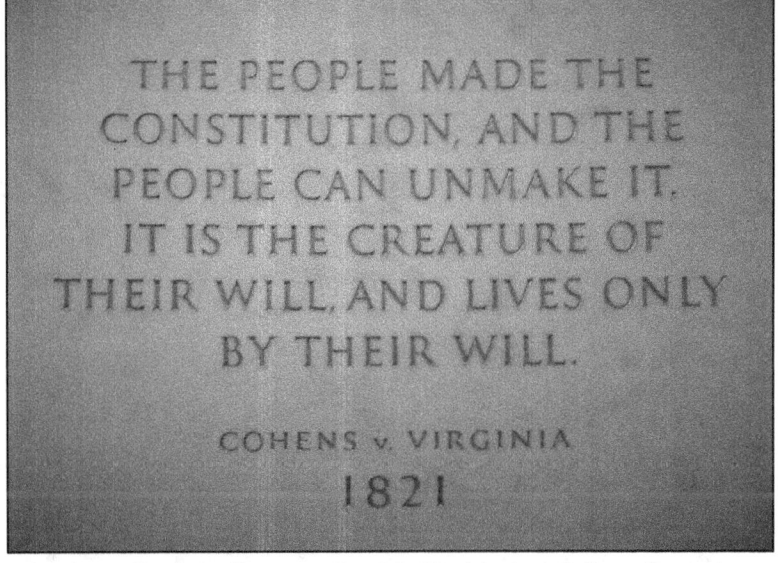

On the walls of the Supreme Court in Washington, D.C. on December 31, 2019. Photo by J.P. Prag.

At the same time, if there are differences between the House and the Senate, the differences will come through Amendments that would move through their own process so as not to stop the individual clauses if there are no threshold objections. More important than all of that, though, is the end of pork packages. It is a common practice for Congress to attach some unrelated spending to a bill as a matter of compromise in order to get a particular person's or group's vote. More often than not these add-ons have nothing to do with the legislation at hand and everything to do with securing funding for the Representative's or Senator's home area and scoring brownie points with the voters.

ALL REPRESENTATIVES AND SENATORS, SAVE FOR VACANCIES OR PHYSICAL INABILITY, ARE REQUIRED TO CAST A VOTE ON ALL LEGISLATION PRESENTED BEFORE THAT CHAMBER OF CONGRESS.

President Barack Obama signed the Patient Protection and Affordable Care Act (which passed without a single Republican vote in Congress) at the White House on March 23, 2010. Photo and base-description by **PETE SOUZA**[177], *Public domain, via Wikimedia Commons.*

---

[177] HTTPS://COMMONS.WIKIMEDIA.ORG/WIKI/FILE:OBAMA_SIGNS_HEALTH_CARE-20100323.JPG

This may seem an odd item, but theoretically a Representative or Senator could just walk out of the room (or never show up to the room in the first place) and not vote on an item. Abstaining (voting "present") is a tool commonly used to avoid the appearance of taking a stand or getting on the record of exactly where a person or organization aligns. Our elected officials must be held accountable, and the only way to do that is to have them on the record. This is how the voters get to check on those representing them because there is a definitive record of not just where they stand on a bill in total, but on each clause and adjustment of that act. The official record can be used for or against an individual that is supposed to be the will of their electorate.

ALL LEGISLATION MUST HAVE AT MINIMUM SIXTY-ONE PERCENT OF THE VOTE OF ALL LEGISLATORS IN THE CHAMBER IN ORDER TO PASS TO THE NEXT PHASE OF THE BILL'S PROCESS.

Here is the biggest rub of all. Today, certain legislation can pass from one chamber to the next and up to the President with a simple majority. As the last twenty years have shown, this means the bulk of legislation was passed on Party lines. When one Party had control of all chambers of Congress and the Presidency, they were able to get their special interest items through. This includes recent massive items like the Affordable Care Act of 2010 and Tax Cuts and Jobs Act of 2017.

Poignantly, Congress used to believe they should reach a higher level of acceptance. This was especially true in appointments to the Supreme Court where Senate Rules required a "super majority" of 60 votes (also known as the "filibuster"). As discussed in the introduction, though, with stonewalling and no discussions between Parties, this requirement was removed in favor of a simple majority. Other concerns may yet remove this legislative hurdle with the shoe on the other foot.

We need to take that choice out of their hands and make sure legislation that has passed already has at least a "super majority" so that it is not just a constant batter-up position. Engraving in the Constitution a 61% requirement for any bill to pass will be closer to getting real legislation into law and limit individual party power. Couple this with the **PREVIOUS DISCUSSIONS ON LIMITING PARTY POWER** and the total impacts will be future-proofed.

CONGRESS SHALL MAKE NO RULES OR EXCEPTIONS TO CIRCUMVENT THE PROCESS OF SCHEDULING AND CONDUCTING A VOTE.

This one sentence expresses the thought: do not try to create loopholes! The bureaucracy in Congress is self-inflicted, but that does not mean that all of it is without value. These rules were created to bring order to what can be a chaotic process within a large body of people. The problem has been that over time these rules have mutated from helpful elements to weapons of war that prevent Congress from functioning in order to push (or suppress) a specific agenda. Here we have a Clause that is ambiguous as well as wide, making all of those rules reviewable under a single criterion: does it stop legislation from flowing naturally? If a rule does not, then there is no worry. If it does, then there must be consequences.

> **FAILURE TO FOLLOW THE GUIDELINES OF THE CONSTITUTION AND ANY FUTURE AMENDMENTS FOR THE CONDUCT OF CONGRESS SHALL BE CONSIDERED TREASON OF THE UNITED STATES OF AMERICA. THE VICE PRESIDENT OF THE UNITED STATES IS RESPONSIBLE FOR ENFORCEMENT OF THIS CLAUSE AND BRINGING FORTH CHARGES OF TREASON AGAINST INDIVIDUAL MEMBERS OF CONGRESS.**

The point of this last Clause is to remove the shield of invincibility that members of the government have. If they do not follow the rules or abuse their positions, what is the consequence? Most of the time it is nothing at all, and at worst it is loss of their job when the voters get a chance. There needs to be a real and tangible consequence for trying to abuse the trusted position of a Representative or Senator.

Therefore, the recommendation is to make it treason to try to stop legislation using rules and procedures and underhanded tactics. There are succinct responsibilities and functions that the leaders of each chamber and the members within have, and if they refuse to do their duty then they need to be punished. For the sake of democracy, the unabashed impudence must end.

DEMAND MORE THAN JUSTICE

Demand a Constitutional overhaul of the entire Judicial Branch

Outside the Supreme Court of the United States of America on December 28, 2019. Photo by J.P. Prag.

» Key Points

- *Just trying to pack the Supreme Court and force potentially un-Constitutional rules like term limits around justices is not enough to fix the systematic issues within the Judicial Branch.*

- *Only a set of Constitutional Amendments that fundamentally redefine the courts, realign their relationship with the other branches of government, and create a deference to the people they serve can bring about any real and lasting change.*

- *Modifications cannot be limited to the highest institution in the land; they must be deployed and enforced at all levels.*

On Thursday October 14, 2021, a commission established by President Joe Biden via an Executive Order unveiled their draft findings. While the final paper was not expected to be released until November 14, 2021—and subsequently was **DELAYED UNTIL AT LEAST DECEMBER 15, 2021**[178]—every side had already expressed their grave disappointment.

The commission was created to evaluate potential changes to the Supreme Court, though not to make any recommendations. Republicans and other conservative-leaning groups scoffed at the very existence of the panel as a scheme to usurp the power of the Courts—a power they have spent the past two decades massaging to meet their tastes using every legislative tool at their disposal. But they should not have feared because the scholarly assembly found that:

- Increasing the size and membership of the Supreme Court would be unwarranted and would create a dangerous precedent;

- Term limits for Supreme Court Justices might be useful, but have no Constitutional basis and therefore could not be implemented;

- The court controls its own process and therefore can release rulings and opinions any way they see fit, including through the so-called middle of the night "shadow docket"; and

---

[178] HTTPS://THEHILL.COM/HOMENEWS/ADMINISTRATION/579814-BIDENS-SCOTUS-COMMISSION-PUSHES-BACK-RELEASE-OF-FINAL-REPORT

- Congress could change the nomination process for judges, but the Legislative Branch is too polarized to make that happen.

Democrats and other liberal-minded groups derided these findings and the process that produced them. With almost all of their dreams dashed, Brian Fallon—Executive Director of **DEMAND JUSTICE**[179], an organization dedicated to changing the makeup of the Supreme Court—**TOLD THE HILL**[180]:

> **THE PARALYSIS-BY-ANALYSIS REFLECTED HERE IS EXACTLY WHAT YOU WOULD EXPECT FROM A COMMISSION MADE UP MOSTLY OF ACADEMICS, INCLUDING SEVERAL DIEHARD CONSERVATIVES WHO ARE FULLY CONTENT WITH THE STATUS QUO.**

Further, Chief Counsel for **Demand Justice** Chris Kang **TOLD CBSNEWS**[181]:

> **YOU WOULDN'T HAVE A CLIMATE CHANGE COMMISSION WITH CLIMATE SKEPTICS. HERE WE HAVE A SUPREME COURT COMMISSION WITH PEOPLE WHO DON'T THINK THE SUPREME COURT IS BROKEN.**

---

[179] HTTPS://DEMANDJUSTICE.ORG/PRIORITIES/SUPREME-COURT-REFORM/
[180] HTTPS://THEHILL.COM/REGULATION/COURT-BATTLES/576867-BIDENS-SUPREME-COURT-REFORM-STUDY-PANEL-NOTES-CONSIDERABLE-RISKS-TO?RL=1
[181] HTTPS://WWW.CBSNEWS.COM/NEWS/SUPREME-COURT-COMMISSION-REPORT-COURT-PACKING-TERM-LIMITS/

Unfortunately for **Demand Justice** and their supporters, this commission has a much more solid argument than they do. Though their heart, morality, and sense of fairness may be in the right place, the cold reality of our current law is against them. The reason for that is **Demand Justice** is simply focusing on the symptoms of a much greater problem and trying to resolve those instead of asking more probing questions—such as:

- Where do the rules of the courts even come from?
- Why is there a prosecution and defense?
- Why are juries a certain size?
- Why does court happen at certain times and places?
- What does a "speedy and public trial" even mean?
- Why is the appeals process the way it is?
- Why does it take years to work through the system?
- And so on and so forth...

The bottom line is that the Constitution is very light on details on how the Supreme Court and all "inferior" courts (as the Constitution likes to call all those layers below the Supreme Court) are supposed to function. While Congress has the right to create those "inferior" levels, that is where their sovereignty and responsibility ends. Nothing in the Constitution has told the Judicial Branch how to act and what it can and cannot do. As such they have made up all of their own answers to the above and much more, which in turn has put us in the quagmire we are in. Even the ability of "judicial review" to determine if a law is Constitutional or in violation of another law is an authority the Judicial Branch has granted itself and has no basis in the Constitution.

Just outside the Supreme Court of the United States on January 2, 2020. Photo by J.P. Prag.

Therefore we can surmise that the silence of the Constitution is the real deterrent to progressive change within the Supreme Court and all echelons below it. If we want a better court system, the only way we can improve it is with a set of Amendments to the Constitution of the United States.

♫ You don't wanna change the world like you say

The problem we are really trying to resolve is the politicization of the courts. Attempting to just add members that lean towards a certain set of beliefs actually has the opposite impact because—as the commission noted—*"Court expansion is likely to undermine, rather than enhance, the Supreme Court's legitimacy...."* As such, we have to take a different approach in order to minimize the impact of politics. Please note that this is not "eliminate" because that is impossible; but mitigation is well within our means. We can start that by first adding an Amendment to the Constitution that defines how the various layers of the Judicial Branch look:

> **The Trial of all Crimes and civil pursuits, except in Cases of Impeachment, shall be presided over by a Panel of Judges. The Panel shall consist of an odd number of Judges. The lowest inferior courts shall consist of three Judges, the appeals courts shall consist of five Judges, and the Supreme Court shall consist of seven Judges.**

Inside one of the stairwells of the Supreme Court of the United States on January 2, 2020. Photo by J.P. Prag.

Here, we have simplified and solidified what should be expected of any level and eliminated much of that political interference. Instead, we break it down into a few easy levels with an odd number of judges in each. In the lowest level—where it is important to note that some courts are specialized in specific topics—the courts would expand from a typical single judge to instead have three. In the middle appeals layer, everything would be standardized with five judges. While this does not particularly address how appeals work today, it does force going to a full appeals court instead of an intermediate level before the full panel that currently exist, thus speeding up the process. Finally, the Supreme Court would cap out at the seven-judge panel.

These maximums, though, are only the beginning of several necessary limitations to make the courts closer to impartial while also keeping the working groups to a reasonable enough size. How then, though, if we have these limiting sizes of the courts do we then enforce what we are looking for? After all, within the Federal system the President nominates judges and the Senate confirms them, so they could still pack these positions any way they desired. For that, we will need several more Amendments:

ALL JUDGES SHALL BE IN A COMMON POOL BY AREA OF THE COURT OR BY TYPE OF COURT AS DETERMINED BY CONGRESS.

First and foremost is the new concept of a "Pool" of judges. Instead of assigning judges directly to a seat, they would instead be part of a "Pool" that is part of an "area". For instance, there is a court that focuses solely on bankruptcy, another on patents, and others that are just general concerns but are separated by geography. These would be the various "Pools" created for each type of inferior, appeals, and Supreme Court—the latter being only one, but worth noting as its own "Pool". Still, it cannot end there:

> EACH PANEL OF JUDGES SHALL BE FILLED FROM THESE POOLS; SHALL SHARE CASES EXCEPT WHEN A SUBSTITUTE IS NEEDED DUE TO A CONFLICT OF INTEREST, MOVEMENT TO A DIFFERENT POOL, PERSONAL LEAVE, DEATH, RETIREMENT, OR ANY OTHER REASON DETERMINED BY CONGRESS;
>
> THE POOL MUST CONSIST OF MORE JUDGES THAN NECESSARY TO FILL PANELS IN ORDER TO HAVE JUDGES IN RESERVE IN CASE A SUBSTITUTION IS NECESSARY.

Think of it this way: perhaps there are 15 "inferior" courts that would require 3 judges each. In total, that means we would need 45 judges. We should then have a "Pool" of, say, 50 judges available so that we can assign the 45 judges we need and keep 5 in arrears for when a substitute is needed. That may happen because there could be some type of conflict of interest or the judge had to leave for whatever reason (i.e., illness, vacation, death, or anything else that may come up). Reasons beyond what is listed in the Amendment would be determined by Congress as the check, but the idea is that an alternate should be able to be pulled in when necessary so that there is always a full "Panel". Currently in the appeals and Supreme courts, when a judge recuses themselves there is no one to replace them, and this can end up with an even number and a tie vote.

The ceiling in the reception hall of the Supreme Court of the United States on January 2, 2020. Photo by J.P. Prag.

Now where this gets particularly interesting is how judges would be assigned to a "Panel":

> **ASSIGNMENT FROM THE POOL TO A PANEL SHALL BE AT RANDOM IN A METHOD DETERMINED BY THE PRESIDENT.**

Here is the beginning of the end of gamesmanship. Though the President would control the methodology, that is just a check on the system to make sure the Judicial Branch is not controlling it themselves. If people felt the procedure was not truly random, they would have a basis to sue via a violation of the Constitution.

With randomness, nevertheless, we will not know which judges are going to end up on a "Panel". If we take the Supreme Court as of January 2022 and assume our "Pool" would continue to be just the same 9 Justices, then we could end up with any combination from "4 Conservatives and 3 Liberals" to "6 Conservatives and 1 Liberal". On the other hand, if President Biden and the Senate added 4 more like-minded people to the "Pool", then the "Panel" could end up being any combination starting at 7 Liberals down to just 1 with all other positions filled by Conservatives. Even if each President/Senate combination kept adding in additional members, the randomness would not guarantee a preferred outcome.

Yet allowing each successive administration to keep adding judges to the "Pool" would create an untenable situation. There needs to be limits on service in order to continually sweep away the more politically charged appointments. This, of course, would come through further Amendments:

EACH PANEL OF JUDGES SHALL SERVE FOR A TERM OF FIVE YEARS.

AT THE END OF A FIVE-YEAR TERM, JUDGES ARE TO RETURN TO THE POOL FOR RE-ASSIGNMENT OR MOVED TO ANOTHER POOL AND MAY NOT AGAIN SERVE IN THE SAME PHYSICAL OR SPECIALIZED AREA.

The ceiling inside the chamber of the Supreme Court of the United States on January 2, 2020. Photo by J.P. Prag.

With this component, a judge would serve a 5-year term with the rest of their "Panel". At the end of those 5 years, everyone on a "Panel" would return to the "Pool" for random re-assignment. Further, that same judge could not again serve in the same physical or specialized area. In the case of our Supreme Court Justices, that would mean that they would be done with the highest court in the land after a single 5-year cycle, unless they had only been sitting in waiting as a substitute.

And this extends much deeper than just the Supreme Court. For instance, if a judge served in bankruptcy court, they could no longer be on that same court and have to move on to somewhere else. If it is desired to make a judge an appeals or Supreme Court justice, once approved by Congress they might be moved into those "Pools". But if they are staying in their assigned "Pool" and the "Pool" is more general or part of appeals, they must then move to a different physical area.

Between the randomness of assignments and being forced to move on to a different physical district, no court area could have a certain style to it that lawyers could use to game the process. Today, lawyers file their cases in specific districts that they feel are more open to their arguments. This would reduce that by having a complete re-shuffling every 5 years. Yet this is not nearly enough; there needs to be one final limit on a judge's tenure:

> **A JUDGE MAY ONLY ACT AS A PERMANENT MEMBER OF FOUR PANELS OVER THE COURSE OF THE JUDGE'S SERVICE.**

Since each "Panel" times out at 5 years, this Amendment means a maximum of 20 years serving in the courtroom. With the randomness from before, a judge could end up in 4 panels in a row or no panels ever or any combination in between. It is not something the judge should have control over, nor any other member of the government. Here we have created the final sweep out of any sitting judge, very similar to the term limits some have suggested.

♪ You've played by their rules, now it's their turn to try

However, this is just the beginning of the process. In order to further reduce politicization of the Judicial Branch, we must put their self-appointed power in check. As the courts are now, they act almost as the single endpoint to all questions—far from the checks and balances of having two other co-equal Branches. While there are already Constitutional methods for the other Branches to hold the Judicial Branch in line, they must be expanded to make sure the Courts do not step over it:

> **Congress shall have the ability to create law that governs the proceedings of the Supreme Court and all inferior federal courts. This includes, but is not limited to, designating where trials may take place, how long a person may be detained before trial, how much time may be spent on arguments, and how long trials may proceed.**

Before, we asked the question of what a "speedy and public trial" even is. Currently, the Judicial Branch has decided it for themselves, and that answer is a process that is excruciatingly slow and debated behind closed doors. Certain legislatures pass laws that cause immediate harm, yet the courts refuse to act until the damage is done—sometimes permanently—and oftentimes release those decisions in the middle of the night (the aforementioned "shadow docket").

A long, spiral staircase inside the Supreme Court of the United States on January 2, 2020. Photo by J.P. Prag.

This Amendment would explicitly give Congress the ability to make decisions on how the courts should function so that they cannot continue to go off on a rogue process. If Congress says each witness has 10 minutes to testify or that the prosecution and defense will be held to a clock like in chess, then that is their prerogative. In the same vein, if Congress says that once someone has been sued civilly or arrested criminally that the trial must begin within a week, then that is what should happen. Just as Congress is to work for the people, so, too, are the courts supposed to do the same. The Supreme Court is still inferior to the people of the United States, and the will of the people should be reflected in how they operate.

This Amendment is open and gives great leeway, but also allows significant change. If something is not working out, the system can be updated easily by Congress. With this Amendment, the courts would no longer be able to run (or slowly trot) amuck and expansive judicial reform could happen much more easily. But the Legislative Branch is not the only one that should have powers over the courts; so, too, should the Executive Branch:

> **THE PRESIDENT OF THE UNITED STATES MAY ORDER THE SUPREME COURT OR THE APPROPRIATE DESIGNATED INFERIOR FEDERAL COURT TO START A TRIAL WITHIN THE TIMEFRAME DECREED BY CONGRESS WHEN THE COURT IS IN SESSION, SO LONG AS THE SUPREME COURT HAS NOT ALREADY RULED ON THE ISSUE AT HAND.**

As an expansion from the previous Amendment, there are

times when the courts just sit on cases because they do not want to get to them in the current session. This can be massively frustrating for those who created the laws and those who enforce them because they have done their part while the last step in the process is refusing to do theirs. Delays like this can go on for years. Thus, should Congress choose, they could give the President the ability to make sure a case gets on the docket within, say, 30 days. That way, if the issue were pressing or involved a Constitutional question that must be resolved, the process could be pushed ahead within whatever other limitations Congress creates for the courts.

At the same time, there have to be limitations. If the Supreme Court has already ruled on a particular subject, the President cannot force their hands. For instance, the Supreme Court had previously ruled that abortion access was legal and Constitutionally protected within the entirety of the United States. Since that was the law of the land, *historically*[182] each time a State passed an anti-choice law the federal courts immediately put it on hold and the appellate courts would rule in favor of the plaintiffs fighting against these laws. The decision had already been made and the law was clear.

---

[182] "Historically" being the operative word because—as of the time of this writing—the "novel" Texas law that used a vigilante bounty system instead of State power had been allowed to remain intact while the arguments worked their way through the system. Because of this ruling, some States began to follow suit with similar laws while others like California planned to use the reasonings to apply it to gun-rights.

Further, while this book was preparing for publication, a draft opinion of the Supreme Court leaked showing that the majority of the bench was prepared to overturn Roe v. Wade and leave abortion access decisions up to each individual State.

Since both are ongoing concerns, we will have to leave them aside for the time being and focus on how to make a system that does not allow radical lifetime appointees to create and destroy rights on a whim.

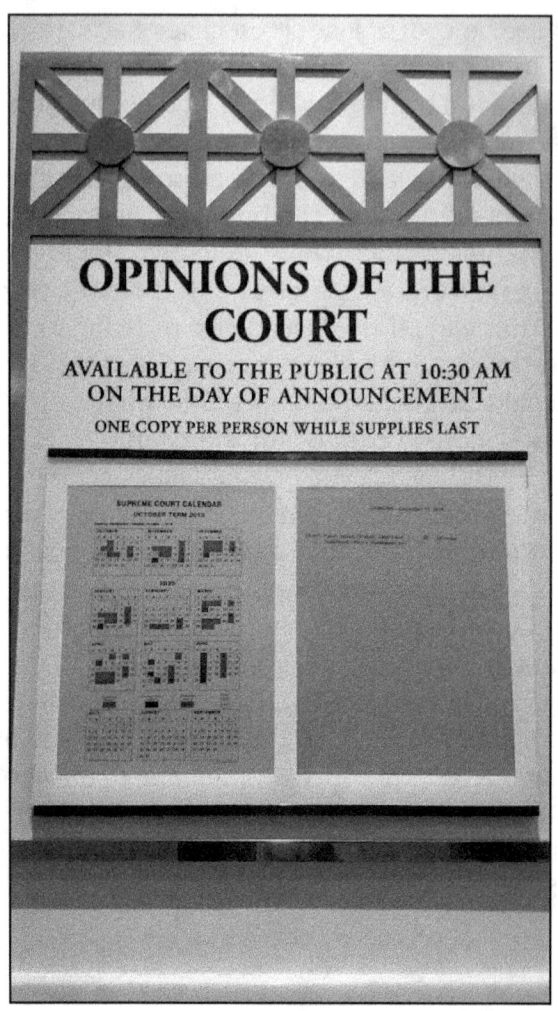

Announcement board inside the Supreme Court of the United States on January 2, 2020. Photo by J.P. Prag.

The hope of these groups is to make it to the Supreme Court and re-raise the discussion again. And let us be clear: there are times when getting back to the Supreme Court is necessary to overturn a poor decision. For instance, in 1883 the Supreme Court ruled against Tony Pace for the crime of being a black man romantically linked with a white woman in Alabama where the State created a law that said the two could not be married. The successful argument was that since the law applied equally to black and white people that it was not discriminatory. It took until the 1967 case in *Loving vs. Virginia* for the Supreme Court to overturn their own handiwork and say that State-sponsored racism cannot be argued as an interest of the government, no matter the "fairness" of the application of the law.

Still, there may be abuse within the Judicial Branch itself, and there needs to be an enforcement mechanism when the courts are in bold defiance. Luckily, we already have an apparatus to do that which just needs a bit of expanding:

> **JUDGES ON THE SUPREME COURT AND INFERIOR FEDERAL COURTS SHALL BE REMOVED FROM OFFICE ON IMPEACHMENT FOR, AND CONVICTION OF, TREASON, BRIBERY, ABUSING THE POWERS GRANTED BY THE CONSTITUTION AND LAW, FAILURE TO FOLLOW THE PROCEDURAL LAW AS SET BY CONGRESS, FAILURE TO START A TRIAL WHEN ORDERED BY THE PRESIDENT, OR OTHER HIGH CRIMES AND MISDEMEANORS.**

The wording here is almost exactly the same as what is written for the Executive Branch in the existing Constitution, with the additions of abusing power, failure to run as Congress has set by law, or failure to start a case under the direction of the President. The Constitution already covers that impeachment can only be started in the House of Representatives and tried in the Senate, and the only punishment is removal from office if voted guilty.

This gives the Legislative Branch the ability to fully enforce all these new powers granted by these Amendments, but still maintain a high threshold in order to do so.

♫ You Gotta Keep 'em Separated

Just because we desire for limitations on the powers of the Judicial Branch to be put in place, it does not mean they do not need an expansion of strength in other areas. The important part is keeping walls between each Branch of government and making sure none holds complete sway over the others. For that, we'll need some additional Amendments, starting with one last removal of a self-granted ability:

> **When standing in judgement of a law or lack thereof, neither the Supreme Court nor any inferior court may create law, modify the meaning of existing law, or remove existing law.**
>
> **The Supreme Court or the designated inferior court must send the law or need for a law back to the appropriate legislature—whether that be Congress or the legislatures of a State or Territory—to create, modify, or remove the law entirely.**

Here, we talk about "standing in judgement", which in this case means when a trial comes along that challenges a law (or lack thereof), we lay out that the courts cannot create their own law to fix or fill in the gaps. Instead, the courts would always have to send orders back to the legislature from whence the law originated and the law must be fixed there. Of note, this also forces legislatures to write law to remove items officially instead of having them just being stricken by the courts. It is a line in the sand that only legislatures can create, modify, or annihilate law.

While a barrier is needed that stops the Judicial Branch from creating law because that is not their job, the courts—as discussed in the **PRIOR CHAPTER**—should have the ability to compel the legislature to create law based upon their discoveries. If the courts find that the law is lacking in a situation or the law as written has flaws, then the courts should have the ability to demand that the law-making body itself revisit and fix this. However, the Courts need a tool to force them to do anything.

> **ANY ORDER BY THE SUPREME COURT OR DELEGATED FEDERAL COURT TO CREATE NEW LAW OR MODIFY EXISTING BILLS AND LAW MUST BE DONE WITHIN THE TIMEFRAME DESIGNATED BY THE COURT.**

The reason these controls need to be specifically laid out in the Constitution is because some would argue being forced to vote for something one does not believe in as induced "speech". Since the 1st Amendment grants the freedom of speech to everyone, a separate part of the Constitution with equal weight would be needed to override that precise idea. With this Amendment, being a member of government restricts rights enjoyed by the masses. Therefore, here, the legislatures must vote and come to a solution or face the potential wrath of the courts. But what would happen if the legislatures just ignored the courts? For that, the Judicial Branch needs some teeth:

SHOULD THE SUPREME COURT OR A DESIGNATED INFERIOR COURT SEND TO CONGRESS OR THE LEGISLATURE OF A STATE OR TERRITORY A DEMAND FOR THE CREATION, MODIFICATIONS, OR REMOVAL OF LAW WITHIN A SPECIFIC TIMEFRAME AND CRITERIA, AND THE LEGISLATURE DOES NOT ACT IN ACCORDANCE WITH THE ORDERS OF THE SUPREME COURT OR DESIGNATED INFERIOR COURT, THE SUPREME COURT OR DESIGNATED INFERIOR COURT MAY HOLD ANY OR ALL MEMBERS OF THE LEGISLATURE IN CONTEMPT AND IMPLEMENT ANY PROCEDURES AND PENALTIES AS DEFINED BY LAW.

Here begins progress! Congress and State/Territory legislatures act with impudence because there are no personal consequences. It is nice that someone wants to serve our government, but that does not give them carte blanche to just do anything they desire. Today, though, that is exactly what happens as it does not matter what legislators do or do not do since the biggest consequence they may face is not getting re-elected.

With this Amendment, the Judicial Branch would have some real power over the Legislative one in that they could fine, imprison, or order both on the members of Congress or the legislators of the States/Territories for refusing their direction. It is still at the discretion of the courts to decide if and how much they want to implement this, and it means that members of Congress and the State/Territory legislatures face the exact same rules as regular people—which is precisely what they are. Congress defined "contempt", including how it can be implemented and what the penalties are. Why, then, cannot the same rules apply to them?

And these controls and power of the Judicial Branch should not end here. Congress and—especially—State/Territory Legislatures have been known to take actions that waste the time and resources of the Courts. If they do so, they should face similar penalties:

> **SHOULD CONGRESS OR THE LEGISLATURE OF A STATE OR TERRITORY KNOWINGLY AND WILLFULLY PASS A LAW THAT IS IN VIOLATION OF THE CONSTITUTION, EXISTING FEDERAL LAW, EXISTING STATE OR TERRITORY LAW, OR PRIOR JUDICIAL INTERPRETATION OF THE LAW—WITH THE EXPRESS INTENT OF USING THE JUDICIAL SYSTEM TO CHALLENGE EXISTING LAW AND JUDICIAL INTERPRETATION—THE SUPREME COURT OR DESIGNATED INFERIOR COURT MAY HOLD ANY OR ALL MEMBERS OF THE LEGISLATURE IN CONTEMPT AND IMPLEMENT ANY PROCEDURES AND PENALTIES AS DEFINED BY LAW.**

Whatever your personal politics, when a State passes a law that is knowingly un-Constitutional, they only pay a monetary price by having to cover the court costs and some of their opponents' costs—all of which are covered by the taxpayers, not the legislators themselves. Yet, time and time again, these legislatures feel it is their duty to pass laws they openly discuss as being created just to bring a challenge to the Supreme Court and overturn some other prior decision.

Sometimes, a State/Territory or Congress is just picking a fight to reinterpret a base definition while the Supreme Court has made it clear: if you want a change, you need to go through a Constitutional Amendment process. These laws are a waste of taxpayer dollars and time. When Mississippi passed a more restrictive version of a law that had been overturned the year before, U.S. District Judge Carlton Reeves exclaimed in disgust:

"HERE WE GO AGAIN..."

"MISSISSIPPI HAS PASSED ANOTHER [SIMILAR] LAW... THE PARTIES HAVE BEEN HERE BEFORE."

"LAST SPRING, PLAINTIFFS SUCCESSFULLY CHALLENGED MISSISSIPPI'S BAN... THE COURT RULED THAT THE LAW WAS [UN-CONSTITUTIONAL] AND PERMANENTLY ENJOINED ITS ENFORCEMENT. THE STATE RESPONDED BY PASSING AN EVEN MORE RESTRICTIVE BILL."

"IT SURE SMACKS OF DEFIANCE TO THIS COURT..."

But what could Judge Reeves do about it? The only thing that was possible was enjoining the defendant again and put the whole law into the same drawn-out process. With this Constitutional Amendment, the Courts could hold legislators in contempt for such an action. Of course, they are not alone in these exacerbations. As such, we need to extend the same controls to the Executive Branch:

> SHOULD THE PRESIDENT OF THE UNITED STATES OR THE GOVERNOR OF A STATE OR TERRITORY KNOWINGLY AND WILLFULLY SIGN A LAW PASSED BY THEIR LEGISLATURE OR GIVE AN EXECUTIVE ORDER THAT IS IN VIOLATION OF THE CONSTITUTION, EXISTING FEDERAL LAW, EXISTING STATE OR TERRITORY LAW, OR PRIOR JUDICIAL INTERPRETATION OF THE LAW—WITH THE EXPRESS INTENT OF USING THE JUDICIAL SYSTEM TO CHALLENGE EXISTING LAW AND JUDICIAL INTERPRETATION—THE SUPREME COURT OR DESIGNATED INFERIOR COURT MAY HOLD THE PRESIDENT OR GOVERNOR IN CONTEMPT AND IMPLEMENT ANY PROCEDURES AND PENALTIES AS DEFINED BY LAW.

As can be seen here, the language is almost the same so that the President and State/Territory Governors cannot simply sign-off or give an order and say they are not accountable. They will follow the same potential penalties for knowingly wasting the time of the courts and the money of the taxpayers.

♫ How can one little street swallow so many lives?

All these changes amount to a redefinition of the courts and its power— but only at the Federal level. Most cases still at least start or take place at the local and

State/Territory levels; and at those stages the rules may be quite different. As such, we must extend all these transformations down to those planes in order to have an impact across all people and systems:

> **THE STATES, TERRITORIES, AND LOCAL GOVERNMENTS SHALL HAVE COURT SYSTEMS SET UP IN THE SAME MODEL AS THE FEDERAL COURT SYSTEM AS LAID OUT IN THE CONSTITUTION AND ITS AMENDMENTS. ANY AMENDMENT TO THE JUDICIAL BRANCH AT THE FEDERAL LEVEL SHOULD BE REFLECTED AT THE STATE, TERRITORY, AND LOCAL LEVEL.**

What this means is that all the modifications above and any further evolutions through future Amendments must also happen at the State, Territory, and local level. What it does not do is dictate how these non-Federal governments must set up their Judicial Branches; it just makes it clear that they should mimic the Federal system as laid out in the Constitution. It can then become a point of challenge if a State, for instance, is not following any of these rules and can be sued in Federal court to make that happen. It is a guidance, but these lower governments could come up with their own language and address their own unique concerns.

With the Federal and Local courts in line, we would have real and permanent change in the judicial system, but still have the flexibility to fix it as time and issues presented themselves.

A bust of the first Chief Justice of the Supreme Court John Jay overlooks those awaiting to be heard in the Supreme Court Building in Washington, D.C. on January 2, 2020. Photo by J.P. Prag.

PART 5: PEOPLE AND THE CENSUS

ONE MORE SEAT AT THE TABLE

How I saved Rhode Island's second Congressional spot in the House of Representatives

Photo by **FERNANDO @CFERDO**[183] on **UNSPLASH**

---

[183] HTTPS://UNSPLASH.COM/@CFERDO

» **KEY POINTS**

- *For years, there had been dire warnings that my State of Rhode Island was going to lose one of its two seats in the House of Representatives when the 2020 Census was completed.*

- *Yet, when the results from the 2020 Census were released, Rhode Island was not in so much danger of losing that seat.*

- *How did this come about? Are there ways that Rhode Island could have lost that seat, both in this universe and others? Did my own actions make a significant impact to save it?*

Late in the afternoon on Monday April 26, 2021, the press release I had been dreading for nearly five years was made public. However, as I read it through, I realized something miraculous had happened; something I had worked feverishly (literally) to prevent from ever coming to fruition. With great joy I jumped up, ran down the hall to my partner's office, and declared with all of the bravado I could muster:

I DID IT! I SAVED RHODE ISLAND'S SECOND SEAT IN THE HOUSE OF REPRESENTATIVES!!! IT WAS ALL WORTH IT!!!!

As my partner came out from behind her desk to give me a congratulatory hug and kiss, a feeling of dread came over me. Was it real? How close to disaster were we? Are we safe from the inevitable lawsuits to come? I had to know...

» BEFORE THE EGGS HATCHED

The press release was from the United States Census Bureau, which revealed the results of the 2020 Census almost five months after the date decreed by law. Although Congress refused to act to change this statute, the delay was inevitable given the challenges during this Census cycle. By the Constitution, every 10 years (*Article 1, Section 2, Clause 3*) the United States must count "the whole number of persons in each State" (*Amendment 14, Section 2*) to be used for many purposes, but mostly for "apportionment", or the act of determining how the 435 members of the House of Representatives are distributed among the States.

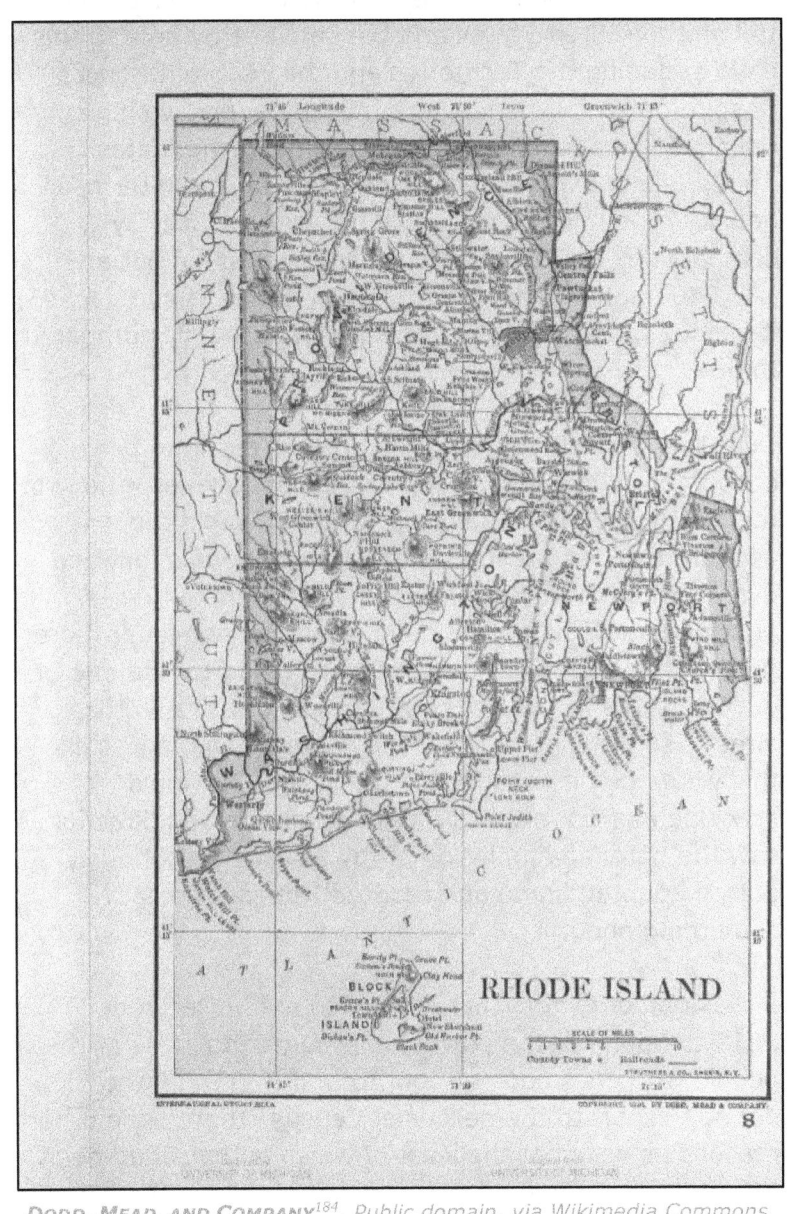

DODD, MEAD, AND COMPANY[184], Public domain, via Wikimedia Commons

---

[184] HTTPS://COMMONS.WIKIMEDIA.ORG/WIKI/FILE:MAP_OF_RHODE_ISLAND.JPG

I live in Rhode Island, the last of the original 13 colonies to join the United States and the smallest by area to this day (excluding the Territories and the Federal District). Despite our small size, over a million people live here. Using 2018 population estimates, among the States Rhode Island was second only to New Jersey in terms of density—the number of people per square mile. By comparison, Montana had a similar population but at 147,040 square miles in contrast to Rhode Island's 1,545, it yielded a density of 7 people per square mile compared to 684.

Over the prior 10 years, we had great reason to be concerned. While other parts of the country—especially in the South and West—were growing at a rapid clip, we appeared to be treading water with our population, and even shrinking on occasion. The signs were very clear: if our population did not rebound or we did not count more people than expected, then we were going to lose one of our two seats in the House of Representatives. With already so little influence at the Federal level, a loss like this would be devastating for the State and would preclude us from a vast array of programs and direction. I saw the potential implosion of my already precariously poised adopted home and realized I needed to do something about it.

It was one of factors that motivated me in December 2019 to apply for the position of Enumerator, one of the people who goes door-to-door to find everyone who did not self-report to the decennial Census. There were other reasons as well, not the least of which is that I had been working remotely and by myself for years and the idea of getting in some nice walks from April through June and interacting with others had a lot of appeal. Over the next several months I was interviewed, conditionally hired, finger-printed, and background checked, all in preparation for beginning training on April 1, 2020 for field operations expected to start late in that month.

And then... well... the COVID-19 pandemic started. Everything was pushed off and communication basically ceased. It was not until late July when someone finally followed up with me and we had a version of hybrid training scheduled. The process was a mess for everyone, the equipment and software difficult, the administration of President Trump unamiable (to say the least), and the timelines and expectations all over the place. It did not help having sweltering weather as I beat the pavement through the hottest Summer months. Thankfully, I did not have to deal with the natural disasters and wildfires of elsewhere. What I did not receive from the federal government, I found in a support group on **REDDIT**[185] of fellow Census peons like me. There were good days and horrible ones, and I still wonder how I pushed myself to hold on until the bitter end. I was finally let go in late October when the Supreme Court allowed the Census Bureau to wrap up operations.

That close-out was bittersweet. Yes, I was delighted to be done, but my own experience made me question the validity of the data. For instance, I would get the same address 4 or 5 different ways (*16 Place Way; 16 Place Way Unit 16; 16 Place Way Apt 16; 16 Place Way #16; etcetera*). At the same time, the Bureau would not support us in trying to just get head counts from multi-unit managers and I was often met with severe resistance. One time late into enumerating I was the first person sent to a housing complex that was majority Latinx and people of color. Although I was shocked to discover no one else had been assigned there yet, I was

---

[185] HTTPS://WWW.REDDIT.COM/R/CENSUS/

able to make great headway. Despite this, the system did not send me back there again for weeks, and I feared for these traditionally undercounted communities.

Photo by **MAX TITOV**[186] on **UNSPLASH**

And here were all my concerns laid bare. If we were so close to the bleeding edge of losing our seat in Congress and I was personally having difficulty getting some of the most undercounted people and areas in the State, was there any hope? These were but a handful of the issues I encountered and there could be a book unto itself on that subject. I'll spare you the details and recommend a read through that sub-Reddit for many tales by myself and others. Suffice to say, things were looking bleak. As the Trump administration continued to attempt to manipulate the data—even after unequivocally losing the Presidential election—I speculated if these results would have to be thrown out. With the Census Bureau continuing to be opaque about when results would be released and States

---

[186] HTTPS://UNSPLASH.COM/@FEARVI

beginning to sue to get them, I wondered if I was going to be back out on that sizzling sidewalk again.

Yet all that fear washed away when I read these words in **THE AFOREMENTIONED PRESS RELEASE**[187]:

> ...[S]EVEN STATES WILL LOSE ONE SEAT EACH (CALIFORNIA, ILLINOIS, MICHIGAN, NEW YORK, OHIO, PENNSYLVANIA, AND WEST VIRGINIA), AND THE REMAINING STATES' NUMBER OF SEATS WILL NOT CHANGE BASED ON THE 2020 CENSUS.

I read those words over and over again before I ran down the hall in jubilation. My eyes did not deceive me; Rhode Island was not on the list! I had succeeded!

» SURVIVAL OF THE SMALLEST

Of course, that is all hyperbole. I did not really do it single-handedly and I may not have had any material impact at all. Over the next day, I read quotes from local politicians patting themselves on the back for a job well done and congratulating themselves for all they did. All I can speak to is my experience where they did nothing for me on a day-to-day basis. On the contrary, I sometimes ran into resistance because their programs were not coordinated with the Census Bureau and resulted in mixed messaging and many people complaining of excessive visits (though to be fair, the latter was also caused by the Census Bureau's scheduling system itself).

---

[187] HTTPS://WWW.CENSUS.GOV/NEWSROOM/PRESS-RELEASES/2021/2020-CENSUS-APPORTIONMENT-RESULTS.HTML

Thus, after letting my partner get back to work, I took a deep dive on how the seats were assigned. Again, I'll spare you the math and computer programs to assign the order, but when looking at the **OFFICIAL RELEASES FROM THE CENSUS BUREAU**[188], it was seemingly not that close:

State	House Seat	State Seat	Priority Value
Texas	426	38	778,290
Illinois	427	17	777,493
Rhode Island	428	2	776,519
Alabama	429	7	776,154
North Carolina	430	14	774,898
Oregon	431	6	774,388
Colorado	432	8	772,675
California	433	52	768,517
Montana	434	2	767,499
Minnesota	435	8	762,998

At 8th-to-last, it does not look like Rhode Island was in any danger at all. However, that is only part of the story. Keeping all other States constant, I figured out to the person how close we actually were. The answer:

19,127

Only **19,127** people separated Rhode Island from losing its second seat in the House of Representatives. Using the 2020 Census figures, this represents just 1.7% of the State population and 0.006% of the entire population of the United States. In this situation, New York would actually regain the seat it lost in this Census. What is

[188] HTTPS://WWW.CENSUS.GOV/DATA/TABLES/2020/DEC/2020-APPORTIONMENT-DATA.HTML

interesting is that Rhode Island's final population figures were 3.6% over 2019's estimates. The prior three years had us growing at an average of 0.1% per year, so things seemed off.

Photo by **ENAYET RAHEEM**[189] on **UNSPLASH**

---

[189] HTTPS://UNSPLASH.COM/@RAHEEMSPHOTO

My first concern was that Secretary of Commerce Gina Raimondo (who oversees the Census Bureau) had pulled some shenanigans. After all, she was the governor of Rhode Island until just a month before these figures were released. But when reviewing the country as a whole (1% growth from 2019 estimates) and individual States, it became clear that there were a few patterns that made all the difference, and it was not the higher-than-expected population in Rhode Island.

When I took the 2019 estimated population and ran it through the apportionment program, it came out exactly the same except Rhode Island and Minnesota each had one less seat and Ohio and Arizona had one more. And therein lies the rub. My brother, his wife, and his wife's mother had all moved to Arizona over the years, along with a plethora of other people. We have been joking for years that they were going to steal our seat (and do nothing with it since they are rather apolitical compared to me). Arizona has been growing at an exceptional clip, but its numbers were the furthest off expectations of all States. As a matter of fact, the Bureau enumerated 1.7% less people than 2019 estimates, or over 127,000 people.

There are two possibilities here. First, the Bureau had been overestimating Arizona's growth rate over the prior 10 years (averaging about 1.5% over the past 8–9 years). The other is that Arizona was the State that was truly hit with what I feared the most: an undercount. It is highly likely that Arizona was undercounted, and that was truly how Rhode Island survived this Census.

» FLEEING TO THE MAINLAND

Still, where did Rhode Island's extra people come from? The answer is the same place that other States got their boosts from: Puerto Rico. Between the 2010 Census and the 2020 one, the United States territory lost nearly 12% of its population, or 440,000 people. The island was already losing population due to a string of natural and man-made disasters before Hurricane Maria hit in 2017, but afterwards nearly 4% of the population immediately left. As the Trump administration bungled the relief efforts, the drain continued. Being United States citizens, the people of Puerto Rico were free to go wherever they wanted in the rest of the country, and they did.

This image by **MORTADELO2005**[190] is licensed under the **CREATIVE COMMONS ATTRIBUTION-SHARE ALIKE 3.0 UNPORTED**[191] license via **WIKIMEDIA COMMONS**[192].

While some have returned, most have remained in other States and made new lives. Florida alone is estimated to have absorbed over 180,000 citizens and Texas over 60,000—these two States also happen to be the big

---

[190] HTTPS://COMMONS.WIKIMEDIA.ORG/WIKI/USER:MORTADELO2005
[191] HTTPS://CREATIVECOMMONS.ORG/LICENSES/BY-SA/3.0/DEED.EN
[192] HTTPS://COMMONS.WIKIMEDIA.ORG/WIKI/FILE:USA_TOPO_EN.JPG

winners in seat gains from this Census, too. Rhode Island appears to have received somewhere between 15,000 to 25,000. Perhaps the exact number is 19,127?

As such, we have an undercount in Arizona and a fleeing Puerto Rican population to thank for saving our Congressional seat. The pandemic has also brought a new set of immigrants to Rhode Island from New York, New Jersey, and Massachusetts. People fleeing congested cities for comparably cheaper housing and open space were not part of the Census count (only people here on April 1, 2020 counted), but will be critical to keeping this trend going in 2030 and beyond. Yet, we will have to support these people in the meanwhile and will need the resources this apportionment brings for the next ten years. In that way, the recent arrivals can thank the people from Puerto Rico for much of what the State will be able to do over the next ten years.

» MULTIVERSE OF MADNESS

That does beg the question of what would happen if Puerto Rico were a State? Using the 2020 Census numbers, Puerto Rico would gain 4 seats in the House of Representatives. Despite this, Rhode Island would still hold on to its second seat! California, Colorado, Minnesota, and Montana would all donate a single seat each to Puerto Rico while Rhode Island would drop from eighth to fourth-from-the-bottom on the priority list. It is much closer the edge, but still safe with the current population numbers.

The hubbub right now is on Washington, D.C. becoming a State after the **HOUSE OF REPRESENTATIVES PASSED**

LEGISLATION[193] to make it so. While this bill stands no chance to make it through the current Senate, it does bring up an interesting "what if" scenario. Still, with a population of around 690,000 people, the District of Columbia would be the third smallest State by population after Wyoming and Vermont (although it would steal the title of smallest State by area from Rhode Island, and would be the densest). Because of this, they would just gain one seat at the expense of Minnesota, who would drop to 7 representatives. And this, of course, would only knock Rhode Island down one spot in the priority order.

Photo by **STEPHANIE KLEPACKI**[194] on **UNSPLASH**

There seems little concern that Rhode Island was in that much danger of losing a seat in the House of Representatives this cycle. Years of hand wringing on my part may have been unnecessary, but that is just the way I am. And to assuage any last doubt I had, I looked through the population percentage gains between the

---
[193] HTTPS://THEHILL.COM/HOMENEWS/HOUSE/549569-HOUSE-PASSES-DC-STATEHOOD-BILL-FOR-SECOND-TIME
[194] HTTPS://UNSPLASH.COM/@SKLEPACKI

2010 Census and the 2020 one. While the United States as a whole (including the Territories) increased 7.1%, the Northeast Region was just 4.1%. With Rhode Island itself coming in at 4.3%, it seems right in line with the rest of the area. Even if the growth rate were just 4.1%, that would only be a difference of 1,657 people; hardly enough to make an impact. Actually, the growth rate would have needed to be less than 2.5% to cause the loss of a seat.

With all of this data and analysis, it seems that—at least as of April 26, 2021—Rhode Island was safe for the next ten years, and perhaps even longer. As such, it was time to bask in my victory.

YES, I CERTAINLY DID IT!

"Bronze Statue of Female Figure on Newel Post Holding a Torch of Electric Light" as part of the exhibit "Celebration of American Contributions to Science" on display at the Great Hall of the Thomas Jefferson Building of the Library of Congress in Washington, D.C. on December 28, 2019. Photo by J.P. Prag.

2022+ IMPLICATIONS FOR 2020 FAILINGS

Revisiting the Census with "Group Quarters: A Play in 3 Acts"

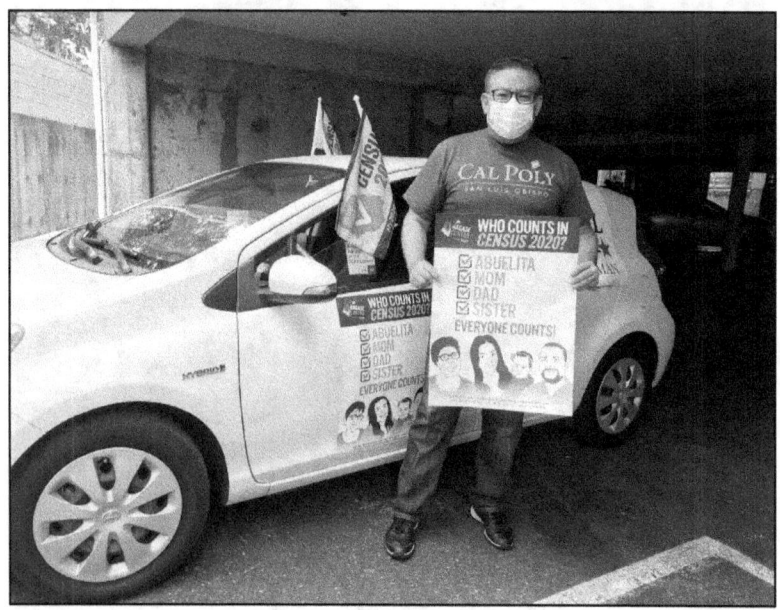

Representative Salud Carbajal (D-CA) attempted to get the word out about the 2020 Census on July 18, 2020. Photo and description by **SALUD CARBAJAL**[195], Public domain, via Wikimedia Commons.

195

HTTPS://COMMONS.WIKIMEDIA.ORG/WIKI/FILE:CENSUS_CARAVAN,_SAN_LUIS_OBISPO_COUNTY,_CALIFORNIA_%28JULY_18,_2020%29_02.JPG

» KEY POINTS

- Many locations have appealed the results of the 2020 Census because they believe there was an undercount in their communities.

- Based upon my own experience employed by the Census Bureau, I can understand their fears, and the decade of consequences to follow.

- While the Census was ongoing, I wrote a piece of fiction to help explain the situation that may add valuable insight to the cases of these municipalities.

> [P]RISONS... BECAME AMONG THE MOST DIFFICULT PLACES TO COUNT—ALONG WITH COLLEGE DORMS, NURSING HOMES AND MILITARY BARRACKS—AS THE CORONAVIRUS SPREAD THROUGHOUT THE U.S. DURING CRUCIAL WEEKS FOR THE [C]ENSUS IN THE SPRING OF 2020. STUDENTS WERE SENT HOME FROM CAMPUSES, AND PRISONS AND NURSING HOMES WENT INTO LOCKDOWNS WHEN THOSE RESIDENTS WERE SUPPOSED TO BE COUNTED.
>
> FROM "'WHOA, THAT'S NOT RIGHT': GEORGIA TOWNS LEAD CENSUS APPEALS[196]" BY MIKE SCHNEIDER OF THE ASSOCIATED PRESS ON JANUARY 22, 2022.

Several fights were going on simultaneously related to the results of the 2020 Decennial Census. However, what they all came down to was a question of undercounts in specific locations. Not having your population correctly counted—especially in relation to minority groups—would lead to fewer representatives in Congress, local legislative bodies, and the Electoral College; less funding from Federal, State and County governments; more expenses at home due to still having to provide services to uncounted people; and many more such issues that would last a decade. As such, by early 2022, various municipalities had already launched appeals and lawsuits to fight the results distributed by the Census Bureau after a laborious "imputation" method to get the numbers as accurate as the agency deemed possible.

---

[196] HTTPS://APNEWS.COM/ARTICLE/CORONAVIRUS-PANDEMIC-HEALTH-BUSINESS-GEORGIA-CENSUS-2020-3FC3EF87B47CBE81CB15A19469841387

2020 US Census questionnaire. Photo and description by M[197], CC BY-SA 4.0[198], via Wikimedia Commons.

Their chances of getting a favorable ruling were not good. A similar process that had existed for appeals had not led to much, if any change. According to Hansi Lo Wang of NPR in his piece "**CHALLENGING CENSUS RESULTS COULD MEAN MORE FEDERAL MONEY FOR YOUR COMMUNITY**"[199]:

> **FOR THE 2010 [C]ENSUS, THE COUNTS FOR ABOUT 1% OF TRIBAL, [S]TATE AND LOCAL GOVERNMENTS WERE REVISED... AND ULTIMATELY... 175 HOUSING UNITS AND 527 PEOPLE [WERE ADDED] NATIONWIDE.**

---

[197] HTTPS://COMMONS.WIKIMEDIA.ORG/WIKI/FILE:2020_CENSUS_QUESTIONNAIRE.JPG
[198] HTTPS://CREATIVECOMMONS.ORG/LICENSES/BY-SA/4.0
[199] HTTPS://WWW.NPR.ORG/2022/01/01/1069610946/2020-CENSUS-CORRECTION-CHALLENGE-RESULTS-COUNT-QUESTION-RESOLUTION

I had a great amount of sympathy for all of these places, and shared their concerns. Having read about their accounts, watched fights over gerrymandered districts, and thought about how the next 10 years would look, I was reminded about my own experiences working as an Enumerator (see below for a definition) during the 2020 Census and the tribulation and failures it entailed. That, in turn, prompted me to recall something I had put together back then; a little capture-in-time that may have had some value to the cases of these localities.

For full disclosure, not only did I contribute to the 2020 Census, but I continue to do occasional work for the Census Bureau and the Department of Commerce, including at the time of this writing as a Quality Control Field Representative for the "Final Housing Unit Follow-Up". Post publication, I may take on additional temporary assignments as conditions and time permit.

» BACKGROUND

Working in the field for the United States Census Bureau is a lonely job. Although your tasks consist of talking to people, most of the time they are not home or do not answer their doors and phones. More so, while your co-workers are out there, you rarely see them, so there is no sense of community or belonging. Supervisors are equally—if not even more—elusive. You truly do feel like you are alone in the world with no support at all.

Thankfully in the 21st century we have many methods and tools for meeting others in the same boat and can commiserate about our experiences. One such place was on the **CENSUS SUB-REDDIT**[200], a message board that my fellow Census workers and I flocked to. It provided the

---

[200] HTTPS://WWW.REDDIT.COM/R/CENSUS/

necessary sustenance and direction we were not getting from all of the many layers above us. While swapping tales of horror and wonder, I was inspired to write a short play to capture a particular experience I and several other people were going through.

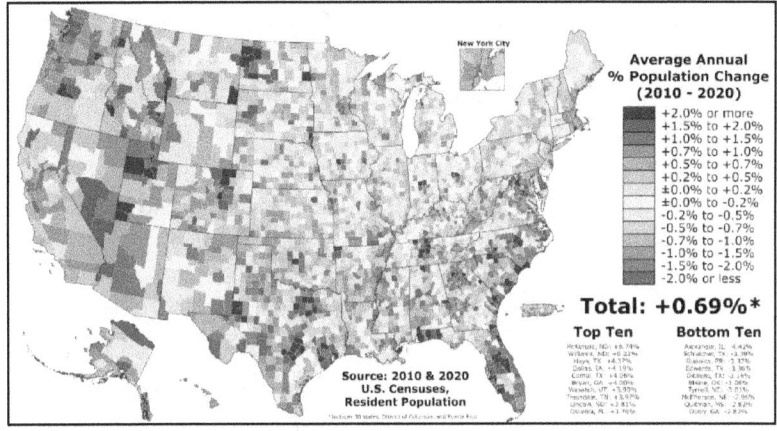

Map showing the average annual resident population growth rate of each county in the fifty States, D.C., and Puerto Rico between the 2010 and 2020 United States Census. Results can be found **HERE**[201] and **HERE**[202]. Description and image by **ABBASI786786**[203], **CC BY-SA 4.0**[204], via Wikimedia Commons.

It is important to note that people who work for the Census Bureau sign a lifetime obligation to never reveal any identifying data or information related to their collection and analysis activities. Any disclosure is punishable by up to five years in jail and a maximum of $250,000 in fines.

---

[201] HTTPS://DATA.CENSUS.GOV/CEDSCI/TABLE?Q=P1%3A%20TOTAL%20POPULATION&G=0100000US%240500000&TID=DECENNIALSF12010.P1

[202] HTTPS://DATA.CENSUS.GOV/CEDSCI/TABLE?Q=P1%3A%20TOTAL%20POPULATION&G=0100000US%240500000&TID=DECENNIALPL2020.P1

[203] HTTPS://COMMONS.WIKIMEDIA.ORG/WIKI/FILE:ANNUAL_POPULATION_GROWTH_IN_THE_U.S._BY_COUNTY_-_2010S.PNG

[204] HTTPS://CREATIVECOMMONS.ORG/LICENSES/BY-SA/4.0

Because of this, it is imperative to be clear that this is a work of fiction. While based on true events; names, places, situations, number of people involved, and any other relevant details have been obfuscated, combined, or completely made up. This piece is a parody and should not be considered any type of official or unofficial release from the Census Bureau, Department of Commerce, or the United States government in general, nor should this be constituted as any type of whistleblower report.

And as I told one of the original readers who did not quite "get it":

> [E]NJOY A LITTLE ARTISTIC LICENSE WITHOUT ALL OF THE REAL DETAILS AND MASSIVE MINUTIAE OF EVERY DISCUSSION WITH ALL THE VARIOUS PEOPLE WITHIN THE COLLEGE ADMINISTRATION, OR THE FACT THAT "ENUMERATOR" AND "CFM" ARE ACTUALLY MULTIPLE DIFFERENT PEOPLE.

» CHARACTERS AND TERMINOLOGY

Enumerator: A person who works intermittently for the Census Bureau during the Decennial (every 10 years) Census. The Enumerator's job is to go door-to-door and get headcount and biographical data from people who have not self-responded to the Census through online, mail, local community drives, phone, or other methods. The Enumerator has no control of their assignments and may be given the same location several days in a row or have an entire apartment building split up between several Enumerators, thus upsetting everyone with multiple visits.

CFS: Short for "Census Field Supervisor", the Enumerator reports directly to the CFS. In turn, the CFS manages a team of roughly 15-20 different Enumerators over a physical area, often one or many "Census Blocks", or ways the Census Bureau has sliced up the country that does not align to any other method, such as districts for the House of Representatives. The CFS has as little training as the Enumerator and almost no power. The CFS may also do some field Enumerator work, too, but is more likely to just be an intermediary from the upper-echelons of the organization.

CFM: Short for "Census Field Manager", the CFM is above the CFS in the hierarchy. The CFM is also as poorly trained as the CFS and the Enumerator, but does

	have the power to override the work both do. Since the CFM has no field training or experience, directives given are often nonsensical and unhelpful. Typically they are one word or short phrase responses in the system that could be summed up as "Just figure it out yourself and do it", despite whatever the situation may be.
FDC:	Short for "Field Data Capture", FDC is a custom app for the iPhone that is used by the Enumerator to record data from respondents. Further, FDC is the main communication method for Enumerators and their CFS and CFM through the note taking system in order to provide relevant details and background. FDC is incredibly unwieldy, specific, and does not allow basic functions like copy and paste. That means that a family of 15 requires manually putting in their 27-character all-consonant name for each person individually.
Person 1:	A typical respondent at the address the Enumerator has been assigned to. Although it is in the middle of the COVID-19 Pandemic (before vaccines even exist) and people have been told

to maintain social distance, Person 1 is still willing to answer the door to an unexpected stranger, although will never wear a mask or stay in their own personal space.

Guard: A person who works at a Group Quarters location—a place where multiple people live under the management of another organization like a prison, nursing home, or university. This is not to be confused with a multi-unit dwelling like an apartment building or condo complex. The Guard here patrols the grounds of one such place.

Phone Proxy: A proxy in general is someone who stands in and answers questions for another respondent. For instance, if someone is not home at Apartment #1, the Enumerator is told by FDC to find three other potential proxies to answer the questions for Apartment #1. This might be going to Apartments #2, #3, and #4, or perhaps talking to the management of the building or even some random person in the hallway. Although it is not standard procedure or part of training, the Enumerator may find valid phone numbers and call people up to get a response. Sometimes, it makes sense to call the manager of a unit, hence the Phone Proxy.

In-Movers: People who moved into a unit after April 1, 2020. The Census records the people who were living there on that date, so the people who have come in since then are In-Movers and do not count there, but instead must be counted where they were on April 1, 2020.

NOV: Short for "Notice of Visit", a NOV is a standard form that the Enumerator leaves at a location when no one answers. The NOV contains directions for responding to the Census, as well as a unique code for that specific location. NOVs must be placed somewhere that can be seen (though not easily from the street by someone just passing by), but Enumerators are not allowed to put them in mailboxes or open screen doors to put them in there.

Breathable Air: Because the 2020 Census was delayed from "April through June" to "July through October", the weather outside is much worse. This includes massive heatwaves, forest fires, hurricanes, and other natural and man-made disasters. Having a good day with breathable air, calm weather, and no other major issues is a rare treat and must be savored.

1940 US Census poster. Image and description by the US CENSUS BUREAU[205], Public domain, via Wikimedia Commons.

---

[205]

HTTPS://COMMONS.WIKIMEDIA.ORG/WIKI/FILE:1940_US_CENSUS_POSTER_%28BORDER_REMOVED%29.PNG

» ACT 1

SCENE 1
Outside a set of row-style houses that are covered in signs for LoCal College

Enumerator: <*Enters from stage right, walks over to door and knocks*> OK, here we go!

Person 1: <*Opens door without wearing a mask and peers out*> Yaa?

Enumerator: Hello, I'm from the United States Census Bureau. Is this 1 Obviously College Dorm Way, Unit 1 of 300?

Person 1: Ummmm... I dunno.

Enumerator: You... don't... know?

Person 1: I just moved in.

Enumerator: Oh, well, do you know anything about the people who lived here on April 1st?

Person 1: I dunno, the college just assigned me here.

Enumerator: Oh, so this is a dorm?

Person 1: I dunno.

Enumerator: OK, thanks for your time.

Person 1: <*Shuts door*>

Enumerator: What do you think, FDC?

FDC: Get me a proxy!

Enumerator: Everyone I talk to says the same thing, FDC. I think this might be a Group Quarters.

FDC: I don't believe you!

Enumerator: All right, for now, I'll just mark everyone as In-Movers, leave NOVs, put my concerns in the notes, and let my CFS know. I'm sure our caring and careful data-driven organization will know what to do with such detailed and well-crafted notes!

Scene 2
3 days later outside same location

Enumerator: Hmmmm... I seem to be back here again. This is going to end up with the same issue. Oh look, there's someone who can help!

Guard: <*Walks towards Enumerator but does not maintain social distance*> What are you doing prowling around this obvious college dorm when you are obviously not a student?

Enumerator: I'm with the United States Census Bureau and signs warding people off do not apply to me[206]. But that's beside the point! Can you tell me about this place?

Guard: It's a dorm. Lots of students live here.

---

[206] By law, signs like "No Trespassing", "No Solicitation", or the like do not apply to Field Representatives of the Census Bureau. They are allowed to and required to enter any property, short of opening a door and entering a dwelling.

Enumerator: What about on April 1st?

Guard: Same thing.

Enumerator: All right, we'll give this a try.

Guard: *<Exits, but continues to glare from the edge of the curtain>*

Enumerator: FDC, I now have confirmation that this is Group Quarters from a Proxy, and you are going to accept it.

FDC: All right, but you are going to record that statement individually 300 times.

Enumerator: Oh FDC, you are such a kidder!

FDC: *<Stares back>*

Enumerator: Oh... I see...

Scene 3
The Evil Headquarters of CFM Central, deep underground

CFM: Oh, let's see what our hard-working Enumerators have for us today. *<Ruffles some papers>* GROUP QUARTERS?! WHY I NEVER! FDC?

FDC: Yes boss?

CFM: Although I have never left this underground layer, I obviously know more about how the world works than any puny Enumerator. Unmark this as Group Quarters and take a memo.

FDC: Ready boss! Everything you say is like ambrosia from the gods!

CFM: Enumerator, just because college students live here, does not mean this is Group Quarters. Get back in there, gain access by any means possible, and E-N-U-M-E-R-A-T-E.

» Act 2

Scene 1
Enumerator's dining room table, where all pandemic home offices are

Enumerator: OK, FDC, what do you have for me today?

FDC: You are going back to 1 Obviously a College Dorm Way.

Enumerator: What, why?

FDC: Here's a note from CFM. *<Hands over note>*

Enumerator: This can't be! No, I have a better idea.

FDC: You aren't allowed to do that.

Enumerator: Hold on. *<Enumerator starts scrolling through the computer screen and picks up a phone>* I've got a solution to this. *<Dials phone>*

Phone Proxy: Hello, this is the Office of Student Housing for LoCal College. How may I help you?

Enumerator: Hi, I'm an Enumerator for the United States Census Bureau.

Phone Proxy: Oh good, I love to help people like you!

Enumerator: Fantastic! Can you tell me about 1 Obviously College Dorm Way?

Phone Proxy: Of course, those are all our student housing.

Enumerator: Was it always student housing? What about on April 1st?

Phone Proxy: Of course! We don't own the buildings, though, we just lease them.

Enumerator: Ah, I see the problem then. And you were leasing them last year?

Phone Proxy: We've leased them for a decade. Our students are the only people who have ever lived there!

Enumerator: Did you include the students who live there in the count you provided to the Census Bureau?

Phone Proxy: Yes, of course. We are actually civically responsible and do everything we are supposed to, double checking all our data so as to not have any issues and make your life much easier.

Enumerator: Well thank you very much, I'll let you go!

Phone Proxy: You are very welcome! Be sure to reach out to me if you have any questions or issues and tell your boss to do the same. I am always happy to help!
<Exits>

Enumerator: You heard it yourself FDC, we now have super confirmation that these are all Group Quarters!

FDC: You know what to do.

Enumerator: 300 times?

FDC: 300 times.

Scene 2
1 Week later, outside a different building

Enumerator: FDC, I'm feeling great! The weather is actually nice, the air is breathable, and I've been assigned to a location I haven't personally proxied a dozen times myself[207]. What could go wrong?

FDC: Incoming message from CFM.

Enumerator: Huh?

FDC: You now have to enumerate 1 Obviously College Dorm Way.

Enumerator: But I checked my entire list! It was not on there! And I've already resolved this situation. What happened?

CFM: *<Walks on stage surrounded by smoke to signify a flashback>* I won't read any of these notes; I'll just say these aren't Group Quarters again and tell them to PROXY HARDER! That will resolve this situation for sure! *<Exits into the smoke>*

---

[207] As it gets later into the timeline, most of the remaining cases are for non-respondents that require a proxy. Enumerators are often sent back to the same location day-after-day and told to find proxies.

Enumerator: No, absolutely not! FDC, get me CFS.

CFS: <*Enters*> Yo, whazzzup?

Enumerator: CFS, look at this situation. There is nothing we could possibly count! You have to stop sending me and the other Enumerators here!

CFS: Well, like, you know, and stuff.

Enumerator: Ummmmm... no?

CFS: Like, it's... umm... a building. And LoCal College, it... uh... ummm... doesn't, like, own it.

Enumerator: They don't have to own it for it to be a Group Quarters.

CFS: Can you, like, ummm... go ask that guy you called for the... ummmm... population count thing for it. Then, like, you can, like, ummm... trust, that it will be, like, fixed later.

Enumerator: No, that would literally be a double count! That goes against everything you ever taught me.

CFS: Oh, like, hadn't thought about, ummm... that. Let me, like, ask CFM what to do.

Enumerator: OK, so while you do that, I'm going to mark this all back to Group Quarters.

FDC: 300 times!

Enumerator: 300... times...

» Act 3
This play isn't over yet! What do you think will happen next? Write your last act and we'll see over the coming weeks which one is closest to reality. The winner receives a shiny piece of **Enumerator Pride** (No Cash Value)!

» Follow-Up
While no one wrote a final act of their own, there were a lot of great responses from fellow Enumerators who had either gone through a similar experience or were extremely sympathetic. Aside from that one person mentioned in the introduction, everyone seemed to enjoy the joke. Here are a few choice responses:

> I GOT TO THE END AND AM JUST GLAD TO FINALLY HAVE CONFIRMATION THAT ENUMERATOR PRIDE HAS NO VALUE.

> THIS IS THE MOST ACCURATE PORTRAYAL OF A **CFM** YET. **10/10**

> WHOEVER IS IN CHARGE OF THE [POSTMORTEM] FOR THIS OPERATION NEEDS TO COME AND MAKE A CASE STUDY OUT OF THIS SUBREDDIT.

Race and Ethnicity are Meaningless Human Constructs

Stop trying to force everyone into predefined categories

Photo by **Clay Banks**[208] on **Unsplash**

---

[208] HTTPS://UNSPLASH.COM/@CLAYBANKS

» Key Points

- *Surveys like the Census that ask questions around race and ethnicity are inherently flawed because they predetermine the possible selections for deeply held personal ideas about identity.*

- *Americans are having more difficulty filling in these fields for a plethora of reasons and are skipping these questions or entering confusing answers, yielding unhelpful data and suppositions based on that data.*

- *Only by allowing free rein responses to questions like these can we get useful data that can be analyzed and re-evaluated over time.*

Racial and ethnic categories are social constructs, defined and designed by those who have historically held positions of influence. Our data collection instruments continue to echo this influence...

From "Separating Race from Ethnicity in Surveys Risks an Inaccurate Picture of the Latinx Community[209]" on the Urban Institute blog on October 15, 2019, co-written by Robert Santos—President Joe Biden's selection for the Director of the United States Census Bureau.

What race am I? If you look at my pictures on my website, you may decide to assign me to a particular race. Yet, did you ask yourself if I feel that way; do I consider myself to be the race you have perceived me to be? Does that race culturally represent what I am? Who do you think you are telling me how I should identify!?! Why don't I have the right to decide what I am?

This is a struggle many—if not all of us—have. While filling out surveys or paperwork for the doctor's office or any such thing, we are presented with predefined fields that give a finite list. Sometimes there is an "Other" or "Refused" option, oftentimes not. Even our own government does this with the Decennial Census (like the one that was completed in 2020) and the regular

---

[209] HTTPS://WWW.URBAN.ORG/URBAN-WIRE/SEPARATING-RACE-ETHNICITY-SURVEYS-RISKS-INACCURATE-PICTURE-LATINX-COMMUNITY

"American Community Survey" that the Census Bureau undertakes in between these larger ventures. The ideas are noble: let us know how many underrepresented people there are and where they live so that we can direct resources there. Unfortunately, the execution has left much to be desired.

*Equipment issued to/purchased by Enumerators working in the field for the 2020 United States Census: Clockwise, black canvas bag with Census logo, hand sanitizer, iPhone 8 with custom software, Notice of Visit forms, Privacy Notice forms, and surgical mask. Photo and description by **DANIEL CASE**[210], **CC BY-SA 4.0**[211], via Wikimedia Commons on October 9, 2020.*

Once again, for full disclosure, I worked as an Enumerator for the 2020 Census, going door-to-door attempting to

---

[210] HTTPS://COMMONS.WIKIMEDIA.ORG/WIKI/FILE:US_CENSUS_2020_TOOLS_OF_THE_TRADE.JPG
[211] HTTPS://CREATIVECOMMONS.ORG/LICENSES/BY-SA/4.0

get population information from those who did not self-report. In normal times it would have been difficult; in a pandemic with politically charged overtones, natural disasters, and a constantly shifting timeline it was nearly impossible. Somehow, though, we got the job done, but not without a lot of questions about data integrity. Further, I continue to do occasional work for the Census Bureau and the Department of Commerce, including at the time of this writing as a Quality Control Field Representative for the "Final Housing Unit Follow-Up". Post publication, I may take on additional temporary assignments as conditions and time permit.

You may say that my experience gives me a bias, and you would probably be correct in that regard. However, I would contend this has also given me perspective to not just my own contentions, but to many other communities who find the question of race one that just does not fit.

» WAVING TO YOUR CAMERA DOORBELL

The quoted Mr. Santos above is one such example. As a Latinx person, he in particular finds it confusing that questions about Hispanic origin are separate from those on race. During my enumerating in communities with large amounts of people of various Latinx descents, a typical interaction went like this...

ME: ARE YOU OF HISPANIC, LATINO, OR SPANISH ORIGIN?

RESPONDENT: YES, I'M GUATEMALAN.

ME: OK, NEXT QUESTION. FOR THE PURPOSE OF THE CENSUS, HISPANIC ORIGIN IS NOT CONSIDERED A RACE. WHAT RACE ARE YOU?

RESPONDENT: *What does that mean? I'm Hispanic, I'm Guatemalan.*

ME: *Options include White, Black or African American, American Indian or Alaskan Native, Asian or Other Pacific Islander, or Some Other Race. You can chose one or more of these.*

RESPONDENT: *I'm Guatemalan.*

ME: *So, "Some Other Race" and fill in Guatemalan?*

RESPONDENT: *Sure, I guess.*

This is not a newly recognized issue. Back on September 30, 2016, the *Office of Management and Budget* (OMB) released the results of a multi-year study about the impact of these questions, **NOTING IN PART**[212]:

> **Nearly half of Hispanic or Latino respondents do not identify within any of the standard's race categories... With the projected steady growth of the Hispanic or Latino population, the number of people who do not identify with any of the standard's race categories is expected to increase...**

---

[212] HTTPS://WWW.FEDERALREGISTER.GOV/DOCUMENTS/2016/09/30/2016-23672/STANDARDS-FOR-MAINTAINING-COLLECTING-AND-PRESENTING-FEDERAL-DATA-ON-RACE-AND-ETHNICITY

In order to alleviate this issue, the OMB recommended combining the two questions about Latinx origin and race together as it better reflected how the people in those communities viewed themselves. This is a position that Mr. Santos supported, as he specifically told Congress during confirmation hearings. Although even after he was confirmed he did not personally have the power to modify the question, he fully supported the OMB's conclusions and said he would strive to see its implementation.

Photo by **JHON DAVID**[213] on **UNSPLASH**

Much to the chagrin of many people, President Trump and his administration chose to scuttle the OMB recommendations and not make them a part of the 2020 Census. In particular, columnist Laura Measher was perturbed because the OMB also made a further recommendation to break out a separate category for people of Middle Eastern and North African origins—one in

---

[213] HTTPS://UNSPLASH.COM/@JACKHAMMER

which she feels she belongs. In the 2020 Census directions, people of Middle Eastern descent were specifically told that they should chose "White" as their race, something that Ms. Measher vehemently disagreed with in her piece "**THE 2020 CENSUS CONTINUES THE WHITEWASHING OF MIDDLE EASTERN AMERICANS**[214]". In a correspondence with Ms. Measher on May 22, 2020, she expressed to me:

> **I KNOW THAT I AND MY FAMILY MEMBERS HAVE DEFINITELY MADE GOOD USE OF THE "OTHER" OPTION ON THE [C]ENSUS. MY MAIN PROBLEM WITH THIS IS THAT IF "WHITE" AND "OTHER" ARE OUR ONLY OPTIONS, MIDDLE EASTERN AMERICANS AREN'T ACCURATELY COUNTED AS A POPULATION (AT LEAST IN THE PUBLICLY AVAILABLE STATISTICS). WITHOUT POPULATION DATA, IT'S DIFFICULT TO CALCULATE ACCURATE STATISTICS REGARDING MIDDLE EASTERN AMERICANS, LIKE POVERTY RATES, ARREST RATES, EDUCATION DATA, ETC. AND WITHOUT THOSE STATISTICS, PREVALENT ISSUES IMPACTING OUR COMMUNITIES MAY GO UNNOTICED.**

Much like Mr. Santos and Ms. Measher, I do not fit in, either. As a mostly Ashkenazi Jew, I find the idea of being classified as "White" to not only be incorrect, but offensive and repugnant. "White" people slaughtered my ancestors for generations and many "White" people still hold prejudice against me today—including bigotry and antisemitism that I have personally had to deal with. That

---

[214] HTTPS://WWW.NBCNEWS.COM/THINK/OPINION/2020-CENSUS-CONTINUES-WHITEWASHING-MIDDLE-EASTERN-AMERICANS-NCNA1212051

is not a group I can belong to; it is an insult to my very being in how I see my identity. Thus—like others interviewed by Ron Kampeas in the piece "**AMERICAN JEWS: ARE YOU WHITE?**[215]"—I chose "Some Other Race" and filled in Ashkenazi. Still, as seen in Mr. Kampeas' piece, that was not a universal response among people who share my origin. Many had no difficulty in choosing "White" and filling in "Jewish" or something similar (or nothing at all), while others endeavored to leave the question blank. All have led to further complications and issues with the data.

» THE HISTORY OF THE WORLD—PART 1

*Photo by **NGUYEN DANG HOANG NHU**[216] on **UNSPLASH***

According to Mike Schneider of the Associated Press in a piece entitled "**CENSUS EXPERTS PUZZLED BY HIGH RATE OF**

---

[215] HTTPS://WWW.JPOST.COM/DIASPORA/AMERICAN-JEWS-ARE-YOU-WHITE-624072
[216] HTTPS://UNSPLASH.COM/@NGUYENDHN

UNANSWERED QUESTIONS[217]", somewhere between 10-20% of questions on the 2020 Census were left blank, a massive increase from the single digits seen in years past. The questions that were most likely to be left blank were around race, Hispanic background, and sex—all questions about identity. What is more, in a separate article five days later ("**CENSUS DATA: US IS DIVERSIFYING, WHITE POPULATION SHRINKING**[218]"), Mr. Schneider noted:

> **SOME DEMOGRAPHERS CAUTIONED THAT THE WHITE POPULATION WAS NOT SHRINKING AS MUCH AS SHIFTING TO MULTIRACIAL IDENTITIES. THE NUMBER OF PEOPLE WHO IDENTIFIED AS BELONGING TO TWO OR MORE RACES MORE THAN TRIPLED FROM 9 MILLION PEOPLE IN 2010 TO 33.8 MILLION IN 2020. THEY NOW ACCOUNT FOR 10% OF THE U.S. POPULATION.**

Meanwhile, all those questions left blank and many of the "Some Other Race" selections were filled in by the Census Bureau in a method known as "imputation". The statisticians at the Census used a court-approved method of trying to guess people's race based upon other available government or public forms that have been filled out, what other members of the household put in as race, what their neighbors entered, what race their name most likely aligns to based on other respondents, and many other techniques.

---

[217] HTTPS://APNEWS.COM/ARTICLE/TECHNOLOGY-HEALTH-CORONAVIRUS-PANDEMIC-CENSUS-2020-5E0DD5B710F1AB0FF23A8272078D5528
[218] HTTPS://APNEWS.COM/ARTICLE/RACE-AND-ETHNICITY-CENSUS-2020-7264A653037E38DF7BA67D3A324FC90D

The point is, Americans are expanding their own definitions of race, ethnicity, and identity; while the government and society are not keeping up. NPR's Hansi Lo Wang did a deep dive on the numbers with those selecting more than one race in his piece "**THE CENSUS HAS REVEALED A MORE MULTIRACIAL U.S. ONE REASON? CHEAPER DNA TESTS**[219]" and found that those selecting "White" in combination with "Some Other Race" increased 1,010% between 2010 and 2020—going from 1.7 million to 19.3 million respondents. As the title suggests, the proliferation of personal DNA tests has given people the ability to further define themselves based upon historical origins. My own DNA results show a previously unknown Mediterranean component:

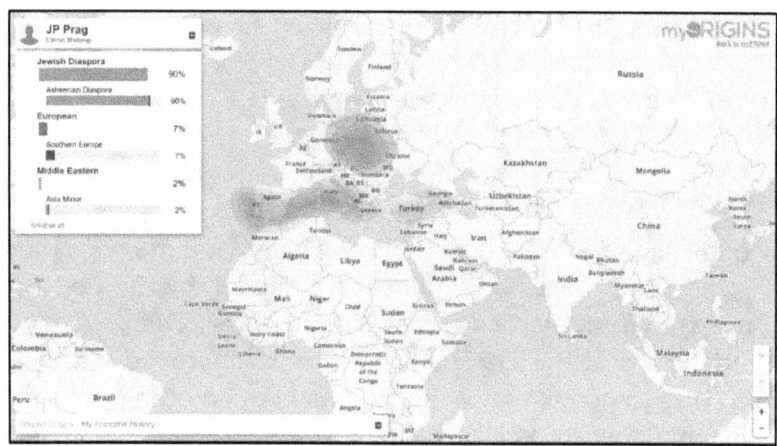

Ethnic origins for the author J.P. Prag according to his DNA results. Screenshot by J.P. Prag via Family Tree DNA on September 1, 2016.

In case you are wondering, my missing 1% comes from my Neanderthal DNA, which is far below the 2.1% average for people of European and Middle Eastern ancestry.

---

[219] HTTPS://WWW.NPR.ORG/2021/08/28/1030139666/2020-CENSUS-RESULTS-DATA-RACE-MULTIRACIAL-DNA-ANCESTRY-TEST-MIXED-BIRACIAL

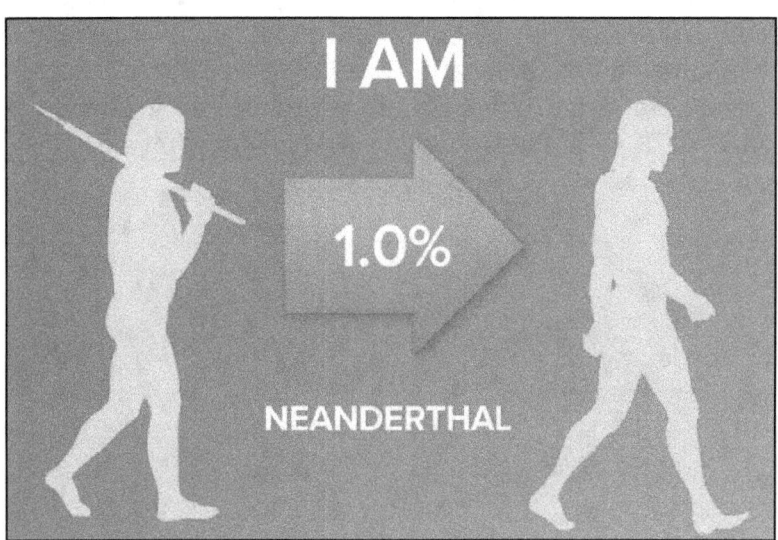

Screenshot of non-Homo Sapien[220] DNA for the author J.P. Prag. Screenshot by J.P. Prag via the National Geographic Genographic Project on September 1, 2016.

While getting a question to tease out non-Homo Sapien origin would be out of the purview of the Census Bureau, DNA tests have at least contributed to the 276% increase in those selecting two or more races.

However, these DNA tests have created a fracturing that is not based in scientific reality. What is being shown in these results is gene flow—how people migrated through time and passed their genes down. It is a probability game of where you are most likely to find pools of these same genes, meaning that they have a common ancestor; it is not an expression of actual race. All studies over the past 25 years have failed to find any part of DNA that is a "race" as we mean it. Skin tones, types of hair, eye shapes, and all of those phenotypes do not align to any part or sections of DNA. Most of it comes from the

---

[220] See prior footnote on "Sapien" versus "Sapiens".

expression of certain genes, not the genes themselves. In other words, genetically, humans are pretty much exactly the same across the board. Everything we think of as "race" and "ethnicity" are as concrete as "religion" and "belief". They are less than constructs; they have no material basis.

*Image provided by **POPULAR GRAPHIC ARTS**[221], Public domain, via Wikimedia Commons.*

A better example might be to look at dogs. Whether a Dachshund or a Bernese Mountain Dog, genetically they are exactly the same. As dogs, they are compatible with each other and can have viable offspring (as impractical as that mating may be). We call them "breeds", but again humans created those through selective reproduction. Finding traits we desired in our companions, we put

---

[221] HTTPS://COMMONS.WIKIMEDIA.ORG/WIKI/FILE:CARNIVORA,_OR_FLESH-EATING_ANIMALS._FAMILY-DOGS_LCCN2003664022.JPG

similar ones together until the trait became more pronounced, and then inbred them to keep that trait. And for analogous reasons, my two short parents preferred to be with a similarly heighted mate, which in turn produced two short offspring.

As such, am I also not just a "breed" of human? What am I but a specific expression of physical traits as homogeneous communities procreated together for millennia? Nothing is physically stopping me from having a baby with any other human on the planet, nor with many other types of extinct hominids like Neanderthals and Denisovans. All these ways of slicing us up have no scientific basis; they are mostly about how others want to prescribe labels to us in order to describe various bodily components and historical origins.

» FLY ME WITH BALLOONS

So if race and ethnicity are meaningless, should we still collect data on them?

IN A WORD: YES!

This again goes back to personal identity. How people view their own being and what communities they assign themselves to is important. All of the reasons we have gone through above and all of the uses the government and other organizations have for these figures is still valid. The problem we have is the method by which they try to generate the data. Being pigeonholed into predefined categories is chaffing at the very least and painfully disrespectful at the worst.

Photo by **Eugene Zhyvchik**[222] on **Unsplash**

---

[222] HTTPS://UNSPLASH.COM/@EUGENEZHYVCHIK

Instead of trying to create categories and shove people into them, is not the simple solution to just ask people what they want to be identified as? Can we not simply ask:

How do you identify your race and/or ethnicity?

It would be an open field and as people typed suggestions could pop up based on what others have previously entered (mostly to try to help with spelling issues), but nothing should stop them from entering their own. Actually, it could actively be encouraged to fill in as many as they feel, whatever makes sense to them. Once we have that data, then we can do an analysis to see what the largest groups are, where they are, how they identify as multiple groups, and all other concerns.

The data could also be expressed as a **Word Cloud**. As an example, a survey asking for a single word would yield a large array of answers. Those results could then be shown where those that have more responses are bigger and bolder while those with fewer results are shown as smaller and lighter.

This visual representation gives a quick idea of where people stand on any topic, including their identity. Statisticians at the Census Bureau could make suppositions on top of this data instead of trying to fill it in. For instance, they may group "Black", "Brown", and "African American" together into a single category for presentation purposes. That is a fine use of taking raw data and transforming it into something useful, while not telling people how they should see themselves.

Example of the findings of an open survey with the results presented as a Word Cloud. Image by TAGCROWD[223], CC BY-SA 4.0[224], via Wikimedia Commons.

Does that mean that they would still group Ms. Measher, me, and others under "White"? Perhaps, or perhaps they would finally see these large groups of people who do not want to be in those categories as unique and interesting. Maybe they would figure out new and different sets. Either way, it is impossible to do now because the base data does not exist. You cannot re-evaluate old data if it does not exist because of your collection method!

Gathering data is only the first step in a long process of analysis and debate to get to action. In between, you

---

[223] HTTPS://COMMONS.WIKIMEDIA.ORG/WIKI/FILE:FRAM_COMMUNITY_DISCUSSION_WORD_CLOUD.PNG
[224] HTTPS://CREATIVECOMMONS.ORG/LICENSES/BY-SA/4.0

make data into information and then information into knowledge. Only through this meticulous process can you come to any meaningful decisions about what to do with all of this. But if the data continues to be garbage at the beginning, then the actions of the government and other similarly situated organizations are only going to be a misrepresented gobbledygook for yet another decade to come.

PART 6: APPROACH

DO 10 MINUTES OF RESEARCH

Even the most frivolous topics deserve effort

Photos from a **HOUSE LISTING IN DALLAS, TX**[225], *captured and put into a collage by J.P. Prag on August 5, 2021. The listing seized the imagination of many people wondering what an industrial-looking interior was doing inside this 5,786 sqft residential dwelling.*

---

[225] HTTPS://WWW.ZILLOW.COM/HOMEDETAILS/13229-SOUTHVIEW-LN-DALLAS-TX-75240/118222349_ZPID/

» **KEY POINTS**

- *Though a subject matter may be ridiculous and only meant for fun, writers should still treat it with dignity and respect.*

- *Being in the world of news and analysis means buckling down and doing the necessary detailed research to get real answers and not just posting quick nonsense to compete with social media.*

- *This is the attitude I take into my own work and expect of others.*

As with every morning, I scrolled through my news feed and pulled up tabs of articles I wanted to read. One came up that was innocuous enough and seemed like it might be a bit of fun. The headline from the *Fort Worth Star-Telegram* declared "**Perplexing interior of Texas house listed for $1M has 'Zillow Gone Wild' creeped out**[226]" and was accompanied by a photo of a seemingly normal—though overlarge—house.

Perplexing interior of Texas house listed for $1M has 'Zillow Gone Wild' creeped out
Fort Worth Star-Telegram · Jul 27

Screen capture of the Google News feed of the aforementioned article.

Since Google has certainly learned my idiosyncrasies, they provided the perfect fodder to tickle my imagination. And the article did not disappoint in this regard! Author TJ Macías posted the peculiar photos of the house (appropriated from Zillow) showing a strange and brightly lit industrial interior inside an apparently ordinary house in a residential neighborhood. I followed the links back to the listing and saw even more, such as the lack of exterior windows. Ms. Macías further expounded on the suppositions from those on the **Zillow Gone Wild Facebook Group**[227], to which she attributed the finding. Their speculation and quips were equally as amusing as

---

[226] https://www.star-telegram.com/news/nation-world/national/article253071263.html
[227] https://www.facebook.com/zillowgonewild/posts/226333319387605

the original premise, and I was satisfied with a little entertainment.

However, the article then just ended right there. "Wait," I thought, "what about the real story? We cannot just end this on rumors and jokes, right?" But that is exactly what happened. Sure, I had a good chuckle, but there was an actual truth to be revealed here. For Ms. Macías and the *Fort Worth Star-Telegram*, that was enough. They had done all the work they were ever going to do.

Since this is the 21st century, the story then propagated outward to other and repeat news services. Briana Zamora-Nipper for *KPRC* declared in her headline "**'A PROPERTY UNLIKE ANY OTHER': THIS TEXAS HOME ON THE MARKET LOOKS TOTALLY NORMAL. IT ISN'T.**[228]" and basically cribbed the entire article Ms. Macías wrote with some minor modifications. The story even crossed the pond where Sandra Salathe of the UK's *Daily Mail* proclaimed "**CREEPY $1M DALLAS HOME HAS HUGE CONCRETE ROOMS AND FAKE WINDOWS**[229]". Ms. Salathe did at least try to do some research stating in part:

> **DAILYMAIL.COM HAS CONTACTED REAL ESTATE AGENT COMPASS FOR FURTHER INFORMATION.**

Yet that is where it ended for them, as well. When they did not immediately hear back, there was no decision to

---

[228] HTTPS://WWW.CLICK2HOUSTON.COM/NEWS/TEXAS/2021/07/29/A-PROPERTY-UNLIKE-ANY-OTHER-THIS-TEXAS-HOME-ON-THE-MARKET-LOOKS-TOTALLY-NORMAL-IT-ISNT/
[229] HTTPS://WWW.DAILYMAIL.CO.UK/NEWS/ARTICLE-9835357/CREEPY-1M-DALLAS-HOME-HUGE-CONCRETE-ROOMS-FAKE-WINDOWS.HTML

go any further. These articles would have you believe it is a mystery that could not be solved. Except I was able to solve it all in 10 minutes with minimal resources at my disposal.

» CRITICAL HIT

Does it seem pedantic that I am attacking a fluff piece with such vigor? Is it mean spirited of me to go after these columnists with such acrimony?

*Female factory workers crowded around tables at lunchtime during the First World War. Photo and description by an **UNKNOWN AUTHOR**[230], Public domain, via Wikimedia Commons.*

No, because this is about doing work and how I approach it. To be clear, I am totally fine with lighthearted journalism that does not add to the social discourse. Despite the serious nature of my portfolio, I can

---

[230] HTTPS://COMMONS.WIKIMEDIA.ORG/WIKI/FILE:INDUSTRY_DURING_THE_FIRST_WORLD_WAR_Q54668.JPG

appreciate and delight in the ridiculous—but only if it is done well. Even the use of conjecture and sarcasm can be perfectly fine tools in storytelling, so long as the author is going to use them to make the real point in the end. I employ these instruments, too, to make an argument, and therefore am not dissuading anyone from their use.

What I am discouraging is the absolute refusal to do the work. No part of me would ever allow myself to publish an article like this without diving deeper into the subject matter and doing the necessary research to get complete answers. The drive I feel to review the actual data; synthesize it into a usable format; and read and edit it over and over again until it reaches the level I consider acceptable is overwhelming. Even a chapter such as the one you are now digesting represents days of research, analysis, and editing unto itself, not to mention the plotting and actual writing.

This has always been my approach, even when it leads nowhere. When I was writing my book **NEW & IMPROVED: THE UNITED STATES OF AMERICA**[231], I distinctly remember one part that involved an entire month of reading through thousands of pages of eye-watering government documents all to just fill out a single column on a table. And in the end, after alpha draft readers and my editor provided feedback, I ended up eliminating everything that had to do with it. Was the work a waste? It was not in my eyes. As I was doing it, I thought it was worthwhile, and I still learned things that were used elsewhere, both in that book and in future projects.

Even when I was writing about professional wrestling—as effervescent as a subject as you can get—I took it extremely seriously. Each one of my articles represented

---
[231] HTTPS://AMZN.TO/3KGWO6E

at minimum 15–20 hours of grind. While some (including the people I worked with) may have been satisfied with posting misspelled copy and paste jobs, that is just not my approach. It does not matter if I was employed by the goofiest third-tier website that was more known for posting scantily clad women than breaking news; I had and still have a pride in putting out a product that is as exhaustive as I could possibly make it. My creations are a reflection of my integrity and meticulous approach.

*Photo of the late Owen Hart by **AE! FROM ARLINGTON, USA**[232], **CC BY 2.0**[233], via Wikimedia Commons. This picture was used for the article **IN DEFENSE OF... VINCE MCMAHON IN THE DEATH OF OWEN HART**[234]. Even professional wrestling can be a serious subject when treated with dignity and respect.*

» JOURNEY INTO MYSTERY

Returning to our mystery house, almost every municipality in the country has a tax assessor or similar

---

[232] HTTPS://COMMONS.WIKIMEDIA.ORG/WIKI/FILE:OWEN_HART_1997.JPG
[233] HTTPS://CREATIVECOMMONS.ORG/LICENSES/BY/2.0
[234] HTTPS://MEDIUM.JPPRAG.COM/IN-DEFENSE-OF-VINCE-MCMAHON-IN-THE-DEATH-OF-OWEN-HART-29F0C80652FF

website to explore the real estate of the area. Dallas is no different and I asked Google for "Dallas property records". The **FIRST RESULT**[235] was exactly what I was looking for.

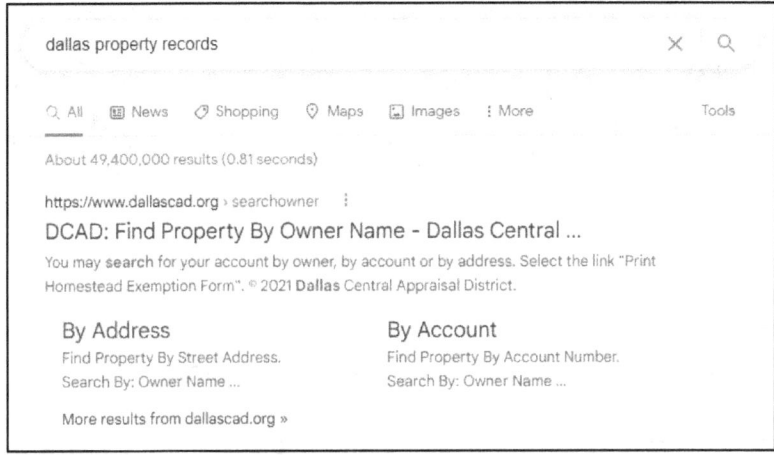

Screen capture of a Google search.

From there I entered the address from Zillow in the search field and got one hit:

Screen capture of the results from the Dallas Central Appraisal District website.

This result presented two interesting tidbits. First was that the "Type" was listed as "COMMERCIAL" instead of "RESIDENTIAL", which told me that this property served some type of corporate or industrial purpose. Pulling up Google Maps and looking at "Street View" further expounded upon the oddness of the estate:

---

[235] HTTPS://WWW.DALLASCAD.ORG/SEARCHADDR.ASPX

Google Street View showing the property that looks quite different than its neighbors.

The neighbors are for the most part small, single-story ranches. The house in question is quite a monstrosity compared to them and completely out of place. Reading through the comments on the Facebook Group that the articles referenced provided some additional direction here. People there mention commercial vans being outside on a regular basis and Dallas codes that say commercial buildings must blend into their surroundings. You see, I was not dismissing the social media aspect of this story, but was not taking it at face value, either, and just copying and pasting it. Instead, I used it as a springboard to further research. Social Media is the perfect place for speculation; news, analysis, and article writing are where we cut through the fog.

Following the links further down the rabbit hole brought me to a **PROPERTY MAP**[236]. When looking at that map, I saw those same single-story ranches, but another property right next door stood out. That plot was also registered as "Commercial" except with one key difference: it was owned by AT&T. Further, looking at that property on street view showed that it, too, appeared conspicuous compared to the neighbors.

---

[236] HTTPS://MAPS.DCAD.ORG/PRD/DPM/?PARCELID=007497002911B0000

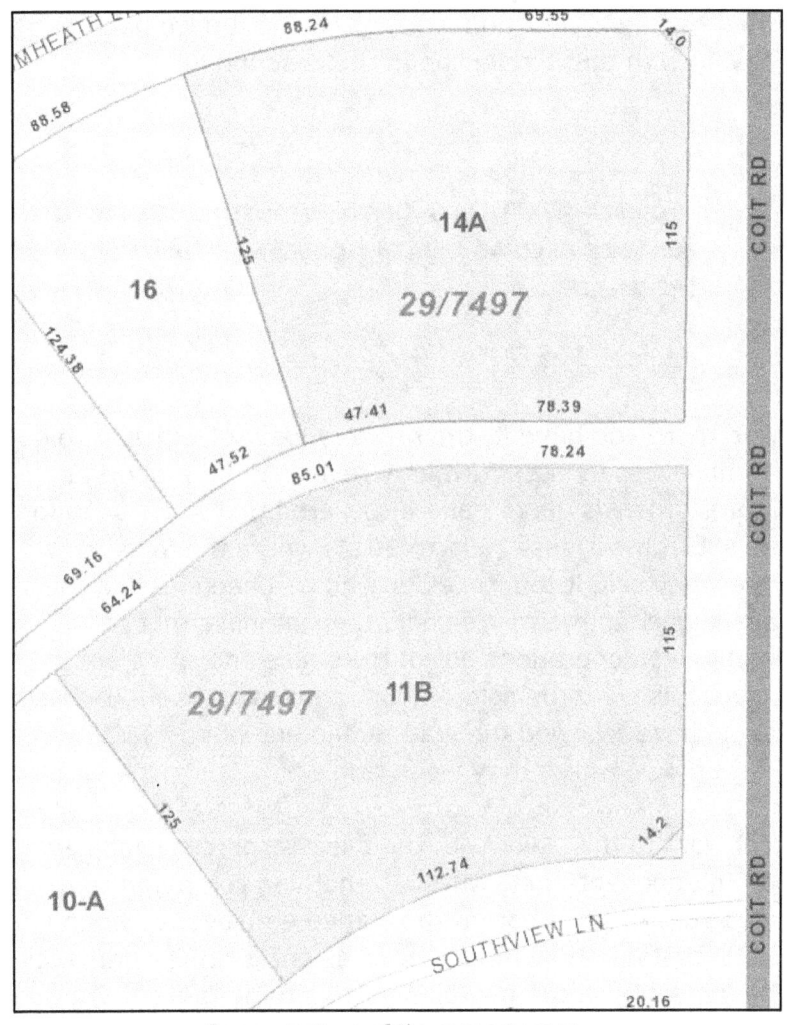

Screen capture of the property map.

Back to the property we are concerned with: the other key point we got was that it was owned by "FELDER NEIL". Another quick search told me that according to LinkedIn (first result), Neil Felder is the owner of "Felder Property Group". Now, a check on the business proved not only that they have a website, but that the site has listings for their properties. And **AMONG THOSE LISTINGS**[237] was the one in question, spoiling all the fun we had been having with this simple line in the description:

> **FORMER AT&T DATA CENTER HOUSE FOR LEASE. CAN ONLY BE USED AS A DATA HOUSE, NO OTHER USE PERMITTED.**

And there you have it, the mystery was solved! Just to go an unnecessary step further, I reviewed the property's **OWNERSHIP HISTORY**[238] and discovered that AT&T used to own it from at least 2001 to 2011, where the following year they sold it to Mr. Felder who had been leasing the space back to them. We could then suppose that AT&T had moved operations out of the space and therefore it was available to be sold off. Or an investigative journalist could have followed the lead to find out when AT&T moved out, where they went, and why.

Yet I got to this point with the basic resources available on the open internet, which are nothing compared to a well-staffed newsroom with salaried employees. I found all of that and may never see one cent for this work; they have people on the payroll available to do this toil. And I was not alone in this approach as Dan Swinhoe of *Data Centre Dynamics Ltd*—a London-based company not exactly in the news industry—did a similar deep dive and **WROTE IN PART**[239]:

---

[237] HTTPS://F-P-G.COM/LISTINGS/SOUTHVIEW-LANE/
[238] HTTPS://WWW.DALLASCAD.ORG/ACCTHISTORY.ASPX?ID=007497002911B0000
[239] HTTPS://WWW.DATACENTERDYNAMICS.COM/EN/NEWS/FORMER-ATT-DATA-CENTER-ON-SALE-AS-POTENTIAL-SAFEHOUSE-OR-WINE-STORAGE-FACILITY/

UK PUBLICATION THE DAILY MAIL WAS ALSO CONFUSED, AND WAS UNABLE TO ASCERTAIN WHAT THE BUILDING WAS USED FOR, THE ANSWER OF WHICH WAS ONE GOOGLE SEARCH AWAY.

Of course, I only discovered Mr. Swinhoe's article because I was further researching the topic for this piece and appreciated the snark.

Inside of a Ybor City cigar factory, circa 1920. Photo and description from the HISTORICAL COLLECTION OF THE TAMPA-HILLSBOROUGH COUNTY PUBLIC LIBRARY[240], Public domain, via Wikimedia Commons.

---

[240] HTTPS://COMMONS.WIKIMEDIA.ORG/WIKI/FILE:YBOR_CIGAR_WORKERS.JPG

» Phoenix Down

What is seen in here is endemic of the modern media in general and the news industry in particular. How many times have you opened an article where the banner was the entire story? What percentage of captions are knowingly misleading clickbait? Why is the same story reposted with just a different heading?

These are indicators of a desire to just get product out the door without being willing to dig in and do the work necessary to make quality over quantity and speed. In many ways, I do sympathize with news sources and other writers who must compete with lightning-fast reactions on social media. And yes, I readily admit that I have professional jealousy that some people can make a living out of posting top-whatever lists, writing seven sentences in response to a tweet, or have others follow their off-the-cuff short responses to everything. Here I will concede there is room enough in the world for these types of writers and content producers. I, though, cannot ever be one of them, and believe there should be more like me.

In a world filled with "who got there first" types, there is actually a unique value proposition in being thoughtful, doing the investigation, knuckling down on the labor, and producing detailed and complete stories. This is the niche where I see myself and how I approach work. It is not just important for me that my work have meaning, but a requirement I have given myself. Without that, I would not have purpose; and without purpose, I might as well be wasting my time in something much more lucrative.

Rotary shop routine at the printing press of the Pravda—the leading Soviet daily—on January 8, 1982. Photo and description by **RIA NOVOSTI ARCHIVE, IMAGE #140640 / VLADIMIR RODIONOV**[241], **CC BY-SA 3.0**[242], via Wikimedia Commons.

---

[241] HTTPS://COMMONS.WIKIMEDIA.ORG/WIKI/FILE:RIAN_ARCHIVE_140640_PRAVDA_NEWSPAPER_PRINTING.JPG
[242] HTTPS://CREATIVECOMMONS.ORG/LICENSES/BY-SA/3.0

EMPATHY // REDISCOVERED

Finding the emotions to be fully human for the first time

Photo by **MATTHEW HENRY**[243] on **UNSPLASH**

---

[243] HTTPS://UNSPLASH.COM/@MATTHEWHENRY

» Key Points

- *One day, something broke... or rather repaired... inside of me.*

- *Suddenly feeling empathy for the first time helped me realize that I had been missing so much.*

- *There is a massive gap between the compassion I did feel and thought was enough and actual empathy for other human beings.*

IT WAS A SCENE I HAD WITNESSED HUNDREDS OF TIMES BEFORE.

After having been a traveling worker for nearly a decade at that point, I had a regular routine when I got to the airport or train station. While going about my humdrum idiosyncrasies, events like this had played out before me a multitude of times without hardly any recognition on my part. All of it was passé—so unremarkable that I barely even noticed anymore. I scarcely even saw the shapes flowing through the airport or train station as individual people; just categories of objects that fell into my self-stylized buckets. Sometimes I was curious about what they were up to, where they were going, or why they had a particular look on their faces. Overall, though, they meant nothing to me.

Sitting there, waiting for my flight to board, I happen to glance up from my book. A little distance away, two people were embracing as they were saying goodbye to each other. One was boarding a flight while the other would remain here, left behind. It was no different than all of the other occasions I had seen such an event—whether it was lovers, parents and children, long-separated friends, or any other such thing. Yet, something inside of me broke. Or, more correctly, something inside of me finally repaired.

Very suddenly, I felt complete empathy for these people. I sensed their emotions at being torn apart from each other, experienced it so deeply that it was as if it was happening to me. Through my head ran all the times something like this did or could have happened to me, seeing myself literally in the shoes of one of them and the other person replaced with the person I held most dear. These were not nondescript blobs; they were fellow human beings who mattered in the same way I did. I was them and they were me; one ball of shared humanity.

Photo by **Suganth**[244] *on* **Unsplash**

» Mind the Gap

It is not as though I did not care about the plights of others before this. While discerning in what I chose to give my energy to, I was concerned about people in all sorts of straits—whether dire or not. This extended not

---

[244] https://unsplash.com/@suganth

just to those closest to me, but groups of people flung around the world, even complete strangers in far off lands. I am not saying that I was lacking in emotions entirely; just that I was not experiencing them to their fullest.

Photo by **DUNCAN SHAFFER**[245] on **UNSPLASH**

Also, I was caring *about* them, not feeling what they were going through. There is a massive gap between compassion and empathy that I have only come to understand over the ensuing years since that strange moment. What I had before was more akin to sympathy and consideration. Not that these emotions and intents should be discounted, but they are a long way from commiseration and identification. I was an exterior force who was completely separate from what they were undergoing. Starting that day, I became an internal conspirator. They were not alone; we were in it together.

---

[245] HTTPS://UNSPLASH.COM/@DUNCAN_SHAFFER

What had happened to me? Why did I suddenly change?

Well, in reality, it was not so abrupt. Without going on a long journey through my entire psychological profile, let us sum it up by saying I lacked stability and guiding influences in my earlier life. From a young age, I learned the only person I could depend upon was myself and used that weapon to keep most other people at arm's length. Through neglect, I raised myself up from my origins into a successful, mostly functioning human being. I was actualized to the point of even recognizing the scars of my childhood and how I could overcome them, or at least work with them so they did not paralyze me. Altogether, I was doing basically fine.

And that level of triumph breeds complacency. I was not only surviving in life; I was thriving. What I was doing and how I lived had proved successful, so much so that I thought the work I had done on myself was complete. You see, I did not recognize that a chasm like this even existed. I had no idea I was still repressing emotions and not experiencing them as I should.

> **How could I know that I had cut off so much of my humanity?**

» The "L" Word

What changed for me is the tritest answer of all: I found someone to love. For the first time in my entire life, I had a stable relationship. Not only did I let someone in, but I also allowed her through my walls and secret passageways. Even my own brother joked that I permitted her into my "Fortress of Solitude". While I thought I was being so sly, others in my life were quick to recognize where I was lacking. Was I lonely before? I do not know because I had cut off my ability to feel and recognize such a thing. How could I emote for others when I could not even do it for myself?

Photo by KÜLLI KITTUS[246] on UNSPLASH

My now partner unlocked all of the remaining dams inside of me. I tell her all the time that she broke me, but in reality, she helped repair me in a way I did not even know I was shattered. She guided me on my reentry into humankind. It was not an immediate thing; it took years of learning to trust and open myself up to the potentialities. And then—after that fateful day when some synapses clicked together for the first time—I had to keep working at it. Recognizing what was possible was only a first step; I had to learn how to harness my emotions and empathy on a regular basis. Today, I still have to work on

---

[246] HTTPS://UNSPLASH.COM/@KYLLIK

it and will always have to do so lest I forget and regress again.

In order to be a fully formed person, my first step was to recognize and accept the failings of my past. But they do not define me; they are just a reference point to acknowledge how far I have come. Now I can see and understand how far I have yet to go, when before it was a world beyond the pale that might as well have been like trying to picture a 17-dimensional object.

And if you, reading this now, are not feeling this as if you are me, then I want you to know that there is something more, something you may not even realize you are missing. But there is no need to agonize over it! Just learning that it exists may be all that is necessary to help you take a small step towards that healing realm.

Just know: you do not need to be walled off from the world and alone inside in order to survive.

AGREEING WITH MY ENEMY

Why we should listen to "those people" who are against us

*Photo by **NIKOLA JOHNNY MIRKOVIC**[247] on **UNSPLASH***

---

[247] HTTPS://UNSPLASH.COM/@THEJOHNNYME

» KEY POINTS

- *When someone who was perceived as my adversary and I teamed up and learned to understand where the other one came from, we were able to create lasting and important change.*

- *This is a lesson that our representatives in government need to learn.*

- *Is there someone who is willing to reach across the aisle and discover that more can be accomplished together?*

WE WERE ON A CONFERENCE CALL AND TONY WAS TAKING A SHELLACKING.

All the managers seemed to be completely against Tony's recommendations and approach. It was then that I spoke up. Not only did I vigorously defended Tony's point of view, but provided further evidence from the field about why he was correct and how it would impact the work we on the front lines actually did that the managers seemed to be disconnected from. There was a noticeable pause from the others.

You see, it was well known in the company that Tony and I did not get along. Some might even describe us as enemies; perhaps even Tony himself would agree. Our personalities were completely contrary, and our arguments—oftentimes in front of co-workers—were well documented. Tony had even told an apocryphal story about me to a filled-to-capacity room during a breakout session at a company meeting. I was furious when I found out afterwards, but the damage to my reputation was done.

Thus, when I came to Tony's defense, it caused a bit of a stir. If the two of us were not only in agreement about something, but were working in tandem to make it happen, then there might be something to it. It seemed the others were beginning to doubt their own positions, but the victory was short-lived. The rest of the people in the meeting picked their jaws up off the floor, gathered their wits, and summarily dismissed and overrode our concerns. Our fledgling alliance was already destroyed.

After everyone left, Tony called me up directly. Apparently, my coming to his aid has struck a chord within him and he wanted to thank me. I told him, "Tony, it's no problem. What you were saying was the truth, and I will always come to the side of truth."

Photo by **GOUTHAM GANESH SIVANANDAM**[248] *on* **UNSPLASH**

Our relationship fundamentally changed that day. Though we had lost the battle, something much more valuable was gained. We never stopped having differences and disagreements, continued to take distinctive approaches

---

[248] HTTPS://UNSPLASH.COM/@WINKNCLICK

to work and life, and were never even close to what anyone would consider friends. However, Tony and I came to an understanding of each other and recognized where the other one was coming from. From these seeds blossomed a functioning and beneficial association, one that did result in real and actual progress. Some years later, Tony was given the reins to head up a new division for the company. He invited me to join him and create the role he knew I had spent my career pitching the need for—giving me every resource I would ever need, including his full support. And I would have taken him up on the offer... if I did not already have plans of my own to leave the organization. As such, we parted ways, but on the best of terms.

» THAT WEIRD UNCLE AT THANKSGIVING

The approach I took with Tony is the same as I take with everyone and everything in life. I will not dismiss people out of hand just because I do not like them or we are diametrically opposed. From my perspective, not listening to someone just because they belong to a different tribe is why we make so very little progress in the world.

This, too, is my standing on politics. Just because I argue against the unnatural oligopoly power of the Republican and Democratic Parties, it does not mean that I contest and resist everything they do. I take a look at each proposal on its own merits and make up my mind about it—whether in the end I am proven correct or not.

So yes, I could hate 95% of what came out of Donald Trump's mouth, but that meant there was 5% that I wholeheartedly supported. For instance, I agreed with him about the need to pull our troops out of Afghanistan and backed the lowering of personnel levels. Or, due to my own background, I was a proponent of moving the embassy in Israel from Tel Aviv to Jerusalem—which was also a requirement of a 1995 law that passed in an overwhelming bipartisan manner 347–37 in the House of Representatives and 93–5 in the Senate. Others, even my own friends, disagreed with these decisions. And that is okay because we can diverge on specific policy beliefs and still appreciate one another. What I could not tolerate was dismissing these pronouncements just because of who they happened to come from.

Photo by **JEREMY BEZANGER**[249] on **UNSPLASH**

This also means I do not blindly follow people who are more agreeable to me. Just because I found Joe Biden's agenda generally more palatable than Donald Trump's, it does not mean I unconditionally bowed to his will. In reality, though I aligned with Joe Biden more than Donald Trump, that number was something like 15–20% of the time. Going back to that Afghanistan example, while I supported the removal of soldiers, the methodology (or

---

[249] HTTPS://UNSPLASH.COM/@JEREMYBEZANGER

lack thereof) by which it was done and the abandonment of people who aligned with us there was untenable to me. Similarly, Joe Biden restored funding that Donald Trump took away from the UNRWA on just the promise that the organization would stop providing to schoolchildren materials that contained components that incited violence and spread antisemitism—a promise they had made and broken multiple times in the past.

Again, though, these are policy beliefs; neither right nor wrong. You may believe the UNRWA's overarching mission is critical despite its flaws and therefore want that funding restored. Or you may believe the United States should not have combatants deployed abroad under any circumstances and therefore pulling out immediately is the preferable route, no matter the consequences. While we may disagree on the actions that should or should not be taken, I can still listen, learn, and respect where you are coming from.

Can you do the same for me?

» WHAT DO YOU WEAR TO THE BEACH?

Unfortunately, the "Tony Approach" is not widely followed in the halls of Congress or anywhere in government circles. If we return back to the aforementioned Afghanistan withdrawal, what we often see are politicians not fighting for a steadfast belief, but against the positions of those who wear an opposing-colored shirt or cheer for a specific animal.

On June 22, 2011, then President Barack Obama let the world know the United States was done with Afghanistan and was preparing to start drawing down the troops. The plan would take three years, wrapping up in the summer of 2014. Representative Nancy Pelosi (D-CA) was not satisfied with this timeframe and stated, *"It has been the hope of many in Congress and across the country that the full drawdown of US forces would happen sooner than the president laid out, and we will continue to press for a better outcome."* In other words, Mrs. Pelosi was closer to the camp of those who wanted to get the soldiers out of Afghanistan, damn the consequences.

Yet in November 2020—more than six years after the withdrawal was supposed to be complete—when President Donald Trump announced his plans to get all combatants out of Afghanistan, Mrs. Pelosi had a harsh response. In her **PRESS RELEASE**[250], Mrs. Pelosi wrote in part:

> **OUR MILITARY AND ALLIES DESERVE STRONG, SMART AND STRATEGIC LEADERSHIP TO PROTECT AMERICA'S SECURITY AND THAT OF THE REGION... WE CAN ILL AFFORD TO LOSE THE HARD-WON GAINS IN THE PILLARS OF SECURITY, ECONOMIC DEVELOPMENT AND GOVERNANCE MADE IN AFGHANISTAN.**

In particular, she attacked the lack of planning, coordination with allies, and consideration for those who provided support on the ground. Yet a mere nine months later when Joe Biden was President and oversaw a chaotic, humiliating, poorly planned, uncoordinated retreat that left behind all those "hard-won gains", Mrs. Pelosi put out a tonally divergent **PRESS RELEASE**[251] that said in part:

---

[250] HTTPS://WWW.SPEAKER.GOV/NEWSROOM/111720-0
[251] HTTPS://WWW.SPEAKER.GOV/NEWSROOM/81421-1

> **ONCE AGAIN, I WANT TO ACKNOWLEDGE THE CLARITY OF PURPOSE OF PRESIDENT BIDEN'S STATEMENT AND THE WISDOM OF HIS ACTIONS.**

Of course, she is not the only one to change her tune. After Mr. Trump's November 2020 announcement, Senator Josh Hawley (R-MO) was one of the loudest cheerleaders calling for the immediate and expeditious withdrawal from Afghanistan, going so far as to **WRITE A LETTER TO THE ACTING SECRETARY OF DEFENSE CHRISTOPHER MILLER**[252] that could best be summed up as: "Hurry up!" And this was hardly a new position for the Senator; a year prior he gave a speech on the subject of the "endless wars" of our times:

Senator Josh Hawley (R-MO) gives a speech on America's approach to international politics, economics, and military intervention in November 2019. **HTTPS://YOUTU.BE/GP0NYHI1XXG**

---

[252] HTTPS://WWW.HAWLEY.SENATE.GOV/HAWLEY-PRAISES-PRESIDENT-TRUMPS-PLAN-BRING-TROOPS-HOME-AFGHANISTAN

His opinion seemed resolute as in April 2021 he disparaged President Biden for extending the deadline for the full withdrawal past the May 2021 endpoint set by his predecessor. However, when the day came that President Biden gave him everything he had always asked for, he had nothing but criticism, going so far as to ask for the President's resignation.

Photo by JEAN WIMMERLIN[253] on UNSPLASH

We could go on with these flip-flopping illustrations for eternity, and there are plenty of counter-examples with politicians who have maintained a position for 20 years— even denouncing their own Party when they failed to acquiesce. Regrettably, these non-team players are not the loudest voices, and they are steadily being replaced by those whose only ambitions are that their Party has more power than the other one. They stand for nothing.

---

[253] HTTPS://UNSPLASH.COM/@JWIMMERLI

» Separating the Art from the Artist

In December 2021, a fight was ongoing about the debt ceiling. Virtually no Republican (there is always an anarchist or pyromaniac in the bunch) wanted the United States to default on its debt payments for the first time in history. To do so would have been economically and politically suicidal and would have immediately sent the world plunging into a recession—potentially even a depression. And that type of economic collapse, on top of a worldwide pandemic that was hardly under control, could have taken decades to come back from.

Photo by *James Lee*[254] on *Unsplash*

Yet despite not wanting to default on our debts, for optics reasons—optics they created by knowingly lying about what was causing the need to raise the debt ceiling—Republicans, save a handful, were unwilling to vote for the necessary legislation. To wit, the compromise appeared to be that they would allow a change in

---

[254] HTTPS://UNSPLASH.COM/@PICSBYJAMESLEE

procedure that would make it possible for Democrats to raise the debt ceiling on their own without a single Republican vote, if necessary. Though Republicans desired the end result, they refused to be the harbingers.

Moreover, when Republicans attacked Democrats for their hypocrisy on the issue, they were also accurate. Though President Joe Biden claimed that raising the debt ceiling was traditionally a bipartisan measure, as recently as 2006 then Senator Joe Biden (D-DE) and the rest of the Democratic caucus forced Republicans to raise the debt ceiling on a Party-line vote. All the reasons, tactics, and politically charged recriminations were the same.

To vote with their conscience would have been tantamount to showing tacit support for the other Party, their sworn enemies, not their co-workers that just approached things from another standpoint. Yet it is still not beyond hope that one day someone from across the aisle will stand up for Representative Tony; someone who appears to be his nemesis. Then on that day they will realize that they are not opponents, but that they can fight...

TOGETHER

AFTERWARDS

ABOUT THE AUTHOR

J.P. Prag is a Pisces, even though that does not mean anything. However, ten of the stars in Pisces are known to host planets, though these stars are nowhere near each other. One of the planets (GU Pisces b) takes around 80,000 Earth years to circle its sun. Of note, some of the stars are not stars at all, but are entire galaxies! Further scientific examination has discovered many other faint galaxies, nebulae, stars, and other stellar objects within the Pisces general area. A couple of those galaxies are on a collision course, so look out for that over the next several hundred million years or so.

When not observing the stars at the Ladd Observatory, J.P. Prag can be found several blocks away at his home and office in Providence, RI, U.S.A. with his partner Caroline and their many tall ferns and philodendrons, lazy lying down cacti, outside pet squirrels (including Squirrel the Raccoon), and a stuffed pet sloth named Peeve.

For more irreverent details (and perhaps some pertinent ones, too?) and contact information, please visit **WWW.JPPRAG.COM**.

Other Works

Please visit **WWW.JPPRAG.COM** to see all upcoming works, prior works, general articles, and current status.

Prior works include:

- **New & Improved: The United States of America**
  Is there a way to save America and ensure justice and freedom for all? There is... if you are willing to rethink and rebuild the entire Constitution!
  HTTPS://AMZN.TO/3KGWO6E

- **In Defense Of... Exonerating Professional Wrestling's Most Hated**
  Parts of wrestling history have been presented with overtly critical comments and outright lies. It is past time to bring truth to the wrestling fan!
  HTTPS://AMZN.TO/2DUBSI8

Upcoming works include:

- **254 Days to Impeachment: The Story of the First Independent President**
  What happens when an idealist sits in the most powerful chair in the world while an entire bureaucracy fights to stay relevant?

- **Compendium of Humanity's End**
  Should humanity populate the stars and find no other life, what does that mean? What happens when those sent out to find life are met with nothing but constant failure?

DEDICATIONS AND NOTES

Mary Rockwell (center) is flanked by Caroline and J.P. Prag at their elopement party on June 23, 2018

As if this age needed another loss, Mary Rockwell passed away on January 5, 2022. Mary was my partner Caroline's very close friend, and had become mine as well. Not only that, she was editor for my first two books and was prepared to be the editor for this one. I feel her loss in every word in these pages, and will always try to remember the lessons she taught me with her keen, critical, and unapologetic eye. Though she is not here to accept it, this book is dedicated to her memory.

With her own pain fresh in mind, this book is also dedicated to Caroline herself. I love you[3], and will be there to support you as you are there to support me.

And as always, I am grateful to you, the reader, who without your existence these would just be silent words on a page. Please be kind out there, and leave a review!

VERSION HISTORY

Version Number	Version Date	Version Notes
0.00	2020-12-01	Draft Started
0.10	2021-12-21	Shell Outline Transfer Complete
1.00	2022-01-26	Alpha Draft
1.50	2022-03-01	Alpha Draft – Edited
2.00	2022-03-06	Beta Draft
2.50	2022-04-07	Beta Draft – Edited
3.00	2022-04-19	Final Release Form
4.00	2022-05-04	Minor corrections and updates before publishing

COPYRIGHTS AND DISCLAIMERS

Copyright © 2021-2022 J.P. Prag

All rights reserved. No part of this publication may be reproduced, distributed, or transmitted in any form or by any means, including photocopying, recording, or other electronic or mechanical methods, without the prior written permission of the copyright holder, except in the case of brief quotations embodied in critical reviews and certain other noncommercial uses permitted by copyright law.

This is a work of nonfiction. No names have been changed, no characters invented, no events fabricated except for hypothetical situations. The advice and strategies found within may not be suitable for every situation. This work is sold with the understanding that neither the author nor the publisher may be held responsible for the results accrued from the advice in this book.

First Edition May 2022

Printed everywhere in the world on an on-demand basis from the nearest regional printing and distribution center.

Edited by Jessica Schmidt
Proud proofreader and editor on Fiverr since 2014
HTTPS://WWW.FIVERR.COM/CURIOUSWOMAN271

Cover art by John Bell
HTTP://WWW.JOHNBELLART.COM
HTTPS://SELFPUBBOOKCOVERS.COM/JOHNBELLART

Ebook, Hardcover, and Paperback cover design by Xee Designs
HTTPS://WWW.FIVERR.COM/XEE_DESIGNS1

ISBN 978-1-7353287-6-8 // ebook
ISBN 978-1-7353287-7-5 // hardcover
ISBN 978-1-7353287-8-2 // paperback

Basil Junction Publishing
7 Knowles Street
Providence, RI 02906

WWW.JPPRAG.COM